MODERN DUBLIN

OXFORD HISTORICAL MONOGRAPHS

Modern Dublin

Urban Change and the Irish Past, 1957–1973

ERIKA HANNA

OXFORD
UNIVERSITY PRESS

OXFORD
UNIVERSITY PRESS

Great Clarendon Street, Oxford, OX2 6DP,
United Kingdom

Oxford University Press is a department of the University of Oxford.
It furthers the University's objective of excellence in research, scholarship,
and education by publishing worldwide. Oxford is a registered trade mark of
Oxford University Press in the UK and in certain other countries

First Edition published in 2013

Impression: 1

British Library Cataloguing in Publication Data

Data available

ISBN 978–0–19–968045–0

Printed and bound by
CPI Group (UK) Ltd, Croydon, CR0 4YY

Acknowledgements

The Dublin I first got to know as a child was a small place, bounded by the route of the 14A bus, a small sliver of the city stretching from the south Dublin suburbs to Grafton Street. However, returning to the city as an adult, and equipped with a bicycle, I travelled more widely, and became aware of a city which had been both very near and almost completely unknown to me—Mountjoy Square, Henrietta Street, Blessington Basin. This book was inspired by my love of Dublin and its architecture, and my desire to know more about the city, and understand its relationship both to the national story and to my own sense of identity. During its long gestation from Dublin, to Bristol, Oxford, and most recently at Leicester, I have accumulated a lot of debts. My very deepest thanks go to Roy Foster. I am very grateful to him for sharing his knowledge of Ireland and architecture, and for his tremendous intellectual generosity, kindness, and rigour in supervising the thesis and advising on the subsequent book. I was also very lucky to have two excellent examiners in Senia Pasêta and Simon Gunn; they provided invaluable insights and suggestions, and have been very supportive since.

A number of people who know and understand more about the city than I ever will, and whose first-hand experiences have shaped the narrative of this book, have been incredibly generous to me during the course of my research. They include Mairin de Burca, Sheila Carden, Harold Clarke, Francis Devine, Margaret Downes, Terry Fagan, Desmond Guinness, John McBratney, Niall McCullough, John McDonnell, Ruadhán MacEoin, Edward McParland, Valerie Mulvin, David Norris, the late Kevin Nowlan and Knight of Glin, Duncan Stewart, Ronnie Tallon, Johnnie Walker, Simon Walker, and the late Knight of Glin. The staff of the Irish Georgian Society—including Donough Cahill and Emmeline Henderson—have pointed me in the right direction on numerous occasions, and the staff at the Irish Architectural Archive have also been incredibly helpful, in particular with sourcing images. It has been wonderful to meet so many people who care so much about Dublin, think so carefully about urbanism, and give up so much of their time to improve and protect the environment of the city. This book would never have been possible had they not shared their memories and opened up their private archives.

This project has benefited immeasurably from colleagues and friends who have been very giving with their time and knowledge. At Bristol and since, Josie McLellan has been unendingly generous with her time, advice, and knowledge of history. The Irish history community at Oxford provided a wonderful environment in which to conduct research: Richard Ansell, Gemma Clark, Frances Flanagan, Ultán Gillen, James Golden, Marc Mulholland, Simon Prince, Colin Reid, Mark Williams, and Tim Wilson all offered suggestions, criticism, and came to the pub. My ideas have also benefited from comments and criticism from John Davis, Matt Kelly, and Ian McBride. John Gold and William Whyte read the manuscript for Oxford University Press, and provided many perceptive suggestions and practical advice. This book was finished at the Centre for Urban History at the University of Leicester, my colleagues there, Colin Hyde, Prashant Kidambi, Katy Layton-Jones, Toby Lincoln, Rebecca Madgin, and Rosemary Sweet, have been wonderfully encouraging during the project's final phase, and have helped me to push my understanding of cities much further. Conducting this research has only been possible thanks to funding by Arts and Humanities Research Council Masters' and Doctoral Awards. Hertford College and the British Association of Irish Studies also supplied additional funding for travel and research in Ireland.

I have also been very lucky to have a wonderful group of friends who have kept me going throughout the long process from thesis to book. Eleanor Austin, Tom Browning, and Seán Quinn were there when this all started, and have believed in me ever since. Thanks to Lu Hiam for two decades of friendship across many locations. At Oxford, Ludivine Broch, Mike Finch, Charlotte Greenhalgh, Chloe Jeffries, Daniel Lee, Eloise Moss, Tamson Pietsch, and Ryan Thoreson all made Oxford a very enjoyable place to study and live. Thanks to Dora Osborne for cake and theory. Almost since the day I arrived at Oxford, Rob Priest has been the best friend anyone could hope for—thanks for the long lunch breaks, mid-afternoon pints, and for assiduous criticism of my work. Big thanks to Matt Houlbrook for being so generous, kind, and patient, sharing so many happy days with me, and showing me what the world looks like from over the handlebars of a bicycle. Finally, my biggest thanks of all are to my family, who have provided an enormous amount of support over the course of the project: David, Rosalind, Rebekah, Josh, Adam, Logan, and Ivy.

Contents

List of Figures

List of Maps

List of Abbreviations

CPI	Communist Party of Ireland
DCG	Dublin Civic Group
DHAC	Dublin Housing Action Committee
DT	Department of the Taoiseach
ESB	Electricity Supply Board
GPO	General Post Office
IAA	Irish Architectural Archive
ICO	Irish Communist Organisation
IGS	Irish Georgian Society
IRA	Irish Republican Army
NAI	National Archives of Ireland
NLI	National Library of Ireland
PDDÉ	Printed Debates Dáil Éireann
RAGE	Radical Action for a Good Environment
TCD	Trinity College Dublin
UCD	University College Dublin

Introduction

Modern Dublin and the Irish Past

> And so it was that I stood on the Cruagh with Seán Ó'Faoláin and looked down over the grey, silent desolation of the city and spoke of what I, as an architect, had liked amongst that pile of bricks and stone. 'Perhaps', said Seán Ó'Faoláin, 'there will rise out of that great waste a city such as we have only dreamed of!' I wondered. I thought of prophets all over the old and new worlds—Aalto, Oud, Gropius, Corbusier, Wright. I thought of townplanners burning their midnight oil on the top floors of Baggot Street. I thought of architectural schools bursting with students and ideas. Yes, like a phoenix, Dublin would reappear, new and perfect and beautiful, planned with vision, rebuilt with knowledge. Not quite the same thing of course as Dublin, 1941, in all its magnificent and shoddy detail.[1]

Standing on the Cruagh, a peak in the Dublin Mountains, Raymond McGrath surveyed the city spreading into the distance beneath him. From his vantage point Dublin had taken on the form of a map, allowing McGrath to visualize the future overlaid on 'that pile of bricks and stone'. The city, like the nation, was a phoenix, ready to arise renewed from the ashes of what had gone before. The excitement and ideas of the architecture schools, the skill of Dublin's town planners, and the inspiration of the 'prophets' of modern architecture meant that within the city itself there existed the potential and capacity for its rejuvenation as something 'new and perfect and beautiful'. McGrath was not alone in prophesying that sweeping changes would take place to the city in the post-war years; indeed, he was part of an active architectural community that saw the techniques and technologies of modern architecture and urban design as heralding prosperity and emancipation for all.

[1] Raymond McGrath, 'Dublin Panorama: An Architectural Review', *The Bell* 2/5 (1941), 48.

Twenty years later, McGrath's urban visions of the 1940s seemed to be about to come to fruition. In this period, the government began to invest in town planning, new opportunities arose for the country's architects, and the old buildings of the core began to be replaced by modern structures. These visible manifestations of urban modernization—including Busáras, the new Liberty Hall, and the Sugar Company building on Leeson Street—were in general well received, understood to be the first, visible signs of prosperity and broader social and economic modernization (Fig. 0.1). However, this attitude was short lived. In the following decade, the city of Dublin underwent dramatic physical changes, but alongside this, conceptions of the value of the city were also evolving, and a disparate movement of architectural preservationists, housing activists, students, and architects emerged to oppose the developments in the city. By the end of the 1960s, popular support for urban change had shifted, indeed reversed. The new buildings and urban forms had not brought a promised new way of living; instead, rapid destruction of the extant city had come to be seen as symbolic of corruption and the failed promise of modernization. An exploration of this story provides a new approach to social and cultural change in Ireland in the post-war period; the

Fig. 0.1. Dublin's quays, showing the newly completed Liberty Hall, 1967.

publications, debates, and ideals of the architectural profession show how the 1950s were a period not of monolithic malaise but when there was lively and internationally engaged debate regarding the future of the city. Similarly, the developing conservationist agenda provides a view of the 1960s which is more multifaceted than previous emphases on prosperity have allowed, revealing Dublin instead as a place of complex exchange between a variety of interest groups with different visions for the built environment, and thus for society and the independent nation. An exploration of these themes shows how the city became a site where a multiplicity of identities and agendas were visualized, debated, and given a concrete reality, and how modern Dublin took its form at the intersection of these tensions.

Since the eighteenth century, the city has been understood to be the key site of the emergence of modernity, and this focus has been followed in recent historical scholarship on urban life. This modernity has conceptualized in a number of overlapping ways, with different interpretations placing varying degrees of emphasis on physical, social, economic, and cultural shifts. The series of spatial changes, including zoning, segregation, suburbanization, mass-transit systems, sewerage, and lighting, through which the state aimed to make the physical spaces of cities knowable, legible, controllable, and the conduit to a better future for their citizens, has been central to ideas of the emergence of the modern city.[2] This 'rationalization' of urban space has taken many guises: in Dublin, for example, this has progressed through many different forms, from the circular roads, canals, and widened roads of the eighteenth century, which imposed a geometric unity on the medieval street plan, to the tower blocks and green spaces of Ballymun, opened in 1966. During the twentieth century, architectural modernism, a disparate movement pioneered by theorists and practitioners such as Le Corbusier, Walter Gropius, and Mies van der Rohe, has provided much of the inspiration, aesthetic, and ideology for these developments. Spanning the century, this movement has had different emphases in differing contexts and different eras; however, it has been broadly united by an aesthetic based on clean lines, bright spaces, functionalism, and new technologies.[3] However, these physical changes have had an import which has transcended changes in urban governance and fashions in design, as the physical manifestation of

[2] James Scott, *Seeing like a State: How Certain Schemes to Improve the Human Condition have Failed* (New Haven, 1998).

[3] Nicholas Bullock, *Building the Post-War World: Modern Architecture and Reconstruction in Britain* (London, 2002); Robert Elwall, *Building a Better Tomorrow: Architecture in Britain in the 1950s* (Chichester, 2000); Alan Colquhoun, *Modern Architecture* (Oxford, 2002).

processes of economic modernization: the city has always been the locus of trade and exchange, but throughout the nineteenth and twentieth centuries the spaces of the city were re-orientated to suit the urban demands of a more vigorous form of capitalism as it developed through the expansion of transport networks and the separation of places of work and residence. These interlinked aesthetic, intellectual, and economic shifts were witnessed by writers and artists, who sought to understand the city as it was seemingly remade in front of their eyes. Figures such as Walter Benjamin, James Joyce, and Georg Simmel were united by their characterization of their respective cities as paradoxical sites of crowds and isolation, transience and immutability, and perils and pleasures, and their work has played a defining role in shaping the study of urban culture during the later twentieth century.

The focus of work on urban modernity has often been on the state's ability to destroy and recreate with seemingly no regard for what has gone before, with examples such as Haussmann's Paris and Peter the Great's St Petersburg used to explore the grandeur and scale of these civic visions.[4] However, the constitution, creation, and institutionalization of tradition has also been a fundamental part of the process of urban modernization. John Pendlebury has described conservation as 'a reaction to the threat caused by progressive modernity... it is bound into a complex dialectic with change and used to affirm the continuity and stability necessary for nationhood'.[5] During the nineteenth century, authors and practitioners such as John Ruskin and Eugène Viollet-le-Duc led a renewed interest in the historic environment, and explored, in very different ways, how ancient buildings should be conserved or restored. The French architect Viollet-le-Duc saw restoration as a process, underpinned by scholarship and historical knowledge, which could lead to almost complete reconstruction; he sought to achieve a 'unity' of style through restoring buildings to a state which reflected one historical moment but 'which may have never existed at any given time'.[6] Indeed, his most famous projects, such as Notre Dame and Carcassone, reflect this approach, having been almost completely reconstructed at his instruction. In contrast, Ruskin and the Society for the Protection of Ancient Buildings saw the value of older buildings in the connection they had with the past, and emphasized the retention of the original materials as fundamental to the retention of the 'truth' of the ancient structure. The similarities and distinctions between

[4] Marshall Berman, *All That is Solid Melts into Air: The Experience of Modernity* (London, 1983); David Harvey, *Paris, Capital of Modernity* (London, 2003).

[5] John Pendlebury, *Conservation in the Age of Consensus* (London, 2008), 21.

[6] Pendlebury, *Conservation in the Age of Consensus*, 16–17.

these two theorists epitomized themes and fault-lines within conservation which would exist throughout the twentieth century: the extent to which reconstruction should be attempted; the emphasis on authenticity and the problem of its definition; and the links between historicity and aesthetics.

In the twentieth century the emphasis upon an essential authenticity and truth of a building, and the ability of the expert to discern it remained, and was only reinforced by the continued development of qualitative and quantitative tools to understand historic structures. John Summerson's 1947 essay 'The Past in the Future' reflected a cautious and minimalistic approach to conservation which was characteristic of mid-century modernism.[7] Although not against preservation of the best structures from previous eras, he noted that old buildings 'like divorced wives... cost money to maintain. They are often dreadfully in the way. And the protection of one may exact much sacrifice from the community as the preservation of a thousand pictures books or musical scores.'[8] This made decisions on the value of buildings necessary. He identified two broad types of value of older buildings: aesthetic and literary. Literary values were associated with a sense of history and continuity; this included the residences of important figures or sites where events of national significance occurred. Aesthetic values, however, were the more important, as they were not enhanced with the passage of time but rather were 'precious and concrete' qualities and values that a building possessed.[9] These conceptions of value led him to describe five types of building that 'in certain circumstances' deserved preservation: buildings which were a work of art; buildings which possessed in a pronounced form the characteristic virtues of the school of design which produced it; buildings, such as churches, of significant antiquity and of a composition of fragmentary beauties welded together in the course of time; buildings which have been the scene of great events; and 'the building whose only virtue is that in a bleak tract of modernity it alone gives depth in time'.[10] In line with these conceptions of value, he rejected the broad-brush preservation of the older parts of a city: 'it is impossible to preserve the "character" of a place when the life in that place has completely changed... aim at things which have the permanent values of architectural order and real artistic quality'.[11]

[7] John Summerson, 'The Past in the Future', in his *Heavenly Mansions and other Essays on Architecture* (New York, 1963), 219–42.

[8] Summerson, 'The Past in the Future', 221.

[9] Summerson, 'The Past in the Future', 222.

[10] Summerson, 'The Past in the Future', 221.

[11] Summerson, 'The Past in the Future', 229.

However, from the 1950s to the 1970s, there was a slow movement away from the orthodoxy articulated by Summerson, and a range of conservationist agendas came to prominence which interrogated the form that the modern city had taken, and found new forms of history and value in the urban environment. The Townscape movement was developed during the 1940s and 1950s in the pages of the *Architectural Review*, and formalized in a book by Gordon Cullen. It sought to realign modernism with the British tradition of the Picturesque to 'counter the emotional boredom induced by the uniformity and straight-line geometry' of modern architecture.[12] As Nan Ellin has described, this movement 'emphasized the relationship between buildings and all that surrounds them, and encouraged designers to enclose buildings around public space rather than sit buildings in the centre of it'.[13] The movement also had an impact on the nature of urban conservation; in contradistinction to Summerson's assessment, adherents defined 'character' as an essential quality of the historic environment which should be preserved through the retention of large areas of buildings and sensitive building in scale. On the other side of the Atlantic, Jane Jacobs was simultaneously leading the way for a new conception of conservation. In *The Death and Life of Great American Cities*, published in the same year as Cullen's *Townscape*, she espoused the need to conserve large areas of the historic environment; however, this was not for aesthetic purposes. She saw the value of cities as residing in the communities they fostered; her emphasis was on the need to retain older buildings in order to create multiple use spaces of home, work, and socialization, and so build urban spaces which were used all day, thus sustaining safe and viable neighbourhoods.[14]

Since their creation as sciences, urban conservation and modernization have developed in dialogue. During the nineteenth century, there was little division between past, present, and future in architectural theory; just as new types of building such as railway stations and apartment blocks took on the motifs and forms of imagined previous ages, so the restoration of older buildings was also often a process of complete reinvention. However, as architectural modernism moved from an elitist, avant-garde art to the mainstream during the twentieth century, this relationship between future and past in the built environment became more sharply

[12] John Gold, *The Practice of Modernism: Modern Architects and Urban Transformation, 1954–72* (London, 2007), 270; Christopher Klemek, *The Transatlantic Collapse of Urban Renewal: Postwar Urbanism from New York to Berlin* (Chicago, 2011), 83–90.

[13] Nan Ellin, *Postmodern Urbanism* (New York, 1996), 61.

[14] John Gold, *The Practice of Modernism*, 271–2; Klemek, *The Transatlantic Collapse of Urban Renewal*, 109–27.

defined. Urban renewal and comprehensive development reshaped large areas of the city, and simultaneously the mechanisms of urban modernization—planning, listing and zoning—also selected and designated historic buildings.[15] Furthermore, the modernist ideals of authenticity and honesty were also central to the emerging science of architectural preservation. Buildings which had been gradually transformed by changes of use and changing needs over their lifetime were restored to their original state at the time of their construction, while a whole industry also developed around manufacturing and delivering 'authentic' building materials and techniques. Promoters of change and preservationists alike worked within the same conception of historicity, and definitively separated past and future through a mutual adherence to a common set of principles. These relationships and cultural values remained constant, even as theorists such as Cullen and Jacobs reconceptualized what and how much should be preserved; the emphasis on planning, the role of the technocrat, the notion of authenticity as the fundamental value upon which the worth of a building was judged, and a modern conception of historicity remained key parts of modernization and conservation. In the words of John Pendlebury, the rise of a conservationist agenda 'was not a break with modernity, but an adaptation of it'.[16]

THE MODERNIZATION OF IRELAND, 1957–73

During the twentieth century, Ireland was slow to adhere to a European model of economic and social development. In the period after independence, the country had entered a long period of entrenched poverty and isolation; during the years of Éamon de Valera's leadership (1937–48, 1951–4, 1957–9), national economic policy had been shaped primarily by the desire to foster and reconstruct a native, Gaelic culture based on agriculture and small-scale native industry, a 'collective dream of a moral community which was authentic, pious, static and intellectually homogeneous'.[17] From the 1930s to the 1950s, successive governments enacted a range of economic policies in pursuit of this vision, such as tariffs on

[15] Simon Gunn, 'The Rise and Fall of Post-War Modernism: Planning Bradford 1945–70', *Journal of British Studies,* 48/3 (2010), 849–69; Peter Mandler, 'New Towns for Old: The Fate of the Town Centre', in Becky Conekin, Frank Mort, Chris Waters (eds.), *Moments of Modernity: Reconstructing Britain 1945–64* (London, 1999), 208–27.

[16] Pendlebury, *Conservation in the Age of Consensus,* 80.

[17] Tom Garvin, *Preventing the Future: Why was Ireland so Poor for so Long?* (Dublin, 2004), 27.

imports and the Control of Manufacturing Acts, which restricted the foreign ownership of domestic firms.

However, in the later 1950s, there was a sudden, tangible, and visible break with what had gone before. A growing sense of crisis regarding the future of the state, caused by a long economic slump and mass emigration, forced the government towards a series of radical policy decisions which amounted to the modernization of the Irish economy in line with global economic trends.[18] The cornerstone of these changes was the Programme for Economic Expansion of 1958, based on a policy document by T. K. Whitaker, which introduced economic planning, switched state investment from social to industrial expenditure, shifted focus from protection to free trade, and encouraged foreign investment in Ireland through grants and subsidies.[19] Following on from the Programme, there were unilateral tariff reductions of 10 per cent in 1963 and 1964, while in 1965 the Anglo-Irish Free Trade Agreement was agreed, which envisaged the removal of all tariffs by 1975.[20] The changes in policy precipitated a structural shift from farming to industry and services, and initiated a reorientation of the economy from autarchy to globalization. Between 1949 and 1968, the proportion of the population of the Republic of Ireland employed in agriculture declined by 13.5 per cent, from 43 per cent to 29 per cent; this fall was matched by a corresponding rise in employment in industry and services. This meant that by 1968, industrial employment almost equalled agricultural employment, whereas in 1949, the sector had only employed half as many people.[21] While the importance of agriculture waned, trade liberalization instead became the central plank of Ireland's shifting economic base.[22] Multinational companies such as Potez Aerospace, Verolme, Westport Textiles, and Chipboard Ltd were among the first to set up, drawn by generous state grants to open their operations. For a time, the results seemed very successful: during the first half of the 1960s, outputs, employment, productivity, and exports all grew.[23] Between 1959 and 1963, total exports increased at a rate of 9 per cent a year, while the rate of increase for industrial exports was 13 per cent. This meant that in 1964, industrial goods accounted for almost 25 per cent of total export value; in the early 1950s, the figure had been around

[18] J. J. Lee, *Ireland: Politics and Society 1912–85* (Cambridge, 1989), 373.

[19] J. J. Lee, *Ireland,* 344; Cormac Ó'Gráda, *A Rocky Road: The Irish Economy since the 1920s* (Manchester, 1997), 29.

[20] Ó'Gráda, *A Rocky Road,* 52.

[21] Kieran Kennedy and Brendan Dowling, *Economic Growth in Ireland: the Experience since 1947* (Dublin, 1975), 11.

[22] Ó'Gráda, *A Rocky Road,* 46.

[23] Ó'Gráda, *A Rocky Road,* 114.

6 per cent.[24] Indeed, by 1973, overseas firms accounted for almost one third of all employment in manufacturing.[25]

These changes combined with a buoyant global economy, and a new sense of confidence caused by the new leadership of Seán Lemass (1959–66), to create a tangible shift in the country's fortunes.[26] Indeed, Lemass's own leadership style and mentality have often been credited with playing an important role in ushering in a new era: J. J. Lee described his governing style as a 'combination of functional ruthlessness with ideological magnanimity... energy, efficiency, even impetuosity'.[27] During the period from 1959 to 1964, GDP growth averaged 4 per cent, ownership of cars and consumer goods rose, and emigration was lower than at any time since independence. However, the changes of Lemass's premiership are understood not only to have remained confined to the economic sphere; during the 1960s, the cultural ethos of the country also underwent noticeable shifts. The totems invoked in support of this view include Ireland's announcement of its intention to apply for EEC membership in 1961, the launch of Télefis Éireann at the end of that year, and a new generation, born since the revolution, entering public life. These internal shifts were reinforced by an international sense of optimism and the ethos of the Second Vatican Council.[28] This combination of social, economic, and cultural change has led many historians to see the epoch as crucial to the evolution of the state: F. S. L. Lyons wrote of the situation in Ireland being 'transformed' in the years 1957 to 1961; John Whyte characterized it as an 'axial' period in the country's development; and Fergal Tobin, writing in 1984, viewed the 1960s as 'the best of decades', seeing prosperity and affluence as providing the material and psychological basis for national recovery.[29]

However, the improvements in the country's economic fortunes began to falter from the mid-1960s. In 1964, there was a sharp rise in prices and deterioration in the balance of payments, while in 1965, the rate of growth of GNP fell to 2.5 per cent, with this being accompanied by a widening of the trade deficit to £45 million.[30] In a seeming retrenchment of economic policy in the same year, there was a tightening of bank credit,

[24] Paul Bew and Henry Patterson, *Sean Lemass and the Making of Modern Ireland 1945–66* (Dublin, 1982), 172.

[25] Ó'Gráda, *A Rocky Road,* 113–14.

[26] Ó'Gráda, *A Rocky Road,* 29.

[27] J. J. Lee, *Ireland,* 372.

[28] Fergal Tobin, *The Best of Decades: Ireland in the Nineteen Sixties* (Dublin, 1984), 60.

[29] F. S. L. Lyons, *Ireland since the Famine* (London, 1985), 582; John Whyte, 'Economic Progress and Political Pragmatism, 1957–63', in Jacqueline Hill (ed.), *A New History of Ireland VII: Ireland 1921–84* (Oxford, 2003), 294; Tobin, *The Best of Decades*, 4–5.

[30] Bew and Patterson, *Sean Lemass*, 172.

a cut in the public capital programme, price controls, and import levies.[31] In 1967, the Second Programme for Economic Expansion, which had been introduced in 1963, was abandoned, with its targets far from fulfilled. Reflecting this stalling of the country's economic fortunes, some of the projects that had been so heavily invested in during the early 1960s collapsed in the latter part of the decade; in 1968, Potez closed without producing a single airplane, despite governmental subsidies, and the Verolme dockyard in Cork also shut, after having been in operation for only a short time.[32]

Despite the promise of the early years of the decade, Jack Lynch (1966–73) presided over a much more economically troubled and politically volatile period than that of his predecessor. The latter part of the 1960s was characterized not only by economic turbulence but a surge of associated civil unrest. Protests regarding housing shortages, unemployment, and the future of the Gaeltacht graphically revealed the extent to which modernization had been circumscribed in its benefits and contested in its aims. Taca, a Fianna Fáil fundraising organization which institutionalized informal links between the party and property developers, was popularly perceived to be indicative of the mutually beneficial nexus of capital and power in the upper echelons of Irish society. In the North, housing protests and student demonstrations slowly led to the re-emergence of violence, which often threatened to spread to the southern state. Indeed, the Arms Crisis, when two high-profile government ministers, Minister for Finance Charles Haughey and Minister for Agriculture Neil Blaney, attempted to import arms for the IRA, and a third—Minister for Local Government, Kevin Boland—resigned in support, was a major constitutional crisis, and revealed the destabilizing impact of northern violence on southern politics. The changes and upheavals which had occurred within Irish society over the preceding decade allowed Terence Brown to describe the mood of Ireland in the 1970s as something very different to that envisaged less than a quarter of a century before, 'that ebullient, vigorous, modernizing society in quest of affluence and success, where real opportunities exist[ed] for the adventurous and energetic, a society disinclined to view poverty as anything but self-inflicted, brash, ostentatious, and not a little callous'.[33] Similarly, in 1988, Joe Lee stated that, owing to the combined weight of the Troubles, corruption, urbanization, and revisionism, during the 1970s there had been a fundamental

[31] Bew and Patterson, *Sean Lemass*.

[32] O'Grada, *A Rocky Road,* 113–14.

[33] Terence Brown, *Ireland: A Social and Cultural History 1922–2002* (London, 2004), 266.

breakdown in the discourses which had sustained the state since its foundation, and that 'no alternative self-portrait…emerge[d] to command comparable conviction'.[34]

Much recent work has been concerned with the question of Irish modernity in the period since independence. Most commentators have seen the arrival of 'modern' Ireland as occurring between the economic reforms of the late 1950s and the accession to the EEC in January 1973, and have pointed to the dialogue between ideas of modernity and tradition between those two dates. In a particularly rich account, Patrick O'Mahony and Gerald Delanty have described Irish culture in the latter years of the twentieth century as consisting of, 'hesitant enclaves of modern values within the traditional, anti-modern order', which 'later began to take its present form with modern values in the ascendant but compromised by the power of tradition'.[35] More recently, Enda Delaney has sought to explore 'who were the "brokers" of this "new" modernity' during the 1960s, where 'the sources of social power and lines of authority rest[ed] in post-war Ireland', suggesting that 'subaltern groups drove on social and cultural change in post-war Ireland, often credited as being the unique achievement of the tiny university-educated liberal middle-class elite'.[36] Dublin's planning controversies have already attracted some interest from geographers and cultural theorists, who—building on the pioneering investigative journalism of Frank McDonald—have sought to read Ireland's move towards modernity through urban change in Dublin in the 1960s.[37] Andrew Kincaid has argued that the destruction of the Georgian city and its rapid replacement with ersatz modern buildings represented the rejection of the national ideals of the founders of the state and an embracing of the international sphere. Indeed, he has argued that the construction projects of the 1960s were the spatial concomitants of the intellectual project of historical revisionism. In Ireland, the term 'revisionism' usually applied to a diverse set of historical ideas, spanning works from the medieval period to the present day, but particularly focused on the nationalist movements of the later nineteenth and early twentieth centuries, which have been united by their attempt to interrogate the inherited narratives of the Irish past. This process gained momentum

[34] Lee, *Ireland,* 653.

[35] Patrick O'Mahony and Gerald Delanty, *Rethinking Irish History: Nationalism, Identity and Ideology* (London, 1998), 167.

[36] Enda Delaney, 'Modernity, the Past, and Politics in Post War Ireland', in Thomas Hachey (ed.), *Turning Points in Twentieth Century Irish History* (Dublin, 2011), 103.

[37] Kevin Kearns, *Georgian Dublin: Ireland's Imperilled Architectural Heritage* (Newton Abbott, 1983); Frank McDonald, *The Destruction of Dublin* (Dublin, 1985); Andrew Kincaid, *Postcolonial Dublin: Imperial Legacies and the Built Environment,* (London, 2006).

during the 1960s as Dublin's skyline evolved; in *Postcolonial Dublin*, Kincaid argues that 'the rewriting of history that was required to naturalise the economic and cultural transition of the 1960s found its spatial manifestation in the flat, rational and concrete structures of international modernism'.[38] Similarly, Hugh Campbell has described the modern architecture of the 1960s as indicative of a new ideology of progress and rationalism in Irish life.[39]

This analysis of the movement from a 'traditional' to a 'modern' Ireland, with the form and tone of the latter inspired by the rhetoric of architectural modernism, is complicated by a close reading of urban change. Rather, this book attempts to map a distinctive Irish urban modernity, and track its emergence through the 1960s. As I explore below, this modernity took its form in relation to several related factors. The evolution of the built form of Dublin during the 1960s was constituted with reference both to international trends in urban modernization and changes within Ireland's economy. However, the clientelism of the state institutions, government, and the professions, combined with local government's bureaucratic inability to direct changes to the city, and its willingness to outsource urban regeneration to private speculators, meant that the project of physical change was always contingent, fragmented, and partial. Moreover, interpretations of Irish modernity to date have not explored fully the problems of the complex and shifting intersections of notions of 'Irish' and 'British', 'future' and 'past', and 'authentic' and 'inauthentic', categories which were often implicit in discursive constructions of the modern state, and which were exposed and debated in controversies surrounding the historic city. In contrast with Kincaid, I see the spatial transformations of the 1960s as far too complex to be understood simply as the physical manifestation of 'revisionism': indeed, the conjunction of the languages of tradition, bureaucratic mechanisms, and international architectural discourses not only evolved as the decade progressed but also aligned differently in the city's different spaces.

In many respects, the transformation of Dublin reflected an international narrative of mid-twentieth-century urban change. A key feature of the evolution of the city was the proliferation of purpose-built office accommodation in the central area. Between January 1960 and December 1970, eighty office blocks were commenced or completed in Dublin, while purpose-built office space in the city increased by 1,570,515 square

[38] Kincaid, *Postcolonial Dublin*, 163–71.

[39] Hugh Campbell, 'Modern Architecture and National Identity in Ireland', in Joe Cleary and Claire Connolly (eds.), *Cambridge Companion to Modern Irish Culture* (Cambridge, 2005), 297.

feet.[40] This reflected the shift in the country's economic profile, which had led to a particular expansion in the service sector and the civil service, and provided a seemingly insatiable demand for office space. Moreover, an unforeseen consequence of trade liberalization was Dublin's entry into a transnational world of financial speculation based on square footage and land prices, where office buildings served as little more than commodities to be bet on and traded; indeed, Frank McDonald has shown how Harold Wilson's 1964 curtailment of office construction in central London led many names associated with that city's office boom, including Harry Hyams, to invest in Irish land.[41] The process of reorientation of the city centre towards commerce, bureaucracy, and international capitalism was accompanied by a rapid increase in vehicular traffic in the city. In 1961, as part of the Karl-Heinz Schaechterle investigations, traffic flow was measured at seventy-three points around the city over a twelve-hour period, the same exercise being subsequently repeated in 1971. While the number of bicycles had dropped by 80 per cent, from 166,000 to 34,000, the number of cars had risen by 111 per cent, from 317,000 to 669,000.[42] In response to increasing car ownership, there was a new focus on transport infrastructure in central and local government. Plans were drawn up and set in train, by experts including Karl-Heinz Schaechterle and the Travers Morgan Partnership, for a series of circumferential motorways encircling the inner city.

The evolution of the social and economic profile of the city was paralleled by changes in tandem at the outskirts of the city. As emigration decreased during the 1960s, inward migration brought people from the countryside to the city, leading to an increase in the population of the county from 718,332 to 852,219 between the censuses of 1961 and 1971. However, this national centripetal tendency was matched by urban centrifugal forces, as slum clearance, suburbanization, and the increasing commercialization of the core resulted in a decline in the population of the city within the canals from 227,613 to 195,840 over the same period.[43] This increase in population of the county, alongside the decrease in residential units in the city centre, created a high demand for additional housing units on the periphery. Large areas of land around the city were requisitioned by Dublin County Council for the construction of

40 Patrick Malone, *Office Development in Dublin 1960–90* (Dublin, 1990), 2.

41 McDonald, *The Destruction of Dublin*, 105.

42 Dublin Corporation, 'Report of the Deputy City Manager and Town Clerk with Reference to Traffic Growth–Dublin City 1961 to 1971', *Reports of Dublin Corporation 1971* (Dublin, 1972), 851.

43 Data from censuses published by Central Statistics Offices available at <http://www.cso.ie> (accessed 9 August 2009).

two-storey cottage developments. While areas at locations including Ballyfermot, Finglas, and Artane had been in construction since the 1950s, the pace and scale of the suburbanization increased rapidly after the 1966 publication of the Myles Wright Report. This scheme created an outline for four new towns to the west of the city, at Tallaght, Blanchardstown, Clondalkin, and Lucan, the decentralization of industry and services to these new nodes, and a system of motorways to link these diffused urban areas.

However, while central and local government had considerable control over the nature of developments on the virgin lands in the hinterlands of the city, it had much less ability to control the development of the city centre. An established bureaucratic mechanism for the contestation of planning decisions was instituted only after the Local Government (Planning and Development) Act came into force in October 1964, while a list of structures requiring preservation or protection was formalized only in 1971. Although reports and plans were commissioned and produced regarding the regulation of Dublin's built environment, they had little traction in shaping the city. Thus the state's role in refashioning the centre of the city was circumscribed; it tended to retreat from taking a leading role in guiding the reconstruction of the capital, preferring instead to defer renewal to private interests. Even after the introduction of limited statist controls, the regulations were frequently broken or disregarded; one northern commentator observed 'a streak of anarchy' in southern society regarding planning laws: 'a common attitude towards law and authority...a combination of a disregard for the rules by some, and a resigned acceptance by the others that the rules will not be enforced'.[44] There was, therefore, a wide divergence between the bureaucratic regulation of the urban environment as recommended in planning documents and the actual changes taking place to Dublin's streets.[45] Indeed, the area where local government had most influence over the built form of the central city was not positive planning initiatives, but was instead with regard to slum clearance, dangerous buildings operations, and traffic planning, which, during this decade, were primarily destructive in impact, and resulted in cleared sites, surface car parks, and planning blight.

[44] *Fortnight*, 30 November 1973, 8.

[45] Myles Wright, *Advisory Regional Plan and Final Report: The Dublin Region* (Dublin, 1965); Colin Buchanan, *Regional Development in Ireland* (Dublin, 1969); Charles Abrams, *Urban Renewal Project in Ireland (Dublin)* (New York, 1961); 'Report of the Planning and Development Committee: With Further Reference to the North Central Area Redevelopment Scheme', *Reports and Printed Documents of Dublin Corporation 1964* (Dublin, 1964), 420.

The limited power of the state meant that the physical evolution of the city was particularly shaped by informal influence. Irish political culture was characterized by the intimacy of elites, informal networks, and clientelism, and these attributes also became part of the city's planning and development. Private speculators were able to acquire prime development land, while planning legislation was also geared towards private funding for urban renewal. Through these channels they played a crucial role in shaping the landscape of the city, as proposed developments were rarely prevented or challenged. These individuals tended to have little interest in the social or aesthetic connotations of 'urban renewal'; rather, their overwhelming interest was in maximizing returns from land prices. This ultimately meant the construction of large office blocks in areas of the city that were already prosperous, only increasing the social differentiation of the city; indeed, the critical mass of new speculative offices were constructed in the axis between St Stephen's Green and Ballsbridge, while sites in the north and east of the city, cleared of buildings through slum clearance or dangerous buildings operations, remained unused. In recent years, similar relationships between politicians, planners, and developers have enabled the unscrupulous and well connected to make vast sums of money from land and property. However, the unsustainable and artificial property bubble that this created during the early years of the new century has also led to an economic crash, the takeover of many of these now worthless properties by the government through the National Asset Management Agency, and the return of emigration and high unemployment.

In 1966, when Nelson's Pillar, which had dominated the vista up O'Connell Street for over a hundred years, was first damaged by a paramilitary bomb and then completely removed by the Irish Army, the continuing symbolic power of the historic environment dominated headlines. But it was not just statuary which still contained unstable memories and meanings. Indeed, just as the state was undergoing a project of modernization centred on a liberalizing economic policy, and the removal of an actively Gaelicizing cultural policy, Dublin witnessed a long-running controversy regarding the cultural provenance of its eighteenth-century buildings, which was seemingly at variance with ideas of the period as a time of increasing cultural plurality. The demolition of eighteenth-century streetscapes was often described as the 'reconquest' of the city which had once been the nucleus of British rule, while the historic city's cultural origin was considered key by both those in favour of reconstruction and preservation in determining its worth. This elision of urban modernization, office building, and the totemic 'de-Anglicization of Ireland', revealed the continued centrality of constructions of the colonial past to Irish modernity. However, this anti-colonial language was not an anachronistic throwback, but was rather inherent to the project of modernization. When modern architecture and town planning finally began to make a noticeable impact on the landscape of Dublin during the later 1950s, it was allied to an economic project of national renewal led by Lemass. The extant terraces of the capital, which had gone through multiple owners and uses since their construction in the eighteenth century, were now diagnosed by current theories of architecture and conservation as the relict remains of the eighteenth century. As such, they symbolized Britain's colonial rule in Ireland, and were in need of replacing with the modern structures of Ireland's new economic project. Post-colonial politics and architectural theory combined in the construction press and debates among architects; not only were the buildings said to be unsuited to Dublin's new status as capital of an independent state and centre of Ireland's economy, but they were not an 'authentic' part of Ireland's cultural heritage, and as such were not worth preservation.[46]

However, from the mid-1960s, the consensus which surrounded this reading of Dublin's modernity began to fracture. This must be understood within the context of the international evolution of architectural theory, which began to emphasize the conservation of larger urban areas for their 'character', and to retain the communities who resided in these places. The new valorization of the landscape of the city allowed for the performance of more diverse narratives in the urban environment than the simple reification of the national story. The city's past, present, and future became an explosive arena of debate, and resulted in demonstrations, occupations, and accusations of corruption, which often dominated the headlines and brought a wide variety of interest groups into coalition. Preservationism tended to attract a disparate set of adherents, characterized by the notable membership of those who were—or saw themselves as—on the margins of society, such as liberals, sexual dissidents, republicans, and socialists. Architectural preservationists marched against the demolitions; republican-socialists campaigned against the displacement of working-class communities; anti-capitalist students, influenced by the global climate of revolt, squatted buildings to prevent them being turned into office blocks; while gentrifiers moved back into the city, purchasing former tenements, and restoring them with brightly coloured wallpaper and furniture from flea markets. David Ley has described gentrification as 'an expression of a critical cultural politics, a rejection of the suburbs and their perceived cultural conformity in favour of the more cosmopolitan

[46] Colin Graham, '"Blame it on Maureen O'Hara": Ireland and the Trope of Authenticity', *Cultural Studies* 15/1 (2001), 60.

and permissive opportunities of the central city'.[47] For all of the people who moved to the Gardiner area in the 1960s and 1970s, preservationism also took on personal significances: in moving to the city centre and becoming involved in social movements, they could find a personal sense of liberation through collective action or anonymity, which the Irish suburb and countryside lacked. Student squatters in Hume Street saw themselves as part of a global movement of students, and sought both to preserve buildings and create a new, radical way of life inside their protest. Similarly, the 'frontiersmen' of the Irish Georgian Society (IGS) who moved to Mountjoy Square and the surrounding area were also characterized by a liberalism and individualism at odds with the dominant culture of the state. Indeed, preservation of North Great George's Street became known as a gay area of the city, in particular after gay rights activist David Norris moved to the street in 1978.

These urban protests were also explicitly political. The growing perception throughout the decade of a nexus of elitism, clientelism, incompetence, and bureaucracy within the state gave the impression that the city was no longer being controlled or cared for in the best interests of its environment or its citizens. Activists used their interventions into the city as a way of articulating their discontent with the nature of independence: housing campaigners and anti-capitalist students were united by rhetoric which accused the government of running the independent state for the benefit of a small group of people, while the majority saw little of the prosperity that modernization was supposed to bring. Whereas, only a decade before, architectural aesthetics and notions of value had been divided between ideas of 'Irish' and 'British' culture, these themes were now overlaid by understandings of the 'vernacular', 'handmade', and 'authentic' nature of extant culture broadly defined, and now contrasted with the globalizing and homogenizing impact of modernization. Moreover, many preservationists also used the city to voice their rejection of the state-sponsored teleology of Ireland's history. In protecting sites which had not been designated as part of the national heritage by the state, these groups were able to invest the cityscape with alternative conceptions of the Irish nation and the Irish past. These sidelined histories played a fundamental role in their vision for the future of the city, and were explicitly articulated in the manner in which they preserved and used the eighteenth-century built environment. The city, caught between multiple conceptions of modernization and tradition, became a forum where the

[47] David Ley, *The New Middle Class and the Remaking of the Central City* (Oxford, 1996), 4.

anxieties and opportunities of Irish life in the 1960s were exposed and debated, and where alternative modernities were explored. Indeed, the unstable meaning of the city streets, which had never been co-opted into the narrative of the nation or represented a unified cultural inheritance, were expropriated by a variety of groups who were able to implant their own meaning on the spaces. Thus the destruction of the city led many to question the truisms of Irish history and to publicly interrogate accepted historical narratives. The city's spaces simultaneously embodied a palimpsest of pasts, and discussion of its future therefore created a debate surrounding this history of the capital—and nation—which was far more complex than that articulated through state-led discourse. Thus the physical modernization of Dublin took place at the nexus of competing demands of change and conservation, and was a key part of the creation of a plural, diverse, modern Ireland.

This book focuses on five preservationist battles regarding eighteenth-century red brick terrace streets which took place in the city within the Grand and Royal Canals during the 1950s and 1960s. In so doing, it reflects how narratives of the city were being constructed by conservationists, developers, and the media. Speculators—the principal drivers of Dublin's modernization—acquired pieces of land for new edifices, while giving little consideration to the coherence of the urban fabric or the new building's relationship to its environment. Preservationists launched flagship 'battles' for important landmarks. Newspapers reported the story of the city's evolution through tightly focused narratives based primarily on these stand-offs between developer, preservationists, and residents. Thus the 'preservationist battle', which was a key feature of the rise of conservation across Europe and North America, was not only a product of how the city was represented but also indicated how representations of the city played a fundamental role in constituting the evolution of the city.[48]

The period under scrutiny is the long 1960s, defined by the tenure of Fianna Fáil in government from 1957 until 1973. This by no means is an exhaustive study of the development of 'heritage' in Dublin in the post-war period. Indeed, the foundation of An Taisce in 1948, a voluntary organization modelled on Scotland's National Trust, dedicated to the preservation of Ireland's built and natural heritage, alongside the controversies regarding the Civic Offices in Wood Quay, the roads through the Liberties, and the demolition of Molesworth Hall during the 1970s all lie

[48] Maria Balshaw and Liam Kennedy, 'Introduction: Urban Space and Representation', in Maria Balshaw and Liam Kennedy (eds.), *Urban Space and Representation* (London, 2000), 1–21.

outside the scope of this study. However, in many ways the 1970s presented a very different legislative and political context. In 1971 Dublin received its first town plan, which institutionalized a policy towards Dublin's historic streets and listed sites for preservation; in 1972 Ireland entered the EEC, bringing Irish heritage policy into a wider European framework; the 1973 Planning Act stipulated the setting up of An Bord Pleanála, in an attempt to remove planning from the jurisdiction of politicians; and in 1975, European Architectural Heritage Year, the Irish Architectural Archive was set up to record and document buildings of historic worth. Related to these domestic shifts, urbanism was also going through a global crisis of both ideology and capital; by the mid-1970s, because of the collapse in the property market and the rise of townscape planning, the era of planners' belief in comprehensive redevelopment as a solution to all urban ills was largely over. Rather, this study concentrates on a close reading of urban change in the 1960s in order to facilitate an examination of the evolution of notions of urban heritage from the foundation of the IGS until the introduction of a formal listing procedure as part of the first Dublin development plan in 1971. A focus on this decade also allows for a critical examination of the crucial shifts which took place in Irish mentalities and cultural politics during this period.

The first two chapters focus on the state and the architectural profession's understanding of the future of the city. Chapter 1 begins by narrating the history of the city from the seventeenth to the twentieth century. It goes on to assess the state's vision for the city from the late 1950s to the early 1970s, and considers how ideology was made visible through bureaucratically imposed town plans. As has been frequently shown, 'the plan of a city is bound up with the politics of power and identity'.[49] Through an assessment of state planning from the Second World War until the 1970s, how power functioned through the bureaucratic regulation of the city, in order to create an urban environment which was Christian, Gaelic, and market-led, is explored. In doing so, however, there was a deficit in planning for the city centre, which was fundamental to the area becoming a site of conflict between the government, private finance, and civil society regarding the area's future. Chapter 2 examines the architectural community's visions for the future of Dublin from the 1950s to the mid-1960s, showing the optimism and radicalism of much architectural opinion at this time, and how the profession was actively engaged with international developments regarding the future of modernism. In so doing, it considers how discourses of the 'Georgian' were used,

[49] Yvonne Whelan, *Reinventing Modern Dublin: Streetscape, Iconography and the Politics of Identity* (Dublin, 2003), 22.

exploring how Irish architecture was often framed in direct contradistinction to neo-classical or eighteenth-century architecture. These ideas, emanating both from the state and architectural profession, coalesced to create an atmosphere where there was little desire or will to preserve the eighteenth-century core.

The following two chapters examine the early development of a preservationist movement. Chapter 3 first studies the debates which surrounded the future of the Royal Hospital Kilmainham in the mid-1950s, then goes on to discuss the first high-profile controversy regarding the destruction of a vernacular Georgian building in Kildare Place, and the resulting formation of the IGS. This group was initially dominated by the former Ascendancy, and throughout the 1960s was instrumental in efforts to preserve the city, through this medium retaining the cultural life of a sidelined and deposed minority community. Chapter 4 then considers the reconstruction of the longest Georgian street in Europe, which was prospected in the early 1960s, and resulted in a long-running debate regarding the relationship between modern architecture and national identity, drawing in such international figures as Walter Gropius, John Summerson, and Albert Richardson. The chapter shows how the ideas debated in abstract in the 1950s took on a concrete reality in the early years of the 1960s: modernism became the form through which a new nationalism, eliding economic progress with traditional motifs, was articulated. Accordingly, the extant city was constructed as the legacy of a foreign, colonial elite.

The final chapters deal in detail with how reconstruction of the central area was resisted and subverted during the later 1960s, when preservationism received much media attention and widespread support. Chapter 5 analyses the politics of city centre housing. It examines the crisis which followed housing collapses in June 1963 and how, throughout the decade, the loss of city communities was eulogized by middle-class commentators and studied by sociologists. It then goes on to assess how the campaign of the Dublin Housing Action Committee later in the decade sought to preserve working-class accommodation in the city, invoking nostalgia for the communal life of the tenements to raise support for republican socialism. Chapter 6 discusses efforts to preserve the former Gardiner area of the north city. Focusing on the IGS's campaign in Mountjoy Square, Harold Clarke's home in North Great George's Street, and Uinseann MacEoin's properties in Henrietta Street, it shows how these new residents viewed this area almost as a 'terra nullis', where those who saw themselves as outside state-led national life could articulate dissonant personal and political identities. This functioned through collection and display of material culture, naming, and the uses of the preserved buildings.

However, the commodification of buildings which had long been working-class accommodation sometimes led them into conflict with the local resident population. Chapter 7 narrates the story of a group of students who, motivated by anti-capitalism and the global climate of revolt, squatted Georgian buildings for six months in 1970 to secure their preservation, failing in their aim but finding a new sense of liberation and their place within a global youth movement. Their justification for the preservation of the houses, not because of their intrinsic worth but as part of a broader campaign to retain the customs and cultures of Dublin city, captured the public mood, and engaged with a widespread disaffection with the broader project of modernization. For the first time, a conservation battle attracted massive media attention and popular support. The battle for the future of Dublin was not won by preservationists in 1970, but the protest at Hume Street marked a turning point in how the future of the city was conceived.

1

Planning and the Eighteenth-Century City, 1955–75

In the 1950s Dublin seemed pervaded by gloom. For the city's writers and visitors it coated everything in a decrepit charm; in the half-light the glimpse of crumbling ironwork and decaying brick was evocative of a previous age. However, this depression and dereliction represented something very different for those who lived in the city: it presented a very visible reminder that the profound social problems the state had faced upon independence were still largely unremedied. Moreover, as the administrative capital of the new state, the city did not project an image of a successful polity. From the 1920s there were efforts to deal with these issues; politicians and experts began to plan for a new capital which would both articulate the power, prestige, and identity of the new state and successfully house its citizens. During the 1960s, these visions of Dublin's future took on a new potency and precision, owing to the introduction of the tools and approaches of an international scientific town planning.

Dublin has been shaped by its location as a nexus point of British, Irish, and European culture (Map 1.1). The original medieval walled city was centred on Christchurch Cathedral on the southern bank of the Liffey, and for a long time after its foundation the city remained a small settlement; as Maurice Craig memorably records, at the beginning of the seventeenth century the population was less than 9,000, the total area was one-ninth of a square mile, and the city had little political importance.[1] However, from the arrival of James, Duke of Ormond as Viceroy in 1662, the city began to expand and, alongside this growth, its nucleus began to move eastwards. In 1592, Trinity College was founded on land acquired in the dissolution of All Saints' Priory to the east of the city, and in the mid-seventeenth century the Irish Parliament also met nearby. Following these institutions, aristocratic families also began to build houses around Hoggen Green (now College Green).

[1] Maurice Craig, *Dublin 1660–1860* (first published 1949; rev. edn Dublin, 1980), 4–5.

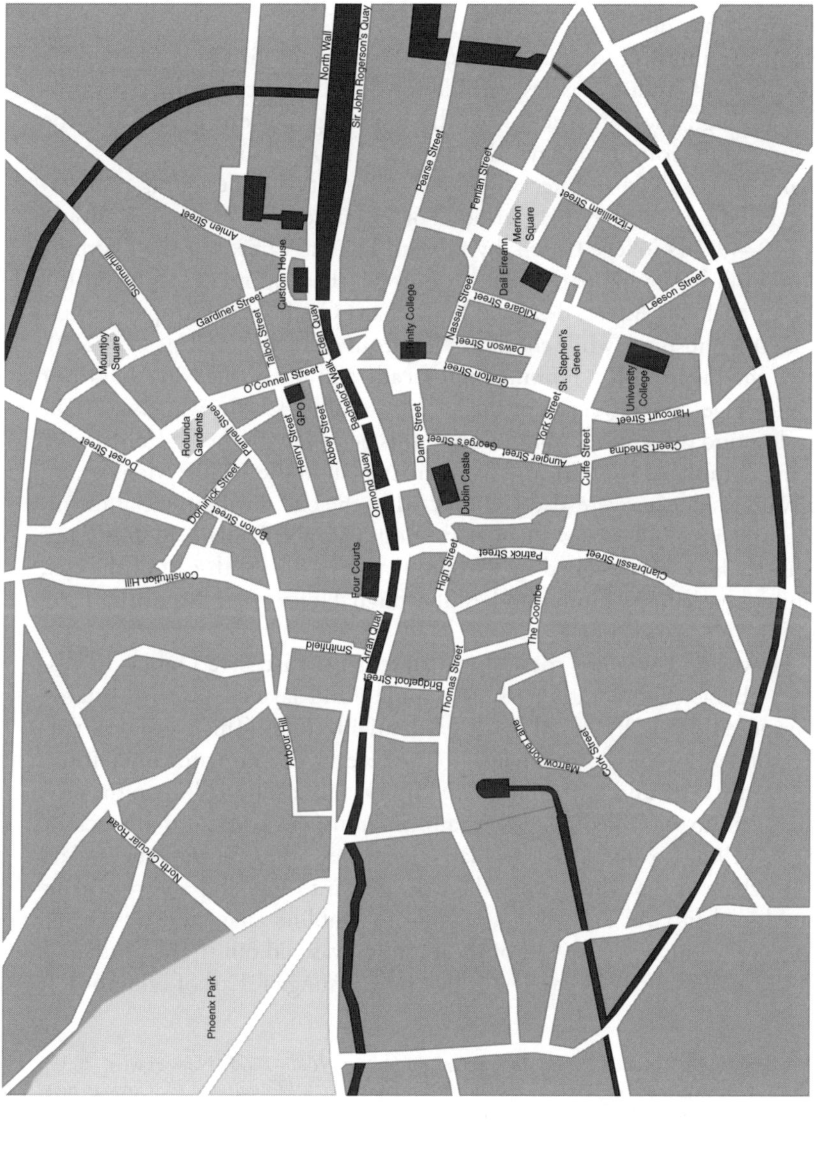

Map 1.1. Map of Dublin.

During the eighteenth century, the population of Dublin doubled from 100,000 to 200,000.[2] Prosperity also led to a prodigious rate of building. This included almost all the monumental public edifices which define the axes of the city to the present day; indeed, one architectural historian has described the buildings of this period as 'the triumph of elegance': almost a military assault of taste.[3] More than any other architect, James Gandon was responsible for this revolution in the city's profile, through the construction of the imposing Custom House and the Four Courts on the quays during the 1780s.[4] However, there were many other skilled architects working in the city and designing pioneering buildings during this period. For example, the Parliament House (1729–39) in College Green, by Edward Lovett Pearce, was the first purpose-built bicameral parliament in Europe; the Rotunda Hospital at the top of Sackville Street, designed by Richard Castle, was Europe's earliest maternity hospital; while the large west front of Trinity College (1752–9), gave the institution a monumental façade still unequalled in Oxford or Cambridge. The residence of the Viceroy, Dublin Castle, was also rebuilt in slow and piecemeal fashion during this period, with the Bedford Tower being completed in 1761 and St Patrick's Hall in the 1780s. Many grand private residences were also constructed in the city during the eighteenth century; in 1745 James Fitzgerald commissioned Kildare House (later Leinster House), designed by Richard Castle in the south-east of the city, while Charlemont House and Aldborough House were begun in 1763 and in 1792 respectively.[5]

However, it was not these grand statements that gave Dublin its distinct character, but rather its overlapping and layered planned estates, composed primarily of red-brick residential terraces. This piecemeal pattern of development arose thanks to the absence of a monarch or an interventionist state and so the failure to impose a totalizing vision on the city; this vacuum was filled instead by a prosperous and audacious aristocratic class, willing to invest in speculative ventures. These entrepreneurs laid out urban forms which were then divided into lots and sold on to be developed in twos and threes, leading to Dublin's characteristic uneven streets and squares. The first of these estates was laid out to the south-east of the medieval city in the 1670s by Francis Aungier, Earl of Longford. It

[2] Edward McParland, *Public Architecture in Ireland, 1680–1760* (New Haven, 2001); Christine Casey, *Dublin: The City within the Grand and Royal Canals and the Circular Road including the Phoenix Park* (London, 2005), 44; Peter Somerville-Large, *Dublin: The Fair City* (London, 1979); Desmond Guinness, *Portrait of Dublin* (Dublin, 1969).

[3] Somerville-Large, *Dublin*, 152.

[4] Craig, *Dublin*, 236–58.

[5] Craig, *Dublin*, 33–4.

centred on the 70ft wide Aungier Street, which subsequently became the principal entrance to the city from the south. Following his example, the Corporation also began its own urban development schemes. In 1664 it annexed 60 acres of grazing land to the east of the Aungier estate and laid out St Stephen's Green, the earliest and largest of Dublin's residential squares, with ninety-six freehold plots being set around the central park. In this period it also laid out Smithfield market-place, Essex Bridge, Ormond Bridge, and Capel Street. These constructions were matched by other ambitious civic schemes, including the reclamation of land north and south of the river to the east of the city centre, and the creation of the 2,000 acre Phoenix Park by Ormond in 1662.[6]

However, it is the Gardiner and Fitzwilliam Estates, facing each other on the north and south sides of the river, which came to define the aesthetic of the city. While they are in many ways similar to each other, they also have different characters formed by their distinctive spatial structures and histories since their erection. Niall McCullough described the Gardiner estate as 'an estate made by negotiation and agreement on land bought up in segments rather than owned for centuries; thus interrupted by other land holdings, it consists of several urban set-pieces made without reference to one another... of the two it is older, larger, looser—and more dynamically original in scale and vision. It is also more truly in the Dublin tradition.'[7] It was begun by Luke Gardiner, who acquired several landholdings in the north of the city in the early years of the eighteenth century. He focused on catering for aristocratic housing: his first venture, Henrietta Street, was intended as a prime quarter.[8] His descendants continued his grand ambition; the estate's most impressive residential set piece was Sackville Street (now O'Connell Street) laid out from 1749, 150ft wide with a central tree-lined avenue flanked by a pair of carriageways.[9] Later in the century, the Gardiner surveyors also set out Mountjoy Square (1792–1818), and linked it via Gardiner Street to the new Custom House. On the south side of the Liffey, the Fitzwilliam Estate developed from the mid-eighteenth century. Its starting point was Merrion Street, begun in the 1750s, and continued by the first set piece, Merrion Square, which was laid out from 1762. From here the estate spread ever south and eastwards, forming Pembroke Street, Fitzwilliam Square, and Herbert Street. This eighteenth-century grid was imposed on top of the existing medieval radial routes out of the city—Baggot Street, Denzille

[6] Craig, *Dublin*, 22–6.
[7] Niall McCullough, *Dublin: An Urban History* (Dublin, 2007), 114.
[8] McCullough, *Dublin*, 114.
[9] Casey, *Dublin*, 43.

Street, and Leeson Street—which disrupted the plan and brought the area into conversation with the overall structure of the city.[10]

Alongside these speculators whose designs for the city were led largely by profit motives, the Corporation of Dublin aimed to rationalize the growing urban form. From 1763 the North and South Circular Roads were laid out, confining Dublin into an oval shape of about 12 square miles and providing 'a strongly articulated framework around the eighteenth century city'.[11] This shape was reinforced when the two canals, the Grand on the south and the Royal on the north, were also brought around the city, parallel with the circular roads, during the 1790s.[12] Best known, however, are the 'Commissioners for Making Wide and Convenient Streets', who were empowered to purchase land by compulsion, and from the 1760s created and widened many of the most important streets in the city. This included widening and extending Dame Street to link Trinity College with Dublin Castle and Christchurch; the construction of Westmoreland and D'Olier Streets; and the extension of Sackville Street to the river.[13] The combination of these monumental edifices, linked by these grand boulevards, created a city which expressed in its buildings and its spaces the power of its ruling Protestant elite; Dame Street, for example, linked Trinity College, the castle, and Christchurch Cathedral, the intellectual, administrative, and spiritual institutions of state. Similarly, the street names—Westmoreland, Fitzwilliam, Hume, Gardiner, Merrion—spoke of the wealth and authority of the Anglo-Irish landowners.

The nineteenth century has been characterized as a time of 'stasis', in comparison with the monumental schemes of the previous century; however, this contrast has certainly been overstated. Indeed, there were some impressive constructions dating from after the Act of Union.[14] Residential building near the canals, including much of the Fitzwilliam Estate, continued in the flat-fronted style of the previous century. However, monumental public buildings, including the Museum Building in Trinity College by Deane and Woodward, the National Library and Science and Art Museums which surrounded Leinster House, the South City Markets, and the major railway stations, were all built in the more ebullient style of the Victorian era. Large areas of red-brick suburban housing were also constructed in townships, including Drumcondra, Rathmines, and

[10] Craig, *Dublin*, 187–91.
[11] McCullough, *Dublin*, 145; Craig, *Dublin*, 192.
[12] Craig, *Dublin*, 193.
[13] Craig, *Dublin*, 173; Casey, *Dublin*, 42.
[14] Hugh Campbell, 'The Emergence of Modern Dublin: Reality and Representation', *Architectural Research Quarterly* 2 (Summer 1997), 44–53; Mary Daly, *Dublin, the Deposed Capital: A Social and Economic History 1860–1914* (Cork, 1984), 1–17.

Clontarf.[15] However, the long-term impact of the nineteenth century was as much in the problems that were sown as the constructions that were completed. The prosperous elites upon whose wealth Dublin was built retreated from the city, meaning that many of the eighteenth-century townhouses were subdivided into tenements and became the backdrop to some of the worst slums in Europe. Most notably, the Gardiner Estate was broken up and sold on piecemeal to individual buyers; the loss of unified ownership marked the end of centralized management and led to the area's rapid social decline.[16] This was in marked contrast to the Fitzwilliam estate which remained in unified ownership, becoming the most consistently prosperous enclave within the canals district throughout the nineteenth and twentieth centuries.

In the years after independence, Corporation building was concentrated on reconstructing what had been destroyed during the War of Independence and Civil War. Such landmarks as O'Connell Street, the Four Courts, the General Post Office, and the Custom House required almost complete reconstruction. The other focus for Dublin Corporation was alleviating the conditions in the tenements, which up to this point had been held up as indicative of the mismanagement of British rule.[17] After fatal slum collapses in Church Street in 1913, an inquiry reported that 60,000 residents of the city needed to be rehoused in better conditions.[18] Walk-up blocks were built in central areas, while the Corporation also planned and built new suburban estates in Marino, Donnycarney, and Crumlin.[19] Despite the benefits of this programme of house-building, this deployment of resources was also indicative of a broader economic ideology which, paradoxically, was also symptomatic of the negative impact of the state's policies on the capital's fortunes. These autarkic programmes emphasized social expenditure, but in so doing also removed Dublin's long-held position within a transnational European and global economy; this only served to reinforce the physical and economic decline that had been set in train by the city's curtailed political power in the nineteenth century. Therefore, despite the state's efforts and reconstruction, the physical decline of much of the city continued in the years after

[15] Peter Harbinson, Homan Potterton, Jeanne Sheehy, *Irish Art and Architecture: From Prehistory to Present* (London, 1993), 199–206.

[16] Jacinta Prunty, *Dublin Slums 1800–1925: A Study in Urban Geography* (Dublin, 1999), 276.

[17] Rosemary Cullen Owens, *A Social History of Women in Ireland 1870–1970* (Dublin, 2005), 285–6.

[18] Ruth McManus, *Dublin 1910–40: Shaping the City and Suburbs* (Dublin, 2002), 35.

[19] McManus, *Dublin*, 180–230.

independence; the efforts of the state could not hold back the structural degradation of the core caused by the city's loss of its economic position.

From the foundation of the state in 1922 until the 1960s, there were few efforts to plan for the city's future, or to systematically quantify its development. In this forty-year period only three town plans were drawn up for the city, none of which were implemented. The first town plan for Dublin arose from a competition run by the Civics Institute of Ireland in 1914, which asked for entrants to look ahead to the city becoming once again the political capital of an Irish nation.[20] First prize was awarded to a design led by Patrick Abercrombie in partnership with brothers Sydney and Arthur Kelly, published as *Dublin of the Future* in 1922 in response to the foundation of the Free State.[21] Seventeen years later, Abercrombie produced his second plan for the city. After the Town and County Planning Act of 1934 was passed, Dublin City Council adopted a resolution to prepare a plan for the municipal area, and on the basis of Abercrombie's proposals of 1914 commissioned him, alongside Sydney Kelly and Manning Robertson, to draw up a new scheme for the city. The designs were submitted to the Corporation in October 1939.[22] These grand civic schemes were exceptions in a period when there was little investment or interest in the city; after both Abercrombie's plans there were no moves to implement his schemes or imbue his designs with the weight of law. Dublin sat uneasily between planned and planless; the Corporation was frequently accused by developers of making erratic decisions on planning applications owing to an ill-defined conception of what was 'scheduled'. Indeed, on this basis, the building firm Modern Homes Ltd took Dublin Corporation to the High Court in 1952 in order to force it to produce a formal, statutory town plan.[23] The firm won the case, and the High Court made a ruling requiring the production of a planning scheme by July 1955.[24] Thus in April 1955, Michael O'Brien, Dublin Corporation's Town Planning Officer, submitted a draft planning scheme to the City

[20] Michael Bannon, 'Dublin Town Planning Competition: Ashbee and Chettle's "New Dublin–A Study in Civics"', *Planning Perspectives* 14/2 (1999), 145–62; Civics Institute of Ireland, *The Dublin Civic Survey Report* (London, 1925).

[21] Civics Institute of Ireland, *Dublin of the Future: The New Town Plan, being the Scheme Awarded the First Prize in the International Competition by Patrick Abercrombie, Sydney Kelly & Arthur Kelly* (Dublin, 1922).

[22] Dublin Corporation, *County Borough of Dublin and Neighbourhood Town Planning Report Sketch Development Plan by Professor Patrick Abercrombie, Sydney A. Kelly, Manning Robertson* (Dublin, 1941), 9.

[23] *Architects' Journal,* 14 July 1955, 421, manuscript copy in Niall Montgomery papers National Library of Ireland Accession No. 6475; *Irish Contractor,* February 1952, 15; *Irish Builder and Engineer,* May 1955, 517.

[24] Brendan Clarke, 'The Environment', in J. J. Lee, *Ireland 1945–70* (Dublin, 1979), 102.

Council.[25] Nevertheless, even the limited provisions of Dublin's third town plan since independence were not put into effect. The costs arising from compensation for those whose land decreased in value owing to zoning provisions meant that implementation would be costly; furthermore, the new Minister for Local Government's desire to overhaul the planning legislation meant that the plan was soon considered too out of date to introduce.[26]

Physical planning from the foundation of the state until the late 1950s had been characterized by a descriptive rather than a numerical approach, the leadership of self-trained 'gentleman experts', and a complete inefficacy in shaping the growth of the city. While city government had been shaped by this ignorance about the inhabitants and buildings under its jurisdiction until the late 1950s, from the early 1960s there were increasing efforts to understand and regulate the urban environment using scientific means. As part of the Local Government (Planning and Development) Act 1963, it became compulsory for each borough or county council to produce a development plan. In response to this legislation, reports were commissioned by the Department of Local Government from some leading international town planners. Experts consulted included Charles Abrams, Colin Buchanan, Myles Wright, and Nathaniel Lichfield, figures who had played a defining role in shaping the landscape of post-war America and Britain. These men wrote on urban renewal, traffic management, and regional development, bringing to the city global conventions of town planning. These reports played an important role in the formulation of Dublin's first statutory town plan. This document was drafted by the Planning Officer, Michael O'Brien, and the City Manager, Matthew Macken, and published in 1967. It consisted of a series of policy statements, development controls, and development objectives relating to population, employment, housing, industry, and commercial uses of the city.[27] The Dublin Development Plan was legally implemented in 1971, for the first time instituting a legal framework for the regulation of Dublin's environment.

The move towards a planned urban environment must be understood within the broader context of the growth of the technocratic state in

[25] Dublin Corporation, *County Borough of Dublin Draft Planning Scheme* (Dublin, 1955); Dublin Corporation, *Planning Scheme Book 'A' Land Reservations* (Dublin, 1957); Dublin Corporation, *Articles of the Planning Scheme* (Dublin, 1957); Royal Institute of Architects of Ireland, *Recommendations and Observations on the City of Dublin Planning Scheme* (Dublin, 1957), 1.

[26] Charles Abrams, *Urban Renewal in Ireland (Dublin)* (Dublin, 1961), 17.

[27] *Draft Dublin Development Plan* (Dublin, 1967). Republished without changes as *Dublin City Development Plan* (Dublin, 1968) and instituted in 1971.

Ireland from the time of the Whittaker report.[28] During the 1960s, Fianna Fáil put great emphasis on planning and expertise as conduits of prosperity. Semi-state bodies proliferated, as control of many areas of governance moved from politicians and the civil service to unelected experts, while novel quantitative methods in analytical work lent a new technical orientation to political decision-making. These organizations included the Industrial Development Authority, responsible for attracting external development, and An Foras Forbartha, which organized and coordinated research in all areas of the building industry. Planning came to be seen as an essential part of the effective running of the state in all government departments, as part of what Michael Bannon has called a 'wide range of policy innovations with which a dynamic government was prepared to experiment in an attempt to meet its twin objectives of ending involuntary emigration and creating full employment at home'.[29] This prompted Garret FitzGerald to note in 1965 that 'in practice we now have a vocational-bureaucratic system of government, whose centre of gravity has shifted away from the politicians towards the civil service and vocational bodies'.[30] The most important and best documented of these areas of planning was economic policy, which was codified by the Department of Finance in three programmes for economic expansion between 1959 and 1972.

The subtleties of the science of planning have been given great attention within Ireland's economic history. However, the same forces also had an impact on city management. Physical planning was as much a part of this movement towards 'government by specialists' as the better-known and more celebrated history of economic planning. But the emphases on experts and on the quantitative basis of town planning did not mean that the city's spaces were depoliticized, but rather that the politics of city governance became subsumed within a discourse of science. For example, the forms used to quantify the information on which town planning was based—such as maps, diagrams, and tables—had an impact on how the city was governed and understood. During the 1960s a variety of maps and plans were produced to represent and understand the city. These maps were highly partial; each was a political device in which the presentation of data contained an image of how society should function. This

[28] Brian Girvin, *Between Two Worlds: Politics and Economy in Independent Ireland* (Dublin, 1989), 210.

[29] Michael Bannon, 'Development Planning and the Neglect of the Critical Regional Dimension', in Michael Bannon (ed.), *Planning: The Irish Experience 1920–88* (Dublin, 1989), 122.

[30] Garret FitzGerald writing in the *Irish Times*, 4 February 1965, quoted in Bew and Patterson, *Sean Lemass and the Making of Modern Ireland*, 145.

ideologically based system interacted with a governmental mechanism which was still presided over by human decision-making. The Minister for Local Government retained his position as the highest arbiter of planning appeals until 1973 (when An Bord Pleanála was set up), giving a political overtone to many planning decisions. As Minister for Local Government, Neil Blaney (1957–66) and Kevin Boland (1966–70) both aimed to rationalize and scientifically manage Ireland's landscape. Blaney and Boland were strongly influenced by nationalism and were deeply embedded in political networks, important factors in how they conducted themselves as minister.[31] Indeed, both are remembered in the literature on twentieth-century Ireland primarily for the part they played in the Arms Crisis of 1970. Thus, while the scientific management of the city was presented as a rational and technical activity, implicit in these proposals was a political agenda which sought to mould the social and political life of the city, an effort which is explored below.

DUBLIN AS A NEW CAPITAL

In the first year of the Free State, the Civics Institute published Abercrombie's radical and visionary plan for the city, and thanks to the positive reception of his design he was called upon by Dublin Corporation in 1937 to produce a new plan for the city. In 1922, Abercrombie had begun his statement on the future for Dublin with a description of the challenges the contemporary city posed to the planner and urban manager, being a site of dirt, disease, and disorder: 'Dublin today presents a similar spectacle to Paris prior to the operations of Napoleon III and Haussmann: it is a city of magnificent possibilities, containing features of the first order, but loosely co-related and often marred by the juxtaposition of incongruities and squalor. As in Paris, central areas which should be of first rate commercial importance are occupied by slums and streets of noble architectural dignity are tenement ridden.'[32]

This description of slums and squalor conjured up images of the industrial cities of Victorian England, but Abercrombie looked to the overhaul of Paris during the Second Empire to provide inspiration for the future of Dublin. His invocation of Haussmann was significant. For Abercrombie, Dublin was a city of 'magnificent possibilities'; he presented an image of the future where the city would rise like a phoenix after the devastation of

[31] Kevin Rafter, *Neil Blaney: A Soldier of Destiny* (Dublin, 1993); Paul Sacks, *The Donegal Mafia: An Irish Political Machine* (New Haven, 1976).

[32] Civics Institute of Ireland, *Dublin of the Future*, 3.

the Anglo-Irish conflict, transformed into a bright and modern city. Unlike his later plans for London, he proposed dramatic interventions in the landscape: 'Dublin, noble city as she is, requires complete overhauling down to fundamentals; no superficial patching, though it extended over the whole city region and dealt with every aspect, would meet the case... [to] compose a city that is worthy to be the capital of a modern country.'[33] Abercrombie's two plans for Dublin, consisting of grand new edifices, zoning of land, and wide and straight roads, were resolutely modern designs. Furthermore, the city he envisaged not only took aesthetic inspiration from the Modern Movement, but used the technologies of town planning to socially segregate the city. Both plans looked to the removal of the 'juxtapositions' between rich and poor in the city centre; in 1939, he recommended that the tenements should be reconstituted to form suitable housing for the new 'black coat' population, the present residents of these buildings being moved to new accommodation on the periphery of the city.[34] Through the clearance of the working-class population into cottage-style suburban development, the reconstruction of central areas, and the imposition of wide, straight roads on the complex street pattern, the plans looked to rid the city of the moral degradation and violent threats of the tenements, enabling it to be a fitting ceremonial and administrative centre of government.

But Abercrombie's modernism also had important and visible national and sectarian connotations. Just as the new state sought to create a visual language of symbols and images by which to define itself, so Abercrombie's plan created an image for a new capital.[35] He proposed a wide range of modifications to shape a new ceremonial urban form for Dublin, which both defined the city as the imaginary heart of the nation and articulated the power of the new state. The central area was to be pulled back from its location around College Green and returned to the ancient area of the city to the immediate west of Dublin Castle. At the core of this new city centre would be the new metropolitan complex located at the top of Capel Street, consisting of a Roman Catholic cathedral and a Grand

[33] Civics Institute of Ireland, *Dublin of the Future*, x. On Abercrombie's plans for London see Patrick Abercrombie, *Greater London Plan* (London, 1945); Peter Hall, *Great Planning Disasters* (Harmondsworth, 1981), ch. 3.

[34] Dublin Corporation, *County Borough of Dublin and Neighbourhood Town Planning Report Sketch Development Plan*, 44.

[35] Ewan Morris, '"God Save the King" versus "The Soldier's Song": The 1929 Trinity College National Anthem Dispute and the Politics of the Irish Free State', *Irish Historical Studies* 31/121 (1998), 72–90; Brian Kennedy, 'The Irish Free State 1922–49: A Visual Perspective', in Raymond Gillespie and Brian Kennedy (eds.), *Ireland: Art into History* (Dublin, 1996), 132–54.

Central station centred on a large plaza.[36] The lines of Dublin's principal roads would also be straightened to form a symmetrical geometric pattern, centring on this cathedral and transport hub (Fig. 1.1).[37] Although Abercrombie's second plan of 1939 was considerably less ambitious than

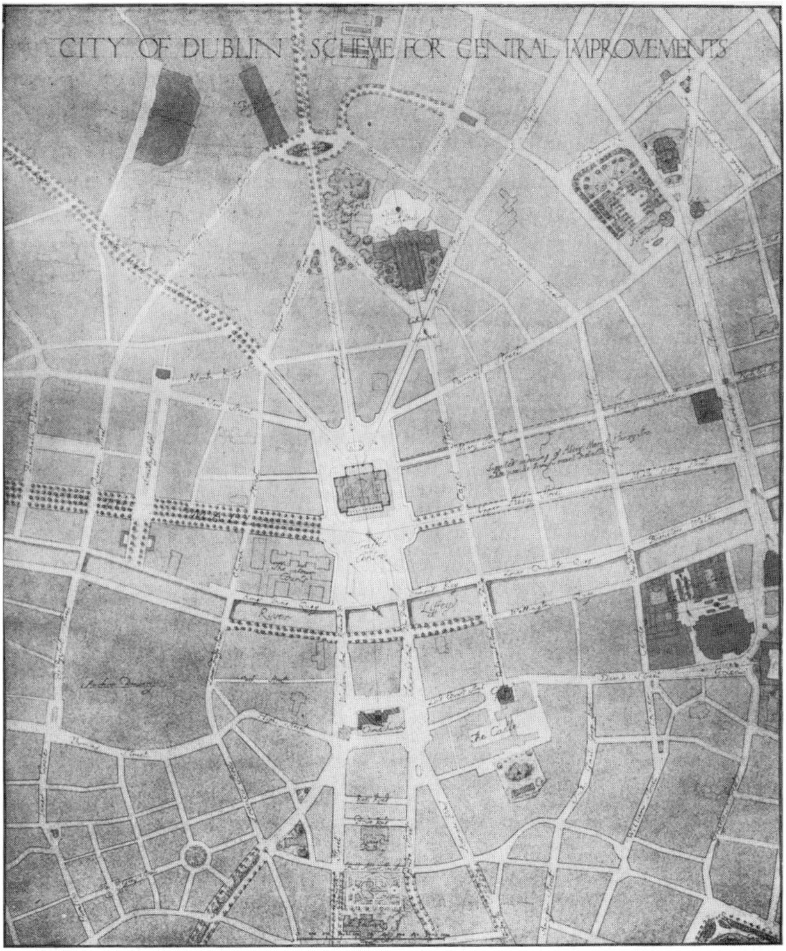

Fig. 1.1. Patrick Abercrombie's design for a new central area for Dublin, including plaza, transport hub, and cathedral, 1922. In Civics Institute of Ireland, *Dublin of the Future* (Dublin, 1922).

[36] Civics Institute of Ireland, *Dublin of the Future*, 39.
[37] Civics Institute of Ireland, *Dublin of the Future*, 37.

his proposals of 1922, it again envisaged a monumental capital for the new state, and contained many similarities with his first scheme. For example, it again proposed a new national cathedral for the area to the north of Ormond Quay, a new transport hub, and a new office complex for Dublin government and for the national legislature, centred on a reconstructed Merrion Square.[38]

The two Abercrombie plans which emerged from the inter-war years were part of a movement within town planning whereby monumental urban forms were planned and constructed as forthright and uncompromising spatial statements of political power.[39] Abercrombie's plans were part of this trend: both were explicitly political in the way that they imagined the city and conceived of urban space. In the relocation of the metropolitan centre back to the ancient, pre-Norman part of the city, and the creation of a national cathedral as the focus of this new centre, it was also the recreation of a 'more Irish' capital city as defined by the Gaelic revival. This combination of rationalization, modernization, and nationalization is also clear in the imposition of a new geometric street pattern on the extant city. Whereas the city bequeathed to the new state by the Wide Streets Commissioners articulated the power and culture of the eighteenth-century Protestant Ascendancy, through the new streets centred on the Catholic cathedral the culture of the new nation was unmistakably carved through the landscape. Thus Abercrombie imagined a future for Dublin which would definitively situate the capital within the story of a Gaelic, Catholic, Irish nation, and create a fresh moral order from the eighteenth-century city. These uncompleted schemes were, however, the highpoint of grand civic designs for the city, as in the post-war years planning would retreat into more achievable goals for a financially constrained state. Although neither of these plans were ever formally adopted, in Abercrombie's conception of radial and circumferential road routes, his policies of dispersed working-class housing, and his uniting of future and past in the streetscapes of the new city, he would have a lasting impact on the policies of Dublin Corporation.

The capital was not only a ceremonial site of political power; it was the foremost site of commerce and industry in the country, and as a locus of population and trade it also posed a moral and social problem for central and local government. For example, in 1954, A. J. Humphreys SJ, author of *New Dubliners,* wrote in *Christus Rex*:

[38] Dublin Corporation, *County Borough of Dublin and Neighbourhood Town Planning Report Sketch Development Plan*, 36–7.

[39] Peter Hall, *Cities of Tomorrow*, ch. 6.

> urbanisation has upset the internal balance of the urban nuclear family, lessened the scope of its traditional functions, weakened inter-familial solidarity and increased dependence on outside agencies. In short, urbanisation in Dublin impairs the life of the primary group. More significantly, it does so without at least as yet destroying the ultimate Christian values so long associated with primary group life in the Western world. Even in Ireland undermining the primary group life may ultimately lead to rejection of those values and to progressive secularisation. But our analysis shows that decline in power of the family, of kinship and of the neighbourhood, so often attributed to loss of religious and philosophical ideals, is initially and extensively the result of modern religious and political organisations. If this be so and if preservation of the primary group is essential to the survival of a civilisation, then our modern problem comes more clearly into focus: how to reorganise the economy and policy in such a way that, while remaining rationally efficient and increasingly productive, it may revitalise the primary level of family and community.[40]

The urbanization of Ireland's population, due largely to inward migration to Dublin, had long been a source of concern for the government and the Catholic hierarchy. The high density population at Dublin's core, living in poverty and in overcrowded conditions, was seen not only as a social problem but also as a potential risk to the state. Urbanization was seen as having the potential not only to lessen church attendance but also to disrupt the familial structures of traditional Irish society. Owing to these perceived threats, Catholic sociological research was conducted into the nature of urbanization, and how to lessen its perceived negative impact.[41] For example, in the 1950s, Humphreys proposed a radical rethinking of Irish capitalist production in order to revitalize rather than diminish the role of the family, thus enabling modernization to contribute to the reinvigoration of Irish civilization. A decade later, the country's political and economic situation had been transformed, but similar concerns remained part of the planning process. A number of reports were commissioned on how to reshape Dublin's central areas to make the city better suited for modern industrial production. In so doing, planners proposed ways to control and rationalize the city centre; to improve the lives of its working-class inhabitants; and to increase industrial productivity. However, they also continued to address the moral problems as set out by Humphreys, and proposed mechanisms to lessen the threats posed by increasing urbanization.

[40] A. J. Humphreys SJ, 'Migration to Dublin: Its Social Effects', *Christus Rex* 4/2 (1955), 199.

[41] For example, see Conrad Arensberg, *Family and Community in Ireland* (Cambridge, Mass., 1948); J. Todd, 'Town and Country', *Christus Rex* 63, 250–6; A. J. Humphreys SJ, *New Dubliners: Urbanisation and the Irish Family* (Dublin, 1966; reprinted London, 1998).

In May 1960, Neil Blaney requested an expert from the UN to advise the Minister for Local Government and Dublin Corporation on how to deal with run-down central city areas which were currently occupied as housing.[42] The UN dispatched Charles Abrams, one of the most prominent American town planners, and in 1961 he submitted *Urban Renewal in Ireland (Dublin)* to advise on the redevelopment of these areas. The area Abrams chose as an exemplar of the problems facing much of the city was the Moore Street district, to the north of the Liffey and just east of O'Connell Street, 'bounded by Parnell Street, Little Denmark Street, McCann's Lane, Sampson's Lane and the rear portions of the Moore Street buildings'. He described it thus:

> There are a number of empty lots as one crosses Riddles Row, while McCann's Lane has a number of old small one-story buildings and a few decrepit two and three story buildings. Contributing to the general drabness are some old slaughter houses and superannuated storage warehouses fronting on walks which serve as the repositories of garbage cans. An empty lot is used for parking, there is the street market on Moore Street, while Cole's Lane, a narrow alley, is composed mostly of old one and two story buildings set among a few vacant lots and shacks. On week days some small scale peddling is done in one of the alleys and there are the push carts on Moore Street with its busy retail shops giving an atmosphere of activity amid squalor . . . the area is definitely decayed—or as the court put it in 1942 "Part of that area is a dreadful blot on the city, and I welcome the evidence that the Corporation is determined on sweeping reforms in a shocking district." Eighteen years later, the buildings still stand, older and shabbier than ever.[43]

Abrams portrayed a dark, uncontrolled urbanism. His description of alleys, slaughterhouses, peddling, and squalor were evocative of a Victorian slum, and stood in direct contradistinction with the light and order characteristic of the idealized twentieth-century city. This jarring of imageries had a particular significance because of the area's location; these streets were directly behind O'Connell Street, the shopping, entertainment, and patriotic heart of the capital. However, Abrams also saw the Moore Street district as indicative of the type of locale which could be successfully redeveloped. Existing laws only allowed for land cleared of sub-standard housing to be replaced by new residential developments, but the report recommended the introduction of legislation to enable the Corporation to use land cleared of housing for a range of commercial and industrial purposes. Further, Abrams recommended that this process operate through partnership between Dublin Corporation and the private

[42] Bannon, 'Development Planning', in Bannon (ed.), *Planning*, 129.
[43] Abrams, *Urban Renewal in Ireland (Dublin)*, 46–7.

sector, enabling property developers to reconstruct these derelict areas, and providing a more cost-efficient means for the state to finance what was becoming known as 'urban renewal'.[44] His suggestions would also have a profound impact on the social and architectural character of the core. Arising from this report, new powers of compulsory purchase were introduced as part of the Planning and Development Act 1963, enabling Dublin Corporation and their commercial partners to redevelop former housing areas for commercial purposes.[45]

In 1964, after these new powers for urban acquisition and modernization had been introduced, Nathaniel Lichfield was invited by the Corporation to draw up new plans for the district to the west of O'Connell Street which had been singled out by Abrams.[46] Lichfield made a series of proposals which would not just redevelop the built stock but completely rewrite the street pattern and transform the character of the area. The scheme reimagined the area as a series of interlinking pedestrian squares on a variety of levels, and as a destination which would be easily accessible to the shopper arriving by car. He recommended the extension of the Henry Street and Moore Street shopping area southwards, with a precinct along the line of Liffey Street; the redevelopment of the west side of Moore Street to form an open market square; the provision of residential flats, a hotel, garden, and entertainments complex along the quays; the allocation of generous car parking and a new bus depot within the area; and the creation of 'flatted factories' (multi-storey factories suited for light industry) to accommodate the displaced workshops.[47] In addition he proposed a pedestrian footbridge over the river flying at a high level over the buildings on the quays, in order to connect the new shopping precinct with Dame Street. This was designed to bring the shopping centre around Henry Street within easier reach of those shopping on Grafton Street to the south of the Liffey, and take the shoppers who walked between the two areas out of the traffic along the quays.[48] These proposals were intended to be only the first part of Dublin Corporation and the Department of Local Government's plan to renew many of the run-down areas of the city centre. In connection with building a shopping precinct for the

[44] Abrams, *Urban Renewal in Ireland (Dublin)*, 38.

[45] Dublin Corporation, 'Report of the Committee of the Whole House', *Reports of Dublin Corporation 1964* (Dublin, 1965), 541.

[46] Dublin Corporation, 'Report of the Committee of the Whole House with Reference to an Introductory Report by the City Manager on the Local Government (Planning and Development) Act 1963 and a Preliminary Report of a Planning Consultant on a Possible Redevelopment Scheme for the Area Bounded by Capel Street, North Quays, O'Connell Street and Parnell Street', *Reports of Dublin Corporation 1964* (Dublin, 1965), 540–54.

[47] Dublin Corporation, 'Report of the Committee of the Whole House', 549.

[48] Dublin Corporation, 'Report of the Committee of the Whole House', 549.

Moore Street area and the new outlying suburban areas, a delegation from Dublin Corporation visited Coventry, Birmingham, Solihull, London, Stevenage, Cambridge, Amsteleen, Amsterdam, Rotterdam, Cologne, Essen, and Düsseldorf in October 1967. Although some of these cities had extensive historic districts, the research group's interest was in their commercial areas and their remodelling of traditional urban patterns.[49]

Similarly, the government's response to the housing crisis of the mid-1960s was also resolutely modernist.[50] In the light of the acute housing shortages (see Chapter 5), Dublin Corporation resolved in 1964 that an additional thousand dwellings a year for the following three years would be required to supplement the programme which was already being carried out by traditional building methods. Following discussions between the Minister for Local Government and Dublin Corporation, they resolved that the National Building Agency, which had been formed in 1961 to facilitate the building of houses for industrial workers and the Civic Guard, would be placed in charge of a house-building scheme at Ballymun, 4 miles north of the city. This would supplement the continuing housing programme of Dublin Corporation in order to increase the provision of housing rapidly.[51] The form of the Ballymun estate was a radical departure for Dublin Corporation, which up to this point had built cottages in the suburbs and walk-up flat blocks in the city. The development, which consisted of 450 houses and 2,550 flats, was influenced by Corbusian theory, mediated through the influence of British planning conventions. The centrepiece of the scheme was seven system-built towers of fifteen storeys, each named after a signatory of the 1916 Proclamation, set within a large landscaped park area. Moreover, this triumphal vision of a modern and patriotic Ireland was the most luxurious accommodation ever provided by the state; central heating was standard in all flats and houses and they were larger than the standard size provided by Dublin Corporation up to this point.[52] The houses had a floor area of about 950 square feet, including three bedrooms and two living rooms, a

[49] Dublin Corporation, 'Report of Group Nominated by the City Council to Carry Out a Study of Central Area Developments, Including Shopping Precincts in England and Certain European Cities', *Reports of Dublin Corporation 1968* (Dublin, 1969), 77–103.

[50] Tony Fahey, 'Housing and Local Government,', in Mary Daly (ed.), *County and Town: One Hundred Years of Local Government in Ireland* (Dublin, 2001), 125; Dermot Keogh, and Andrew McCarthy, *Twentieth Century Ireland: Revolution and State Building* (Dublin, 2005), 277.

[51] Sinéad Power, 'The Development of the Ballymun Housing Scheme, Dublin, 1965–69', *Irish Geography* 33/2 (2000), 199–212.

[52] Dublin Corporation, 'Report of the Committee of the Whole House, with Reference to the Outline Plans and Detail of the Housing Development Scheme on the Former Albert College Lands', *Reports of Dublin Corporation 1965* (Dublin, 1966), 2–4.

toilet downstairs, and bathroom and toilet upstairs, while the flats varied in size from one to three bedrooms, all also with a living room, kitchen, and bathroom.[53]

The Moore Street project slowly diminished in size from the original grand vision because of the protests of local interest groups, and consequently the redevelopment scheme for the area was never executed. Indeed, the Ilac shopping centre on Henry Street was all that was ever built of the imagined series of indoor and outdoor pedestrian precincts.[54] Despite the greatly reduced form in which the scheme was implemented, the formation of this project, alongside the development of Ballymun, represented a moment when Dublin Corporation moved to bring about a comprehensive vision for the city in line with urban renewal programmes taking place across Europe. However, in proposing to demolish these back lanes and replace them with covered shopping centres, while moving the population out to purpose-built estates on the periphery of the city, Dublin Corporation was doing more than simply improving the physical condition of the area. In 1964, Tom O'Mahony, the City Manager and Town Clerk, stated in relation to the Moore Street area that 'For many years the Corporation has been conscious of its lack of legal authority to undertake the clearance and redevelopment of areas, other than housing areas, of which large sections continue to be covered by what are, at their worst, nothing but commercial and industrial slums, and at their best constitute an uneconomic and wasteful occupation of valuable sites by inadequate structures for inadequate purposes.'[55] O'Mahony's description of the 'inadequate structures for inadequate uses', indicated Dublin Corporation's policy not only of removing housing from the central areas but also of rationalizing the city centre; to have each area zoned and designated for a proper, 'respectable' use. Moreover, his use of the term 'slum' was significant. Slums, like dirt, are relational concepts; they could only come into existence with the creation of a scientific town planning which designated the 'right' area for wealthy and poor, or for commercial, industrial, and residential districts. In fictional writing about the city, Dublin was often recorded as a site of sex, opportunity, and liberation in contradistinction to the suffocation of the countryside and its conservative society. This conception of the urban environment was taken up by planners;

[53] Dublin Corporation, 'Report of the Committee of the Whole House, with Reference to the Provision of Space Heating and Water Heating for the Ballymun Housing Project', *Reports of Dublin Corporation 1965*, 351–4.

[54] McDonald, *The Destruction of Dublin*, 161.

[55] Dublin Corporation, 'Report of the Committee of the Whole House, City of Dublin Interim Report on Pilot Scheme of Central Area Redevelopment', *Reports of Dublin Corporation 1968*, 544.

the physical degradation of the environment was seen as linked to the moral denigration of society, and in remedying the former, the latter could also be controlled, improved, and moulded.

The Department of Local Government not only meditated on the localized problem of specific central areas, but also on how to reshape the form and character of the city as a whole. In 1964 Myles Wright was commissioned to report on the future growth of the 'Dublin region'.[56] This report, published in full in 1968, went on to be the most influential document in shaping Dublin's development until the end of the twentieth century, presaging the enormous growth of suburbs to the west of the city which would take place in the following decades.[57] Wright's future for Dublin was based on a car-led traffic structure. However, he was not the first town planner to enthusiastically support a radical remodelling of Dublin's landscape in order to support mass car ownership. The first report on the city's transport policy was Karl-Heinz Schaechterle's *Traffic Investigation Concerning the Future Main Road Network*, commissioned in 1959 and submitted in 1965.[58] This report was influenced by the contemporary drive for urban motorways, and proposed the aggressive intervention of roads into the urban fabric. While Wright followed these proposals for the centre of the city, his scheme was much more ambitious and radical than Schaechterle's proposals. For Wright, cars were an aspirational commodity, and mass car ownership would be central part of Ireland's new-found affluent society. He argued that prosperity was giving the opportunity of greater car ownership in Ireland and that this increased car use could not and should not be discouraged. On the contrary, the car should be wholeheartedly embraced by the state as the foundation of transport policy.[59] This was a substantial paradigm shift for a government which had, only twenty years previously, rejected the idea that Irish families would own their own vehicle.[60]

This car-led transport structure allowed—indeed, required—mass suburbanization of Dublin's population. Since the foundation of the state many new cottage estates had been constructed at Dublin's peripheries, in

[56] Myles Wright, *Advisory Regional Plan and Final Report Part I: The Dublin Region* (Dublin, 1966) and *The Dublin Region: Advisory Regional Plan and Final Report Part II* (Dublin, 1967).

[57] Kincaid, *Postcolonial Dublin*, 158–63.

[58] Karl-Heinz Schaechterle, *Traffic Investigation Concerning the Future Main Road Network* (Ulm/Donau, 1965); this report was modified by An Foras Forbartha, *Transportation in Dublin* (Dublin, 1971) and Travers Morgan Partnership, *Central Dublin Traffic Plan* (London, 1973).

[59] Wright, *Advisory Regional Plan and Final Report Part I*, viii.

[60] Tom Garvin, *Preventing the Future: Why was Ireland so Poor for so Long?* (Dublin, 2004), 94–5.

areas such as Ballyfermot and Finglas, but Wright's proposals went far beyond these modifications in terms of scale and vision. As the road network would not take much more traffic, a radical remodelling of the use structure and social composition of the city was required, to create a diffuse city more suited to the demands of full car ownership. This would enable as many people as possible to live in the suburbs and to commute to work by car, ensure that the road network to the city would not be overburdened, and provide space and transport links for the state's new industries.[61] He therefore recommended the decentralization of much industry, commerce, and population to four new nodes at locations to the west of the city, centred on Blanchardstown, Lucan, Clondalkin, and Tallaght. Wright saw low-density cottage-style housing developments not exceeding fifty persons per net acre centred on these new towns as desirable for the majority of accommodation, and indeed, the Department of Local Government produced specifications for these house-types.[62] Thus Wright envisaged a Dublin where citizens would live in nuclear family units, would have more space in which to live, and more freedom to use their cars, being explicit in his desire to remodel Dublin along the lines of an American city.[63]

After the publication of the Wright Report, Dublin began to grow westwards, an expansion which would continue until the end of the century. The four new towns identified by Wright became large urban centres; the growth of Tallaght was particularly swift, with its population rising from 4,605 to 69,563 in the twenty years between the 1961 and 1981 censuses.[64] Alison Ravetz has described suburban housing schemes as 'cultural colonisation': an attempt by the elite to give working-class people middle-class culture: 'the suburb was more than a place: it was a culture in which the dominant influence was the home, physically and conceptually isolated from other urban activity and the public sphere. It served new patterns of marriage where housework and care of children were not counted as "work".'[65] Thus the city centre was not only the site of architecture that was well over a century old, but was also a space not conducive to the proper formation of the family, with its overlapping of public and private spheres, and the blurring of family boundaries implicit in the tenement life of the eighteenth-century streets. The creation of large suburban housing estates, as envisaged by

[61] Wright, *Advisory Regional Plan and Final Report Part I*, 22.

[62] Wright, *Advisory Regional Plan and Final Report Part I*, 18–19.

[63] Wright, *Advisory Regional Plan and Final Report Part I*, 19.

[64] Online at Central Statistics Office, <http://www.cso.ie>.

[65] Alison Ravetz, *Council Housing and Culture: The History of a Social Experiment* (London, 2001), 3.

Myles Wright, can therefore be read as the physical manifestation of an attempt to create the Christian, family-centred society as inscribed in the constitution. Suburbanization of Dublin's population was made possible through the adoption of modernist urban forms based on universal car ownership, yet it also provided an answer to the problems of the threat to traditional Irish society if it were to experience mass urbanization, as posed by Humphreys.

Since the nineteenth century Dublin Corporation (later in partnership with the Department of Local Government) had approached the city as a social and a moral problem for the state. Although this attitude remained the same during the 1960s, the answers provided differed substantially. An examination of town planning in this period provides an image of Dublin becoming a modern metropolis, but this was a particular Irish vision of the modern city. As shown by the Ballymun project and the plans for the Moore Street area, the state's vision for the city was characterized by an orthodox modernist aesthetic: clean lines, brightly lit precincts, and the use of concrete and steel. However, this modernism also helped to produce a more socially controlled society: the centrifugal pull of suburban developments solidified the structures of gender and the nuclear family, while the renewal of central areas removed the lure of dark alleys, to be replaced by interlinking commercial areas. This would also be a city which would be better suited to the demands of contemporary industry, consisting of new factories close to good transport links and with a large, skilled population nearby. Of fundamental import for the development of Dublin was the role envisaged for the market in these changes. While Abrams' report dealt with a perennial problem for Dublin—poor city housing—his solution, of introducing legislation to allow deficient housing to be bought and replaced by privately financed commercial interests, heralded a change in the composition of the city centre and a new clash between old and new forms of city life. Similarly, government support for car ownership opened up a new arena for the acquisition of mass-market consumer goods. Thus in the 1960s, the government retained its jurisdiction regarding the social and moral well-being of its citizens. However, this became newly interventionist when mediated through new forms of capital and modernist town planning.

While Dublin had long been understood both to be a site of political power and a place of disease and danger, during the 1960s a new way of reading the city began to develop. Owing largely to a clamour of voices from individuals and voluntary bodies, with which this book is primarily concerned, there was a new understanding of the city as a historic site, and there were new efforts to define and protect buildings dating from the eighteenth century. The first legislation to mandate for the preservation of

Ireland's historic environment was the British Ancient Monuments Protection Act of 1882.[66] This Act appointed the Commissioners for Public Works as guardians of a selected list of pre-Christian sites, provided for their upkeep, and made injury to those sites a criminal offence. However, the Act was limited in its jurisdiction to structures that were uninhabited because of concerns about the conflict between collective rights to national heritage and personal rights to private property. This lacuna in legislation was remedied in Britain by the foundation of the National Trust in 1895.[67] But the Trust never operated in Ireland—with the exception of the donation of Kankurk Castle in 1900—and therefore the post-medieval built environment was lacking in any protection from development and despoliation.[68]

The Ancient Monuments Protection Act was inherited by the new state, but repealed in 1930 with the introduction of the National Monuments Act, which in many ways followed the precedent of the 1882 legislation. This Act provided the basis for the protection and maintenance of archaeological sites, monuments, and artefacts for the next fifty years. It enabled the Board of Works to purchase sites by compulsion or to appoint itself guardian of national monuments in private possession. It also made it illegal to demolish, disfigure, excavate, or sell for export any part of a national monument. The Act defined a 'national monument' without reference to a particular time period; however, in practice this was not how the legislation was used. As Ken Mawhinney has described, 'it was very much archaeological in spirit, in the sense that its provisions suited the protection of structures and artefacts of the medieval and earlier ages'.[69] The record of items protected bears this out; in 1964 only one national monument under the guardianship of the Board of Works, Marino Casino, dated from after 1700.[70] Moreover, like the 1882 legislation, the Act of 1930 did not extend to inhabited structures, and therefore had a very limited impact on Dublin, offering no protection whatsoever to the eighteenth-century streets and squares.[71]

[66] *Ancient Monuments Protection Act 1882* (London, 1882); John Delafons, *Politics and Preservation: A Policy History of the Built Heritage 1882–1996* (London, 1997), 25.

[67] Delafons, *Politics and Preservation*, 29–30.

[68] John O'Loughlin Kennedy, 'Introduction', in Valerie Bond (ed.), *An Taisce: The First Fifty Years* (Meath, 2005), 25.

[69] Kenneth Mawhinney, 'Environmental Conservation: Concern and Action 1920–70', in Bannon, *Planning*, 91.

[70] Marino Casino was, however, in a state of serious disrepair in 1960—boarded up, fenced off, and closed to the public—see photo in *RIAI Yearbook* 1951–2; Bord Fáilte, *National Monuments of Ireland in the Charge of the Commissioners of Public Works in Ireland* (Dublin, 1964).

[71] Mawhinney, 'Environmental Conservation', 91.

Until the introduction of the city development plan in 1971, there were no legal provisions for the protection of the eighteenth-century city, and no listing procedure for the conservation of its built stock. Indeed, in the unimplemented 1955 town plan, the only buildings listed for preservation were Fitzwilliam and Merrion Squares (excluding the streets that linked them).[72] Furthermore, the great monuments of the city—the Custom House, the Bank of Ireland, the Four Courts—were owned by the Office of Public Works, and so exempt from the provisions of this plan. Planning permission could therefore be applied for the replacement of any building, in spite of its age or historic associations. Between 1964 and 1968, demolition was exempted from planning permission, meaning that any structure in the city could be knocked down without prior approval of the Corporation; many eighteenth-century areas were destroyed because of this loophole, to increase the value of land they were situated on as office space. These legislative anomalies meant that there were only two 'national monuments', in Dublin city: Portlester Chapel and St Mary's Abbey.[73] However, this absence of historic buildings legislation was slowly challenged by civil society groups during the 1960s.

However, preservation of Dublin as a 'historic' site was problematic. This was not only because preservation clashed with notions of urban modernity and social policy, but because the eighteenth-century city was also seen to be part of a heritage of colonialism, and therefore as a problematic part of Irish history. On many occasions during his tenure as Minister for Local Government, Kevin Boland made pronouncements of this nature. For example, in February 1968 he described the Irish Georgian Society's efforts to secure the preservation of the eighteenth-century Mountjoy Square:

> I appreciate there are a number of people in this city and in this country who see these Georgian buildings as reminders of the days of gracious living—gracious living that was made possible by the fact that there were available to them as slaves the mere Irish who were living in insanitary and overcrowded hovels in the back-lanes or in the damp, concealed basements of these gracious houses. It was possible to live graciously in them. I can appreciate that these people have their nostalgic memories and would like to see these things retained...This campaign for the preservation of our national Georgian heritage would be much more impressive as far as I am concerned, if in many cases the people who are conducting it were not also

[72] Dublin Corporation, *County Borough of Dublin Draft Planning Scheme* (Dublin, 1955).

[73] Bord Fáilte, *National Monuments of Ireland in the Charge of the Commissioners of Public Works in Ireland*, ix.

> activists in the campaign to destroy what the majority of the Irish people look upon as our real national heritage. I have no doubt it would be very pleasant if they could contemplate from outside the pleasant façades of these Georgian buildings and dream of the days when the lower orders knew their place and when it was possible to live graciously in these houses as a result of the financial resources supplied by the serfs on the land.[74]

In many ways Boland's comments paralleled similar derisive comments that critics such as Reyner Banham were making in Britain regarding the preservationist movement.[75] But his description of the 'mere Irish' and his suggestion that the architectural preservationists were also trying to destroy 'our real national heritage', by which he meant the Irish language, revealed a 'national' quality to debate regarding the future of the city which was particular to Ireland. The subtext of his speech was that the eighteenth-century city was not worth saving as it was a relic of British rule in Ireland; a foreign landscape on native soil. Indeed, Boland seemed to suggest that to mourn the loss of eighteenth-century buildings was to mourn the loss of British rule. He was not the only senior politician to express such views; James Gibbons, Parliamentary Secretary to the Minister for Finance, with responsibility for the Office of Public Works, described the Georgian Society's efforts scornfully as 'saving Ireland from the natives'.[76] Boland and Gibbons publicly articulated sentiments which were widely held. Many greeted the preservation of Georgian architecture with antipathy at best. At a time when the rural west and the Irish language were feared to be in a terminal state of decline, concerns for the eighteenth-century architecture of the city's capital was seen to be minor in comparison with the disappearance of this ancient culture, which was still understood to be the wellspring of national identity. Even in the 1960s, the urban, European experience of the nation's capital sat uneasily in official narratives of Irish history. Thus the rapid destruction of the city, which took place along modern, international lines, was defended by the political elite through traditional modes of discourse that related to the Irish nation.

This blindness or antipathy towards Dublin's eighteenth-century built environment was not just the result of a deficit of historic buildings legislation but extended into all areas of town planning. For example, traffic proposals were notable for being drawn up without any assessment of the age of the buildings that would be demolished in order to implement the

[74] Printed Debates Dáil Éireann (henceforth PDDÉ) 232, 28 February 1968, cols 2011–13.

[75] *New Statesman*, 12 April 1963, 529.

[76] *Irish Times*, 16 December 1966, 15.

plans, and during the 1960s, road widening was responsible for the destruction of many extant streets. In his 1965 proposals, Schaechterle imposed a series of radial and circumferential road routes on the city. The innermost level of this series of roads was a 'square tangent' running on the route of Cork Street, The Coombe, St Stephen's Green South, Merrion Square West, over a new bridge east of the Custom House, connecting to Summerhill, Parnell Street, North Kings Street, and continuing to Arbour Hill and Kingsbridge station.[77] This inner tangent was proposed to be four lanes wide, apart from the most pressurized eastern segment between Leeson Street and Butt Bridge, for which six lanes were suggested.[78] He also recommended an 'express traffic road . . . free of crossings' along the Grand Canal and the North Circular Road, to provide the city with an orbital route. With this in mind, he proposed that between Davitt Road, Leeson Street, the Liffey Bridge, and Drumcondra Road this road would be a six-lane expressway, with separated directional carriageways and junctions at two levels.[79] Indeed, the plans for the replacement of the Grand Canal with a motorway hung over the city throughout the 1960s, sporadically gaining popular attention, and were not finally dropped until a sustained popular campaign led by the Inland Waterways Association forced the Corporation into retreat in 1969.[80] After this reversal, Dublin Corporation's traffic policy was modified by the Travers Morgan Partnership in a report published in 1973. Although this report did not recommend the destruction of the Grand Canal, it would similarly have significantly changed Dublin had it been followed in full. It proposed the routing of substantial inner city motorways through residential and historic areas adjacent to the canals, and recommended a high level bridge across the Liffey beside the Four Courts.[81] Unlike earlier plans, the Travers Morgan scheme did demarcate three areas—the cathedrals, the quays, and the Georgian sector—for sensitive traffic planning. Yet, in so doing, it routed large roads on the peripheries of these areas, essentially cordoning them off from the rest of the city, and destroying the character of other areas which had not been listed.

Before 1971, town planning in Dublin took place without reference to a 'historic' city. Each of the town plans discussed above represented the imposition of new forms on old city space, through bureaucratic use of

[77] Schaechterle, *Traffic Investigation*, 44–5.

[78] Schaechterle, *Traffic Investigation*, 84.

[79] Schaechterle, *Traffic Investigation*, 86.

[80] National Archives of Ireland (henceforth NAI) Department of the Taoiseach (henceforth DT) S16904B/95–Canals: Maintenance etc. Grand Canal; Future of Dublin Section.

[81] Travers Morgan Partnership, *Central Dublin Traffic Plan*, 80.

geometric forms. Thus transport planning, office construction, and residential building all had a destructive impact on the extant eighteenth-century city. This was in line with international norms in town planning, which, from the end of the Second World War until the mid-1960s, sought to impose rational, modern urban spaces on older street plans in cities across Europe and America. However, this attitude to the past began to change during the 1960s. For example, by the end of the decade, planning in Britain was heavily weighted against comprehensive redevelopment. In Dublin, the complete absence of any provision for the protection of historic buildings was marked during a time when there were increasing provisions across Europe for the protection both of landmark buildings and townscape areas.[82]

But this cannot be understood solely through the prism of the rise and decline of urban modernism. As preservation rests on culturally constructed notions of authenticity and value, it cannot come into existence unless a society desires it. As Ashworth and Tunbridge have detailed, 'Heritage is, by the original definition of the word, determined by the legatee; all heritage is someone's heritage and that someone determines that it exists. It is thus a product of the present, purposefully developed in response to current needs or demands for it, and shaped by those requirements. It makes two sorts of intergenerational links both of which are determined by the present. The present selects an inheritance from an imagined past for current use and decides what should be passed on to an imagined future.'[83] In Ireland, based on the continued importance of rurality, Catholicism, Gaelic culture, and the history of a continued struggle against a British aggressor, the eighteenth-century buildings of Dublin did not represent an 'imagined past for current use'. Moreover Dublin, as the centre of British administration before 1922, the nucleus of eighteenth-century Protestant culture, and the site of an urban society, represented a counterpoint to the creation of an Irish national identity. However, modernization and preservation decided by planners and urban officials were not reproduced from map to city unproblematically: town plans and legislation were subject to contestation and interpretation by a range of groups, who aimed to subvert urban governance and impress their vision for the city on the urban form.

[82] Sophie Andrae, 'From Comprehensive Development to Conservation Areas', in Michael Hunter, *Preserving the Past: The Rise of Heritage in Britain* (Stroud, 1996), 135–55; Delafons, *Politics and Preservation*, ch. 11.

[83] J. E. Tunbridge and G. J. Ashworth, *Dissonant Heritage: The Management of the Past as a Resource in Conflict* (Chichester, 1996), 6.

2

Georgian Dublin and Modern Architecture, 1950–65

In 1950 the writer, poet, and doctor Oliver St John Gogarty wrote a eulogy to the city of his birth:

> Today on both sides of the river the lea is covered with the most perfect examples of Georgian architecture that remain, now that a great part of London is demolished or replaced. Dublin stands about its river very much as when the City Fathers planned it at the end of the XVIIIth century. True, its principal street is vulgar and bizarre, with plaster palaces and neon lights that make the day tawdry and the night hideous; but in its guarded squares, uncrowded streets and quiet culs-de-sac and along the canals, a loveliness still lingers from a century that is gone. Among rose-red houses, public buildings of white stone rise, crowned with various domes of copper, green with age.[1]

Gogarty recorded Dublin at the start of the 1950s as a place of contrasts: squalid and serene, elegant and vulgar. But what is really striking about this passage is the emphasis he placed on the coherence and integrity of the city. While much of Europe was being rebuilt, Dublin remained the city the Wide Streets Commissioners had mapped out in the eighteenth century, characterized by broad red-brick thoroughfares with vistas terminated by grand grey edifices. Indeed, for Gogarty, this seeming timelessness conjured comparisons with John William Burgon's Petra, 'a rose-red city half as old as time', when he wandered the city's streets. Yet, although his gaze was drawn to the intact remains of the eighteenth century, Dublin was no longer the city it once was. In the intervening century it had undergone radical social, political, and economic changes, and its opulent doorways now hid some of Europe's worst slums. These contrasts and juxtapositions provided many points of debate for architects, who were keen to create a new city and engage with the European architectural mainstream. This chapter takes up these themes, through an examination

[1] Oliver St John Gogarty, *Rolling Down the Lea* (Dublin, 1950), 9.

of how discourses of the Georgian were understood and used within the Irish architectural profession from the mid-1940s until the mid-1960s.

As Gogarty suggested, Dublin entered the 1950s a run-down city with a remarkably complete and coherent urban fabric, which was well over a hundred years old. As London, Paris, and Berlin rose anew from the devastation of war, the pervasive atmosphere in Dublin remained one of decay and fading grandeur. East to Sir John Rogerson's Quay, west to Ussher's Island, and north and south as far as the canals, the city was still a patchwork of eighteenth-century development. Despite the state's attempts to alleviate the conditions in the slums and rehouse Dublin's tenement population, conditions within the canals were still very poor. For example, much of the Gardiner estate had been in tenements for over a hundred years, and was consequently faced by the problems of poor sanitation, overcrowding, and structural decay.[2] The area around the Liberties, which had never been developed on a large scale, was even more tired. When an investigation was conducted into conditions in the Marrowbone Lane area of the city in 1955, the problems were listed as structural defects, extensive dampness, defective natural light, and inadequate lavatory and washing accommodation, compounded by the keeping of piggeries in this already crowded area.[3] However, not all the eighteenth-century city was in this squalid state. In fact, there was great variation in the condition of the built stock, with the Fitzwilliam-Merrion area remaining particularly prosperous. In 1957, much of it was still in single family occupancy or in offices, described by the Council of the Royal Institute of Architects of Ireland as 'well preserved, well-kept and well maintained'.[4]

There were some changes to the city in this period. Importantly, Michael Scott's Busáras, a building of European architectural significance, was completed in 1953 (Fig. 2.1). Central portions of both Dominick Street and Gardiner Street, two of the great thoroughfares of the Georgian era, were removed in 1957 to make way for blocks of flats designed by Desmond FitzGerald, while the crescent-shaped Hardwicke Place, one of the few architectural set pieces of the city, was taken down in 1954, also to be replaced by new Corporation housing.[5] These streets had long been in tenements, and their destruction caused no dissent or tangible nostalgia in the press (in marked contrast to events a decade later), instead

[2] Thomas Bodkin, *Report on the Arts in Ireland* (Dublin, 1951), 55; *Irish Builder and Engineer*, 22 March 1958, 215; *Irish Architect and Contractor*, July 1956, 18.

[3] *Irish Times*, 12 January 1955, 8.

[4] *Royal Institute of Architects of Ireland Yearbook 1956–57*, 17.

[5] *Irish Builder and Engineer*, July 1957, 553; *Irish Times*, 12 January 1955, 8.

Fig. 2.1. Busáras. Image courtesy of *Plan* magazine.

provoking a celebration of the modern, convenient dwellings which replaced them.[6] Despite these piecemeal changes, Dublin stood outside the mainstream of post-war town planning. Unlike many of the capital cities of western Europe, it stood undamaged by the bombs of the Second World War, and did not participate in the large-scale urban reconstruction which was contemporaneously transforming many cities across the continent.

In travel writing, guidebooks, and architectural magazines, Dublin was presented as a crumbling relic of a previous era, and a site of profound poverty. For example, when the first Royal Institute of British Architects (RIBA) conference after the end of the Second World War was held in Dublin, in 1947, the city was presented for the British readers of the *Architects' Journal* as a site of poverty and dilapidation:

> On the north bank, Capel Street, Bolton Street and Dorset Street form a sort of continuous arc leading through a district where fine Georgian houses have become slum tenements, in a state of extreme dilapidation and decay. Graceful doorways are broken and rooted, the bare wood showing through the paint, delicate iron railings are rusty, broken and held together with bits

[6] *Irish Builder and Engineer*, 13 July 1957, 553; *Irish Times*, 19 March 1960, 10; *Irish Architect and Contractor*, February 1957, 16.

> of wire. Women in black shawls stand in the doorways, while children with ragged clothes and bare feet play on the stone steps and swing on the iron work. Such a picture is the most lasting impression of Dublin and, with its combination of grace and beauty with tragedy and decay, it conveys the essential atmosphere of the city.[7]

This description of Dublin echoed long-established constructions of Ireland in the popular press; the women clad in black shawls, the ragged children, and the 'grace and beauty with tragedy and decay' all defined the city in terms of long-established tropes of Ireland. However, these images were also constructed with reference to contemporaneous changes in Britain. During a period when the pages of the *Architects' Journal* were filled by the new commissions of the welfare state, this tour around the poorer streets of Dublin evoked a city which seemed to remain in a bleak, pre-war past recorded by authors like J. B. Priestley and George Orwell. But these descriptions of Dublin were not only emanating from Britain. Taking a similar tone, the same year the writer Frank O'Connor made a journey into the more deprived areas of Dublin in his semi-fictional travelogue *Irish Miles,* and wrote evocatively of Henrietta Street:

> One slum house attracted us because a first floor window had been lifted out body and bones, and through it you could see the staircase ceiling, heavy circles and strapwork which suggested a Jacobean hangover. The poor people sunning themselves on the steps drew aside to let us pass. The staircase had been many times coated with salmon-coloured wash which half obscured the rich plaster panelling, but a ray of light through a ruined window-frame lit a beautiful stair with carved treads and delicate Restoration newel posts. It would have been alright but for the smell.[8]

Irish Miles was not only a travelogue but also a political tract against Irish insularity, against de Valera's premiership, and against the frustrations and disappointments of rural life. In choosing to travel to Henrietta Street for his chapter on Dublin, O'Connor made the choice to represent the capital of the independent state as a dirty, crumbling relic. Furthermore, its decaying buildings became potent, tangible symbols of the failing of independence to provide economic renewal or cultural rebirth for the nation. O'Connor's use of Dublin to represent national malaise also had more famous counterparts in fictional writing of the period. Indeed, there were many literary attempts to capture the city's juxtapositions and contradictions. Novels such as J. P. Donleavy's *The Ginger Man*, Flann O'Brien's *At Swim-Two Birds*, Dominic Behan's *Tell Dublin I Miss Her*, as

[7] *Architects' Journal*, 5 June 1947, 476.
[8] Frank O'Connor, *Irish Miles* (Dublin, 1947), 13.

well as many of the short stories of Seán Ó'Faoláin were all set within a crumbling, suffocating, fictionalized version of Dublin at mid-century.[9] Thus in this period, the physical decay of Dublin, as represented in the artistic production of leading cultural figures, was used to critique broader failures; the slowly decaying capital of the new nation came to symbolize the absence of a broad spectrum of artistic and cultural renewal as expected at the state's foundation.

In this atmosphere of decay and stultification, there were many within the architectural profession who had visions for the city's reconstruction. In 1958, the architect and journalist Niall Montgomery gave a paper at the Architectural Association on his ideas for the city, entitled 'That'll All Have to Come Down'.[10] It received widespread coverage in the press, and an article based on the talk, entitled 'Start all Over Again', was also printed in the *National Observer*.[11] In his desire to reconstruct the city, Montgomery displayed not only a desire to build for the future, but also the destructive atavism which has been a recurrent theme of Irish history: 'Dublin is an ancient monument, not so very ancient really, but as a monument, odd in that it consists of the whole sad heart of a city, not public buildings, churches, statues and great houses only, but whole terraces, squares and crescents of residences also. It's a cenotaph, empty tomb of that really underprivileged figure, the Unknown Nobleman, and it even has its perpetual flame—dry rot.'[12] To replace this 'empty tomb', he called for a Corbusian reconstruction of Dublin, featuring 'houses from fifteen to twenty storeys high, with lifts all the way up, roof gardens and all modern conveniences to make them the last word in efficiency'.[13] He argued that this type of building would bring the countryside right into the city, and maintained that the normal 'green belt' policy was 'content to keep the countryside outside the city'.[14]

Niall Montgomery was not alone in articulating this kind of radical vision of Dublin's future. The minor modifications of the 1955 town plan were roundly criticized in the *Recommendations and Observations on the City of Dublin Planning Scheme*, submitted by the Royal Institute of Architects of Ireland.[15] The Institute condemned the plan, describing it as

[9] J. P. Donleavy, *The Ginger Man* (Dublin, 1955); Frank O'Brien, *At Swim-Two-Birds* (New York, 1939); Seán Ó'Faoláin, *An Irish Journey* (Dublin, 1940); Dominic Behan, *Tell Dublin I Miss Her* (Dublin, 1962).

[10] Correspondence with Radio Éireann and press clippings relating to this talk in Montgomery papers. See also *Irish Builder and Engineer*, 26 March 1955, 297.

[11] *National Observer: A Monthly Journal of Current Affairs,* July 1958, 9.

[12] *National Observer*, July 1958, 9.

[13] *Irish Times Pictorial Weekly*, 30 April 1955, 2.

[14] *Irish Times Pictorial Weekly*, 30 April 1955, 2.

[15] RIAI, *Recommendations and Observations on the City of Dublin Planning Scheme*, 1.

'perfunctory road widenings as substitute for the bright future implicit in the imaginative proposals of Sir Patrick Abercrombie', and evoked Dublin's proud history of civic improvement passed down from the Wide Streets Commissioners in its demand for more imaginative and visionary proposals.[16] Raymond McGrath, the Australian-born architect who came to Dublin at the start of the Second World War to take up employment in the Office of Public Works, also saw Dublin's future lying in the introduction of international standards of town planning and modernist aesthetics.[17] While in Britain, he had been at the forefront of modern architecture; his interiors for Finella in Cambridge being described by Alan Powers as the only example of inter-war British architecture which dealt 'with ambivalence about modernity through a Modernism equivalent to that of Eliot and Joyce'.[18] He was also an early member of the MARS group alongside Wells Coates, E. Maxwell Fry, and Berthold Lubetkin, and he brought these principles with him in his visions for the future of the city. Michael Scott gave a paper to the University College Dublin (UCD) Architectural Society in 1955, entitled 'Towards a New Dublin' in which he expressed his hope that in thirty years Dublin would be a 'dream city'.[19] He wished to see the town plan go much further in looking to the future, and described the attempt to preserve Georgian Dublin as a 'magnificent failure' which was 'magnificent propaganda for the more contemporary and intelligent method of re-building Dublin.' Following on from this, he cited the need for high buildings and new thoroughfares as examples of a more radical approach to the future of the city.[20] Similarly, Andrew Marsh, writing in the *Irish Architect and Contractor*, argued: 'New Dublin should be planning new, as a blue print for the future.'[21] To create this new, aspirational city, he called for the rebuilding of the whole city centre, with the retention only of the set-piece buildings such as the Custom House, the Four Courts, and the Bank of Ireland.[22]

These statements revealed an architectural community whose members were aware of developments in the mainstream of continental planning

[16] RIAI, *Recommendations and Observations*, 1.

[17] See introduction; Raymond McGrath, 'Dublin Panorama: An Architectural Review', *The Bell* 2/5 (1941), 48. Donal O'Donovan, *God's Architect: A Life of Raymond McGrath* (Bray, 1995); Brian Kennedy, *Dreams and Responsibilities: the State and the Arts in Independent Ireland* (Dublin, 1991), 107.

[18] Alan Powers, *Britain: Modern Architectures in History* (London, 2007), 35; Elizabeth Darling, 'Finella, Mansfield Forbes, Raymond McGrath, and Modernist Architecture in Britain', *Journal of British Studies*, 50/1 (2011), 125–55.

[19] *Irish Times*, 18 November 1955, 9.

[20] *Irish Times*, 18 November 1955, 9.

[21] *Irish Contractor*, June 1951, 11.

[22] *Irish Contractor*, June 1951, 11.

and design. These architects were all looking internationally for inspiration, envisaging that the reconstruction of the city would come through large state-led planning initiatives. In the 1950s, many Irish architects trained abroad, and even during this insular decade the profession was transnational both in terms of its networks and intellectual engagements. For example, Robin Walker and Kevin Roche trained with Mies van der Rohe; Michael Scott toured America, and all subscribed to the *Architects' Journal* and *Architectural Review*. Sheila Wheeler, secretary of the *Architects' Journal*, also kept up frequent contact with Neil Downes, Raymond McGrath, Uinseann MacEoin, and Niall Montgomery. Scott, Marsh, and Montgomery had been influenced by developments in British and continental town planning, and by avant-garde theory such as Le Corbusier's Plan Voisin and Frank Lloyd Wright's Broadacre City.[23] Their plans were based on utopian ideals that tended to reject the past and turn towards a new, brighter, healthier future created by a new built environment.[24]

During the 1950s, the failure of the state to build—to create a glorious new capital as envisaged by Patrick Abercrombie—was frequently noted by politicians and architects alike. The decrepit and ageing eighteenth-century city became symbolic of the multitude of failings of the state: to adequately house its people, to solve the problem of poverty, to provide economic opportunities, and to create a new national culture. In this context, architects saw themselves as having a role in solving the nation's problems and simultaneously rejuvenating the city. Figures from within the architectural profession recommended that complete reconstruction of the city must take place as a way of counteracting this combined physical and cultural malaise. In so doing, they reprised the pleas of a previous generation: for Ireland to find its place in the world by looking outwards, and engaging with global trends in urban design. The theories of an international architectural avant-garde provided Ireland with an opportunity to provide housing for all, and to reconfigure the social make-up of society. To Montgomery, Scott, and Marsh, however, the eighteenth-century city played an important role. For these modernists, the extant city represented the past, and the counterpoint to all that the new city would be: it was dirty, constructed by and for social elites, dilapidated, and lacking in light and air. Indeed, the reconstruction of the city along international lines provided the state with an opportunity to fulfil the hopes of the state's founders for rebirth, prosperity, and renewal.

[23] Le Corbusier, *The Radiant City: Elements of a Doctrine of Urbanism to be Used as the Basics of our Machine-Age Civilisation* (London, 1933).

[24] Peter Hall, *Cities of Tomorrow: An Intellectual History of Urban Planning and Design in the Twentieth Century* (Oxford, 1992), 3.

Mirroring debates regarding the overarching form of the city, there was also no consensus regarding the style Irish urban architecture should take. Across Europe, the new buildings which rose anew after the devastation of war were lighter and brighter than the pre-war streets which were being replaced. This style had still been contentious in the 1930s, but in the years immediately following the cessation of hostilities it came to characterize state-led orthodoxy in architecture. In Britain, the arrival of modernism as the style of the post-war welfare state was marked in grand fashion by the Festival of Britain of 1951. This event explicitly linked the cool palette and clean lines of modern design with the arrival of the affluent society, and has subsequently entered not only architectural but also national hagiography. However, modernism was not victorious throughout Europe. In states at the edge of Europe, such the USSR and Spain, heavier, more ornate styles persisted. These were two countries under very different autocratic rules, but both tended to favour a similarly heavy 'wedding-cake' style for public buildings and institutions of state. The post-war modernist transformation of the built environment was also slow in coming to Ireland; if the architectural community and city governors were united in believing that the city must be reconstructed, there was no consensus on what the new buildings of the city would look like.

Although the state tended to favour modernism for projects such as hospitals and schools, Ireland did not participate in the post-war wave of rebuilding that affected most of Europe, and the new style made little impact on the appearance of the capital. During the 1950s, the Catholic Church was a major source of new commissions, but it tended to shy away from modern design, favouring instead a heavy and historicist Hiberno-Romanesque style.[25] When a competition was held for a new church for Clontarf in 1954, and won by a modern design, it was vetoed by Archbishop McQuaid in favour of a design in a Romanesque revival style.[26] This style sought to create an unbroken lineage between pre-Norman Irish Christianity and present-day devotion, through the construction of Romanesque-inspired churches adorned with the symbols of nineteenth-century cultural nationalism. The ungainly churches which peppered the new suburbs were the most ubiquitous architectural legacy of the 1950s: in Dublin, the churches in Clonskeagh, Finglas, and Nutgrove

[25] The retrogressive nature of church design was of great concern to the architectural community, forming much of the substance of the Architectural Association's President's Address in 1958 and in 1961. See *Green Book: The Journal of the Architectural Association 1961*, 23–5; *Green Book: The Journal of the Architectural Association 1958*, 39–43.

[26] *Irish Architect and Contractor*, September 1954, 17; Richard Hurley and Paul Larmour (eds.), *Sacred Places: The Story of Christian Architecture in Ireland* (Dublin, 2000), 14.

are all examples in this style.[27] The simultaneous apotheosis, and terminal point, of the style which had dominated Irish ecclesiastical building since the late nineteenth century was Galway Cathedral, dedicated in 1965 and designed in a jarring mishmash of Romanesque and Byzantine styles, and controversial since its erection.[28]

In this atmosphere of simultaneous economic stasis and retrograde cultural production, there was, nonetheless, debate among the architectural profession as to the direction of Irish architecture. Despite the lack of capital for large-scale projects during the period, Ireland had two very rigorous builders' journals in the *Irish Builder and Engineer* and *Irish Contractor* (after 1954, the *Irish Architect and Contractor*) which frequently discussed the nature and direction of Irish architecture. They took a strikingly progressive and international approach, publishing articles on new architecture worldwide, such as Unité de Habitation, the Seagram Building, and Lever House.[29] They also published extensively on the technological developments which enabled architectural new departures during the twentieth century, such as new uses of steel and reinforced concrete. In this context of rapidly developing constructional methods, and influenced by the global fame of such architects as Mies van der Rohe, Le Corbusier, and Walter Gropius, many Irish architects took an interest not only in the large-scale questions of planning, but also in how an indigenous architectural tradition should articulate itself in the mid-twentieth century.

In 1954, Ailtire (Irish for architect), the long-standing columnist for the *Irish Architect and Contractor*, in a gloomy mood after reviewing a particularly dreary crop of competition entries for the new Port and Docks building, bemoaned: 'really we have not a vestige of native architectural tradition showing as yet, and that (as *they* say about everything), after thirty two years of independence'.[30] He went on to opine that, 'After all, our climate, our history, our social structure, religion, geographical position, economy etc etc should make a difference: *if our architects were interpreting these elements correctly*. But are they? Have they a clue? It's a hard thing to say; yet I don't think they have. There is too much *copyism* going on. Inevitably, we are over-influenced by England.'[31] To Ailtire, national formation and cultural formation were intertwined. He emphasized the importance of casting aside foreign influences emanating both

[27] *Irish Builder and Engineer*, 20 April 1957, 291.

[28] *Irish Independent*, 28 October 1957, 1; *Galway Cathedral* (pamphlet, Galway, 1965).

[29] *Irish Architect and Contractor*, June 1953, 46; *Irish Architect and Contractor*, September 1953, 53; *Irish Architect and Contractor*, March 1959, 11.

[30] 'As I see it', *Irish Architect and Contractor*, March 1954, 18.

[31] 'As I see it', *Irish Architect and Contractor*, March 1954, 18.

from contemporary Britain and eighteenth-century Ireland in developing an indigenous, national architecture of independence. Indeed, Ailtire proceeded to contend that 'we have no separate architectural identity worth speaking about and we never had'. To illustrate this argument, he averred that although Gallarus, the round towers, Glendalough, and Cashel had pointed the way to an incipient tradition, Strongbow had seen to its demise.[32] Glendalough and Cashel were two monastic settlements and sites of political power in pre-Norman Ireland which he perceived to represent the unadulterated spirit of Irish design. He contrasted these buildings with the constructions of the eighteenth century, which he explicitly set outside the teleology of Irish architectural development: there was no native blood in 'Gandon, Ducart, Vallency, Pearce, Cassels, Chambers or Ivory'. While dismissing contemporary, Hiberno-Romanesque church architecture as 'not part of our native tradition', he looked to an architectural future imbued with Gaelic influences: 'Yet just as we are trying to express ourselves through our own revived language, so we must try to formulate ourselves in stone. It is a test of our ability to meet conditions here; to use materials in a distinctly Irish way and to be ourselves.'[33] Indeed, it is of fundamental import that Ailtire chose to invoke the totem of the language; in drawing a parallel between this and native architecture, he indicated that its inspiration should come principally from looking inwards to a Gaelic culture, as opposed to either the legacy of Ascendancy or contemporary developments in America and continental Europe.

A young Arthur Gibney, in an article published in the Royal Institute of Architects of Ireland (RIAI) yearbook of 1956–7, took a very similar view in his conception of Irish architecture, and the problems which faced the creation of a modern, yet distinctive national idiom. He described the Georgian style as 'the nearest thing we have to hand' to a native tradition, but went on to posit that its characteristics were antithetical to the essence of Irish architecture:

> Symmetry and monumentality are foreign to the Irish spirit. All our ancient works show a horror of such obvious and static qualities... Symmetry and monumentality were essential ingredients in the Palladian formula, which depended for its effect on a mathematical perception of geometric ratios which was just as strange to the subjective Celt as the Platonic idea it embodies. Most of our Georgian monuments are of this ideology. It is significant, however, that most of them were actually designed by Englishmen.[34]

32 'As I see it', *Irish Architect and Contractor*, March 1954, 18.
33 'As I see it', *Irish Architect and Contractor*, March 1954, 18.
34 Arthur Gibney, 'Towards a National Architecture', *RIAI Yearbook* 1956–7, 20.

His conception of the differences between the Celt and the Englishman were derived directly from Matthew Arnold, and this difference related directly to the creation of a national architecture. This made Georgian architecture an implicitly foreign creation, while Irish architecture relied on a rejection of these qualities.[35] Gibney went on to speculate about an approach which fused the technological developments of modern architecture with a Celtic inheritance, but admitted that it was 'a difficult synthesis to visualise'. He suggested that although the structural expression of all big undertakings must remain international in form, a distinctive identity could be expressed in decoration informed by past styles and 'based on organic and animated abstraction'.[36] He therefore rejected both the Romanesque revival architecture of much church building of the period and a rigid adherence to an international style.

It is notable that these two architects took such similar views on Irish design, jointly dismissing the eighteenth century as outside the lineage of Irish architecture and looking instead to a style imbued with Celtic influences.[37] However, for Ailtire and Gibney, an indigenous style derived from Irish particularity certainly did not mean Hiberno-Romanesque. As Ailtire wrote, 'I wish the period in which the contemporary idiom has to fight for its life against the sham revivalists was over in Ireland as it is in almost every (other) civilised country in the world.'[38] In similar terms, Michael Scott told a meeting of the Irish Association in Belfast that 'by far the best designed buildings today were industrial buildings; fortunately one can not build Romanesque factories'.

Yet, just as church building attempted to create a new national aesthetic while recreating an unbuilt Irish past, so too did Gibney's and Ailtire's conception of Irish modernism lead to the creation of a new image for the state. Indeed, buildings from this period, such as Busáras and the American Embassy, Ballsbridge, both reveal continental influences while also retaining Celtic decorative motifs. Busáras, designed by Michael Scott and opened in 1953, was one of the first large-scale modern buildings to be completed after the end of the Second World War. It was originally planned as the 'Central Station', to be situated at the top of Capel Street as proposed in Abercrombie's 1922 and 1939 designs. In the event, it was moved eastwards to make travel to England easier, so that those coming to Dublin from the countryside to emigrate would not have to get another

[35] Gerry Smyth, 'The Natural Course of Things': Matthew Arnold, Celticism, and the English Poetic Tradition', *Journal of Victorian Culture* 1/1 (1996), 35–53.

[36] 'Towards a National Architecture', *RIAI Yearbook* 1956–7, 29.

[37] *Irish Builder and Engineer*, 23 February 1957, 131.

[38] *Irish Architect and Contractor*, April 1956, 20.

bus to the dock.[39] The story of its location is indicative of the considerable financial hardships facing the country at the time of its erection; despite this, a considerable amount was spent on the building's design, construction, and detailing. It was extensively modelled on Le Corbusier's work of the 1930s, but was notable for Scott's particular flair for decoration, evident in its rippling roofs and mosaics.[40] Indeed, Clair Wills has discussed Scott's combination of 'a Gaelic Christian past and a modern future' with reference to Scott's famous Irish Pavilion at the 1939 World Fair.[41] It is notable how far these ideas of modernism in Ireland diverged from the ideals of the movement's founders. Irish modernism integrated a functional aesthetic and mechanized production with pre-Norman motifs, creating a seemingly unbroken lineage between independent Ireland and a distant past preceding British arrival. Although internationalism and future-orientation had been fundamental to the movement's foundation, Irish modernism was explicitly 'national' in tone, and consciously sought to link modern design with an aesthetic which predated the twelfth century.

In Britain, Georgian architecture was contemporaneously understood to have provided one of the roots of modernism that made the architectural developments of the twentieth century both progressive and yet uniquely English.[42] The same could not be said in Ireland. The emphasis on a 'Celtic' aesthetic meant that Georgian Ireland was left outside the lineage of Irish architecture. Gibney and Ailtire both positioned Palladianism, and Ireland's great architects of the style, as outside the national architectural canon. But whereas Ireland's eighteenth-century architecture was often unthinkingly derided as 'British', Gibney and Ailtire synthesized this commonly held view into a theorized vision of national architecture based both on modernist doctrine and the aesthetics of the Gaelic revival. However, this architectural theory served to reinforce attitudes to the built environment based largely on sectarianism, post-colonial politics, and social prejudice. Any sense of continuity between medieval and early-modern architecture and town planning, or symbiosis between Irish and European styles, was flattened by a binary discourse which constructed these forms as oppositional. Indeed, carrying on this conception of culture, it is notable how explicitly the structural functionalism, circular

[39] O'Regan, *Michael Scott*, 22.

[40] Casey, *Dublin*, 76.

[41] Clair Wills, *That Neutral Island: A History of Ireland During the Second World War* (London, 2008), 18–21.

[42] William Whyte, 'The Englishness of English Architecture: Modernism, and the Making of a National International Style 1937–57', *Journal of British Studies*, 48/2 (2009), 441–65.

shapes, and sinuous forms that defined Irish modernism were explicitly promulgated in opposition to the architecture of Georgian Ireland. In this schema, eighteenth-century architecture thus stood outside Irishness itself, putting Dublin in the Swiftian position of having a foreign landscape on native soil.

Louis Le Broquy recognized the importance of Busáras's modern style for national self-identification, aligning Georgian Dublin with a past which was now gone:

> The technique and purpose of Georgian architecture belong to another age. Since then we have become a free people, responsible to ourselves for our conduct and our future. This bus station is the first building of European importance to be built by Dubliners, in the city of Dublin, since we became independent. It is to be the greatest single contribution which our nation has made to architecture.[43]

However, the role which Le Broquy envisaged for modern architecture in forging a new, European-facing future for the state was not universally accepted. There was no consensus on the direction that Ireland should take, both in engaging with international developments in architecture and promulgating its own distinctive style. Ailtire and Gibney concurred in seeing the Georgian city as the creation of an alien elite, but both were ambivalent in their conception of how Irish architecture should resolve the division between being modern, which was explicitly international in its definition, while also being Gaelic, for which the inward look was an essential part of its identity. While the architectural legacy of the eighteenth century was disowned and allowed to decay, much that was constructed attempted to fill this gap, being designed in the style of a past which had never existed. This failure to engage with international trends in architecture can be understood as a result not only of a lack of money for substantial building projects but also a consequence of a culture adrift, unsure of how to articulate its identity spatially in relation to both the already extant architecture dating from the eighteenth and nineteenth centuries and also the new developments emanating from Europe.[44] Indeed, this discomfort regarding how Ireland should assimilate or integrate the influences coming from America, Britain, and the continent were part of a greater unease which encompassed every aspect of Irish cultural production. The analogy with debates within Irish literary culture

[43] *Irish Times*, 12 May 1950, 5.

[44] John Olley, 'Weaving the Fabric of the City: Urban Design and Dublin', in Annette Becker, John Olley, Wilfred Wang (eds.), *Twentieth Century Architecture: Ireland* (Frankfurt, 1997), 46.

was noted: Frank O'Connor wrote, 'what *wouldn't* we give for a building done in the mood of Synge's "Playboy" or Yeats' "On Baile's Strand" instead of the sickly imitations of "Hiberno-Romanesque" we get as their equivalent?'[45] This was of fundamental import for the future of the eighteenth-century architecture of Dublin, as, in many ways, the desires to create a new future through modern design or a new past through Hiberno-Romanesque forms were very different articulations of the same impulse: to create a new aesthetic for the new state, an aesthetic which was designed in opposition to the extant eighteenth-century city.

In the late 1950s, the gloom which had enveloped the architectural profession began to lift, and the ideas and debates of the 1950s began to take on a new reality. The Building Centre opened its first Irish franchise in Dublin in 1960, and its in-house journal, *Forgnán*, edited by Niall Montgomery, epitomized this spirit of the age:

> *Forgnán* is not yet in the dictionary: magazine is!–it means 'Store for gunpowder'. Naturally it is hoped that this magazine will be a store for the dynamite of ideas. *Forgnán*, a new word, is a sign of the Centre's pride in its identity, in its youth and in its nationality. The pride is not complacency: *Forgnán* hopes to spread itself, internationally, on all wave-lengths, and ultimately in the major languages. The story needn't be dull. An old nation, a new state, squeezed into part of a small island, dominated by its agricultural industry, has begun to build, to expand its cities, to think in terms of factory production, processing and assembly of goods. The common market is providing the drama. The tariff walls are being undermined: nations are going to learn that the only effective substitute for Protection is Attack. *Forgnán* is with those who believe that for the small nations the weapons of success are Design and Quality.[46]

Forgnán was an invented word, but it was an invented word *in Irish*, representing a dynamism and modernity previously unassociated with the national tongue.[47] Alongside this, the romance and drama Montgomery found in factories, processing, and the common market were also new aspects of political discourse, which previously had elevated tradition and agriculture as the central tenets of national life. These economic and political changes were also manifest in a new upturn in the building industry in Dublin city. The city's skyline was soon broken by the strong verticals

[45] Frank O'Connor, 'Meditation in Clonmacnoise', *Forgnán*, February 1962, 6.

[46] *Forgnán*, January 1962, 5.

[47] Edited by Niall Montgomery, and only published for nine (turbulent) months in 1962, it received contributions from such prominent figures as Garret FitzGerald, Ove Arup, Robin Walker, Patrick Delaney, Frank O'Connor, James White, Percy Le Clerc, Seán Ó'Faoláin, and Patrick Pye. See Montgomery papers for correspondence relating to this journal.

of Ireland's first high-rise buildings, such as Liberty Hall, Dublin's first point block, O'Connell Bridge House, the Sugar Company headquarters on Leeson Street, and the new Bord Fáilte (the tourist board) building on Baggot Street.[48] Competitions were also announced for a new Arts Library for Trinity College, and a new UCD campus at Belfield, which was, with the exception of the new town at Shannon, the single largest building project in Ireland, while Michael Scott designed a new Abbey Theatre and the first phase of the Radio Télefis Éireann (RTÉ) offices at Stillorgan.[49] This was only the beginning of an office revolution in Dublin, which led to an enormous wave of building in the city during the decade.

The new buildings were all constructed in the style and materials of European post-war modernism. Liberty Hall rose above the city, its four large walls of glass creating an elegant silhouette on a sensitive site beside the Custom House. This was matched by the considerably less elegant O'Connell Bridge House, a sixteen-storey concrete office block which stood on the southern edge of O'Connell Bridge, and which, with Liberty Hall, dominated the skyline of the city. Paul Koralek's Berkeley Library in Trinity College was a strong mass of moulded concrete, while Robin Walker's Bord Fáilte building was the first core plan building in Ireland.[50] These buildings used concrete, glass, and steel to create new structural forms previously unseen in the capital. They were unashamedly international in ethos, being very similar in design to the many buildings which were also transforming the landscape of central London at this time. The integration of Gaelic motifs and functionalist construction, evident in many buildings dating from the 1950s, wilted away in this period as these architects looked to a more purely international idiom for the design of the new buildings.

The new buildings of this period, with their strong lines, dominant horizontals, and emphasis on individual edifices rather than street fabric, were immediately noted to be out of place in the low, unified core of the city. For many architects, these new buildings were important symbols of Ireland's transformation. For example, Norman Smyth wrote enthusiastically of O'Connell Bridge House, challenging its detractors by pointing out that:

[48] *Irish Architect and Contractor*, April 1957, 14; *Irish Architect and Contractor*, May 1959, 12.

[49] *Irish Architect and Contractor*, July 1958, 12; *Irish Architect and Contractor*, March/April 1961, 12; Walker, 'Architecture in Ireland 1940–75', 27; Patrick Delaney (ed.), *Architectural Survey (Dublin) 1958–66*; Patrick Malone, *Office Development in Dublin 1960–80* (Dublin, 1981), 54–8.

[50] O'Regan, *Scott Tallon Walker Architects*, 46.

> There are critics who complain that new buildings in Dublin are not in harmony with the rest of the city. This is true at present. But what is forgotten, or ignored, is that the erection of a handful of clean-lined, modern structures is only the first stage in the transformation of Dublin from a rather shabby town dominated by crumbling slum areas, interspersed with dreary Corporation housing estates, into a twentieth-century city with comfortable and hygienic working and living accommodation. The rate of erection of new commercial buildings is relatively slow at present but this is expected to increase as our industrial potential is realised.[51]

O'Connell Bridge House had a layout suited to modern office work, and its design looked to European and American conventions, while in its use of new materials and building methods it reflected Ireland's advancing technological expertise. Standing much taller than all the surrounding buildings, and utilizing new construction methods, it stood in the centre of the city as a beacon of Ireland's modernity. This future for Dublin, prospected by buildings like this, would be international and prosperous, where most would work in comfortable offices, and the city would be hygienic, light, and clean-lined. Buildings such as O'Connell Bridge House thus not only represented Ireland's economic and cultural transformation but also brought it into being.

This emphasis on the transformational potential of spatial reconstruction led architects to look to sweeping changes to the city. Norman Smyth saw the available sites as representing a challenge to town planners, builders, and architects to design a rational, clean, and modern city comparable with those being constructed in Britain and Europe, and urged town planners to discard 'conventional and outmoded ideas' in the creation of a new city.[52] Writing in *Forgnán*, Brian Hogan, one of the most prolific architects of the 1960s, looked to the reconstruction of Dublin as a way of shaping the values and culture of Ireland: 'it is clear . . . that the present cycle in the evolution of the city is coming to an end and a rebirth is required'.[53] He called for a more scientific understanding of the *genius loci*, so that a new Dublin could be created that retained and improved on its particular sense of place, posing the question, 'Do we like ourselves as we are—or, now that our long established environment is decaying, should we take this opportunity of radically changing our milieu, and hence, in the course of generations, changing the attitudes and values of our children and their descendants?'[54] Thus, Hogan had a clear concep-

[51] *Build*, November 1965, 25; 'President's Inaugural Address', *RIAI Yearbook 1964*, 5.
[52] *Build*, November 1965, 27.
[53] *Forgnán*, April 1962, 18.
[54] *Forgnán*, April 1962, 19.

tion of the link between the individual, society, and space, and a belief that in remaking the spaces of the capital city a new society was being forged.

This sense of modernity, positivity, and progress had a concomitant impact on architectural attitudes to the eighteenth-century city. In the 1950s, Dublin had been portrayed as a crumbling, dirty relic. As shown by Smyth's description of the city, these images lived on in the early 1960s, but they were now juxtaposed by an image of the city as a real place of possibilities, transformed by economic advances, technological developments, and Irish expertise. In November 1961, the Architectural Association held a debate entitled, 'This house deplores the repeated attacks on our Georgian Heritage'. It was convincingly lost; the general premise for the motion's defeat was that architects should be building for the present, and reflect the spirit of the age, just as the Georgian builders had.[55] In a series of four forums in the *Irish Times* conducted by Michael Viney on 'The Future of Dublin', Sam Stephenson was determined in his desire to see the city built anew. Indeed, the forum was accompanied by architectural drawings by Sam Stephenson of a visionary new city of precincts, skyscrapers, and high-level urban motorways.[56]

The notions expressed by Smyth, Hogan, and Stephenson, of building for the future and reforming society, were also worked through in great detail by Robin Walker, who provided a 'scientific' analysis of the future of the eighteenth-century city based on contemporary architectural theory. Writing in *Forgnán*, he proposed a radical solution to the problem of the eighteenth-century city, and displayed the influence of having worked with both Le Corbusier and Mies van der Rohe.[57] He provided a 'rational' diagnosis based on scientific architectural principles for the future of the area, believing that the city's 'function has changed and it is clear that any renovation which expresses its new—that is, different—function will fail to harmonize, and it is equally clear that any rebuilding or renovation which does not express its function will fail to function'. In order, therefore, to avoid a 'chaotic and discordant environment' which would be created by piecemeal rebuilding, he suggested that:

> if one can . . . accept that the buildings of the area are structurally and functionally obsolete and to some degree due to their over dense land use, redundant; that the present pattern of land use is unsatisfactory; and that the

[55] *Irish Builder and Engineer*, 11 November 1961, 895.

[56] *Irish Times*, 16 October 1963, 8; *Irish Times*, 17 October 1963, 8; *Irish Times*, 18 October 1963, 8; *Irish Times*, 19 October 1963, 10.

[57] John O'Regan and Nicola Dearey (eds.), *Michael Scott: Architect in (Casual) Conversation with Dorothy Walker* (Cork, 1995), 165.

> street pattern is also structurally and functionally obsolete and likely to become redundant, it should be clear that, contrary to any case for the preservation of the area, a good case can be made for its total demolition and reconstruction. It should be clear that is possible to envisage a total and radical redevelopment of the area to serve the requirements of the present and the foreseeable future in relation to an overall policy and plan for the whole city.[58]

Walker saw the value of the city in its aesthetic rather than historical considerations, and hence saw no reason why these could not be improved, and reconstruction could not take place. He suggested instead of the piecemeal rebuilding of the city a unified cityscape, where industry, residential, and commercial uses of the city would be zoned rationally, housed in appropriate buildings, and constructed as part of a coherent approach to the whole city.

For the architects of the early 1960s, the ideals of progress and prosperity dominated their conceptions of the future of Dublin. They looked to modern architecture as providing the material basis for national renewal as conceived and propounded by Lemass. This language of the architectural profession drew heavily on an international consensus in town planning. However, Lemass's idea of a new Ireland played heavily on a similar vocabulary as that espoused by the founders of modernism: the values of efficiency, progress, and hygiene were central tenets of both discourses.[59] Moreover, the exaltation of the power of the machine which was such a key feature of modernist doctrine in the inter-war period, and was resuscitated again by the New Brutalists in the 1950s, had a parochial analogue in Lemass's exultation of industrialization as a means to an affluent, independent nation. However, in this discourse, 'Georgian Dublin' was constructed as the opposite of everything architectural modernism stood for: it was a dark, dirty, unrationalized past, which had been built for a function that no longer existed. With its cramped streets and low residential buildings, it no longer provided for the needs of the modernising state. Therefore, both for the future city to be created and for the future of the nation to be realized, Dublin had to be reconstructed.

In 1958, Dublin was still the city that Gogarty had described; its principal street was 'vulgar and bizarre', but beyond this, 'rose-red houses, public buildings of white stone . . . crowned with various domes of copper, green with age' still dominated the scene. There was little construction in the city centre during the 1950s, and the vast majority of the city's

[58] Robin Walker, 'The Squares', *Forgnán*, April 1962, 13.

[59] David Pinder, *Visions of the City: Utopianism, Power and Politics in Twentieth-Century Urbanism* (Edinburgh, 2005), 3.

eighteenth-century buildings remained intact. However, this romantic stasis was, for many from the architectural profession, a malaise, characterized by a lack of work, a lack of money, and a lack of scope for experimentation. The continued existence of the city which had once been the centre of the British administration in Ireland was seen by many to represent a wider failure within Irish life for social progress and cultural renewal. Indeed, this deficit of opportunity was palpable: in 1956 every one of UCD's twenty-four final-year architecture students had emigrated within three months of graduating.[60] To add to this feeling of malaise the place of modern architecture was not yet secured. Architects were engaged in debate, not only with an establishment which frequently commissioned buildings in a retrogressive idiom, but also within the profession, as to how new developments should be incorporated into a national style. But this paucity of work did not translate into a deficit of ideas; there was an appreciable sense among architects of the need to remake the city in line with contemporary planning theory, and a real sense of optimism regarding the improvements which could be made to Irish life if the capital was available for large scale reconstruction. There was a unity of opinion, however, in relation to understandings of Dublin's Georgian fabric. The urban environment was seen as a dark, dirty, and crumbling relic; as a monument to an elite which had disappeared; and as the counterpoint to the creation of a new city of light and air. Furthermore, the volumes, masses, and forms of the architecture of this period were also seen to be antithetical to a new Irish architecture, be it modernist or historicist. This combination of factors alongside an ambitious, yet frustrated profession, and a limited, indeed never implemented, plan produced by Dublin Corporation meant that in the construction boom of the 1960s there was little appetite or provision to preserve the decaying city.

The abstract debates of the 1950s took on a new reality in the 1960s. In this decade there was a huge amount of reconstruction in the central areas of the city. In particular, new office blocks were constructed, using international standards and forms. Lemass's vision of a new identity for Ireland, and all it entailed—prosperity, internationalism, and consumption—was understood to be fundamentally constituted through this transformation of the built environment. This meant that in the 1960s there was little will to preserve the eighteenth-century city emanating from much of the architectural community. For this group, the extant city was a dark, unhygienic, poorly functioning slum; it stood for the opposite of everything the new city would be.

[60] *Irish Architect and Contractor*, October 1956, 15.

3

Kildare Place and the Irish Georgian Society, 1957–8

As the previous chapters have suggested, during the 1950s there was little interest in the city as a historic site. However, while many architects and town planners called for a complete reconstruction of the centre of the city, the end of the decade also witnessed the beginnings of a campaigning movement for architectural preservation. During this period, prominent figures rallied to save the Royal Hospital Kilmainham, which was closed up and unoccupied, from further deterioration. The controversy which surrounded the demolition of two eighteenth-century houses on Kildare Place led directly to the foundation of the Irish Georgian Society, a group which would be at the forefront of preservationism and would play a critical role in forming attitudes to the built environment for the following fifty years. Although the form and architecture of Dublin was not the incendiary political issue in the 1950s that it became ten years on, these scuffles not only prefigured the large-scale demonstrations of the 1960s but also set in place the social and cultural codes through which they would be defined.

In 1955, the Royal Hospital Kilmainham had stood empty, boarded, and locked for over six years (Fig. 3.1). Unrepaired and unmaintained, its condition was degrading swiftly; it was becoming unstable, in need either of demolition or of expensive structural work. The building had been completed in 1684 to a design by Sir William Robinson. Constructed on a courtyard plan with arcades on three sides and a chapel and master's lodgings on the fourth, it also featured a hundred yard long great hall, which was topped by a tower and spire.[1] It was one of the largest, most elaborate, and earliest structures in the city, described by Maurice Craig as 'an eloquent building, the most eloquent Dublin was to see until the

[1] Office of Public Works, *An Introduction to the Royal Hospital Kilmainham: Its Architecture, History and Restoration* (Dublin, 1987); Edward McParland, *The Royal Hospital, Kilmainham, Co. Dublin: A National Centre for Culture and the Arts in Ireland* (Dublin, 1985).

Fig. 3.1. Royal Hospital Kilmainham, 1979. Image courtesy of David Davison/ Irish Architectural Archive.

coming of Gandon'. Indeed, it was the largest surviving edifice of its period in Ireland, and the earliest secular public building in the country.[2] From the building's erection in the seventeenth century it had functioned as a hospital for retired British soldiers; however, in the years immediately after independence conditions in the country became unsuitable for the hospital to maintain this use, and the last remaining pensioners were finally transferred to Chelsea in 1927.[3] With the departure of the military personnel it then served for the following twenty years as the headquarters of the Garda Síochána. However, when it was discovered to be suffering from dry rot and insect infestations in 1949, the Gardaí departed, and the vacant building found a new use as a municipal warehouse.[4]

The 270-year-old building was rescued from this indignity in 1955 after Taoiseach John Costello, under pressure from a coalition including Maurice Craig, Patrick Little, and Senators W. B. Stanford and Michael

[2] Craig, *Dublin 1660–1860*, 59.

[3] NAI DT S2123D press clipping from *Irish Press*, 30 November 1954; also NAI DT S2123D, Memorandum for Government from Department of Finance, 19 December 1955.

[4] NAI DT S2123D, Memorandum, 19 December 1955.

Hayes, intervened to prevent its further degradation. But as there was no precedent or legislation to allow for its preservation as a historic landmark, a use had to be found for this large and ancient structure. Costello wrote to all government departments asking if they required the building: Defence proposed using it as its office headquarters; Justice asked for it to be returned to use as the headquarters of the Garda Síochána; Posts and Telegraphs desired to use it for the storage of materials, and the grounds for erection of warehouses; Seán MacBride and members of Dublin Corporation hoped to obtain the site for their new Corporation offices; while Education proposed that the building should be used for a folk museum.[5] Of all the possibilities for the site, the option of converting it into a folk museum was most seriously considered. This proposal led to the government issuing the Royal Hospital Kilmainham (Dissolution of Governors and Revocation of Charters) Order 1955, dissolving the defunct Governors of Hospital of King Charles the Second, which had been incorporated in 1684 to maintain the building, so that the Board of Works could take full control of the hospital and therefore carry out the necessary repairs.[6]

In its time as a warehouse during the 1940s and 1950s, the Royal Hospital had functioned as a repository of imperial flotsam. The seventeenth-century great hall's contents included a former Lord Mayor's coach, Queen Victoria's statue exiled from Leinster Lawn, and an Aran currach, while other rooms housed several portraits and spare office furniture owned by the Board of Works.[7] Indeed, the hospital served as a storehouse for symbols of Empire which no longer had a place in the geography of the city. Moreover, the structure itself was also an imperial artefact, being part of the nexus of sites which had defined British military presence in Ireland. Costello's choice to reuse the hospital as a folk museum was significant: it symbolically reappropriated a site of former colonial and military power, in order for it to serve as part of the project of building the post-independence nation through the collection and display of 'authentic' Irish cultural artefacts. In so doing, it would have recast the building to serve as part of the symbolic geography of the new nation state, and thus overwritten the existing historic associations. However, this conversion was never implemented; owing to Costello's intervention

[5] NAI DT S2123D, Letter from J. P. Keane to John Costello, 3 December 1955; NAI DT S2123D, Letter from Gerald Sweetman to John Costello, 3 November 1955.

[6] The governors were all presumed to be dead. NAI DT S2123D, Letter from J. P. Keane to John Costello, 3 December 1955 and Royal Hospital Kilmainham (Dissolution of Governors and Revocation of Charters) Order 1955.

[7] NAI DT S2123D press clipping *Irish Press*, 28 December 1955. Also Frederick O'Dwyer, *Lost Dublin* (Dublin, 1981), 40.

the hospital was repaired, but the building remained unopened to the public until its restoration as the Irish Museum of Modern Art in 1984.[8]

Despite the age, grandeur, and architectural importance of the Royal Hospital Kilmainham, this was not the most high-profile preservationist debate in the latter part of the 1950s, nor was it the most significant in terms of creating the preconditions for the battles regarding the city in the 1960s. When the destruction of two fairly ordinary houses in Kildare Place began during the summer of 1957, there was a well-orchestrated campaign to secure their preservation; this attracted much media attention and precipitated the foundation of the Irish Georgian Society.

Kildare Place was a small square set back from Kildare Street, just to the south of the National Museum (Fig. 3.2). The square, which was completed in the years before 1750, had originally consisted of four houses, two of which were constructed by Richard Castle.[9] During the 1880s, the National Museum and the Church of Ireland teacher training college were built on each side of the square, entailing the destruction of 1 and 4 Kildare Place.[10] However, the surviving houses remained in residential occupation until 1927 (Thomas Bodkin lived in No. 2 for a decade from 1917 while director of the National Gallery), and were subsequently used as offices by the Fisheries Branch of the Department of Agriculture. However, the terrace had been vacated and left empty in 1955. Although the two eighteenth-century buildings were not included in the sparse provisions for preservation in the 1957 City Plan, the National Monuments Advisory Council and the RIAI had listed them for preservation in their recommendations on the document, owing to their particularly fine, well-preserved interiors (Fig. 3.3).[11] Despite this, in March 1957, the decision was taken by the Office of Public Works to demolish the vacant buildings, with no immediate plans for the site's reuse.[12]

News of the destruction of these houses only reached the public domain after demolition had already begun. Indeed, it received no coverage in the press at all until Lord Wicklow wrote a letter to the *Irish Times* in June 1957, alerting the paper's readership to the demolition.[13] This letter led to a flurry of indignation in the letters pages, and, despite the fact that the

[8] NAI DT S2123D Memorandum on file, 25 August 1958; see also NAI DT S16682B.

[9] O'Dwyer, *Lost Dublin*, 42.

[10] O'Dwyer, *Lost Dublin*, 42.

[11] RIAI, *Recommendations and Observations on the City of Dublin Planning Scheme*.

[12] NAI DT S5004C, Letter from National Monuments Advisory Council to the Secretary of the Office of Public Works, 19 March 1957.

[13] *Irish Times*, 17 June 1957, 5.

Fig. 3.2. Nos. 2 and 3 Kildare Place, 1957. Image courtesy of the Office of Public Works.

Fig. 3.3. Interior of 2 Kildare Place. Image courtesy of the Irish Architectural Archive.

roofs were already being removed, several attempts were made to halt the demolition.[14] Letters were sent directly to the Taoiseach, Éamon de Valera, asking for him to prevent the destruction of the houses; Declan Costello TD attempted, with little success, to have the matter debated in the Dáil; while the Arts Council, the National Monuments Advisory Council, and the RIAI all wrote to the government in support of the preservation of the houses.[15] There was also an effort at a coordinated approach: Terence De Vere White, the novelist and journalist, organized a petition addressed to de Valera, which was signed by many prominent individuals from Ireland's artistic and cultural scene.[16]

However, these various efforts to have the demolition stopped had no effect. De Valera responded to the clamour of voices for preservation with a statement saying that the buildings could not be saved because of their condition.[17] While his press release regarding demolition focused on the structural defects of the terrace, and the unjustifiable amount of money it would cost to put them in order, privately his office also acknowledged the lack of suitability of these structures for modern management techniques—although this reason, present in governmental memoranda, was discreetly removed before release to the press.[18] There was thus no consideration of the buildings as having an aesthetic or historic value; rather their worth was assessed only as offices which had become obsolete. Indeed, when Patrick Beegan, the Parliamentary Secretary to the Minister for Finance, was asked by Declan Costello if the houses should be preserved under National Monuments legislation, he replied that, 'Deputy Costello gave us the definition from the Act of a National Monument and its national importance, and it was only in respect of the architectural design of these buildings that any case can be made, because they have no historical or traditional background whatsoever.'[19]

Notwithstanding Beegan's narrow definition of 'historical and traditional background', this view was not all-pervasive within the government and the Office of Public Works. Even though his name did not appear on the petition, the Private Secretary to the Minister of Finance informed the Department of the Taoiseach that he believed 'that the agitation against

[14] *Irish Times*, 25 June 1957, 4; *Irish Times*, 16 May 1958, 7.

[15] NAI DT S5004C Memorandum on file, 20 June 1957; PDDÉ 163, 2 July 1957, cols 404–6; PDDÉ 163, 2 July 1957, cols 514–22.

[16] NAI DT S5004C, Letter from Terence de Vere White et al. to de Valera, 19 June 1957.

[17] *Irish Times*, 27 June 1957, 9.

[18] NAI DT S5004C, Letter from Secretary to Taoiseach to Terence de Vere White, 25 June 1957.

[19] PDDÉ 163, 2 July 1957, cols 514–22.

the demolition of the buildings had been fostered, if not initiated by the present Inspector of National Monuments in the Office of Public Works, Mr Percy Le Clerc'.[20] Le Clerc's quiet protest against his own organization was indicative of his dissatisfaction with the state's policies concerning the built environment; indeed, six months later he would be a founding member of the Irish Georgian Society.[21] However, despite his intervention, demolition continued, and a few months later only a blank wall remained where the houses had once been.

The significance of the Kildare Place controversy lay in the very ordinariness of the buildings. This was the first time that Georgian red-brick houses, which were neither public buildings nor had any associations with any key moments of Irish history, became the subject of pleas for preservation. The rationale for preservation of these structures rested neither on their having famous architects nor on their being historically significant landmarks, but rather on their character, and the character created by a multitude of similar buildings. Antoin O Maonaigh, of Top Back Room, Fitzgibbon Street (the only exception to the otherwise homogeneously middle-class profile of the preservation campaign), called on de Valera to preserve the terraces of the city as the repositories of 'the soul of Dublin'.[22] Similarly, Terence De Vere White's letter to de Valera also demanded the preservation of the buildings solely for their aesthetic merits, as part of the streetscape which gave Dublin its character:

> These houses have no particular historical associations: they form a part of a great heritage which was allowed to go to waste in the last century and which, if every effort is not made in the present, will be dissipated. The preservation of a few historical buildings do not keep a city's character: it is the total effect of the houses such as these which made Dublin unique.[23]

De Vere White's conception of the importance of preservation in order to retain the 'character' of Dublin mirrored a broader movement from within architectural practice towards preserving the fabric of the city and a sense of place. Indeed, the Kildare Place controversy was contemporaneous with the beginnings of the Townscape movement in the *Architectural Review*. However, as yet these ideas had very little traction within Ireland; the idea that the eighteenth-century domestic terraces of the

[20] NAI DT S5004C, Memorandum on file, 20 June 1957.

[21] See list of committee members in *Quarterly Bulletin of the Irish Georgian Society*, January–March 1959, 7.

[22] NAI DT S5004C, Letter from Antoin O Maonaigh to de Valera, 22 June 1957.

[23] NAI DT S5004C, Letter from de Vere White et al. to de Valera, 19 June 1957.

city, rather than just the set-piece buildings, should be preserved was not widely held.

Despite their differing aims and approaches to the city, those who called for the preservation of the buildings shared with the architects who wished to see the city's reconstruction a common sense of pessimism regarding the present and future of the Irish state. For example, Uinseann MacEoin, the editor of the *Irish Architect and Contractor*, was vituperative in his attack on the government's decision to demolish the terrace, contrasting the 'history and tradition' of the houses with the poverty of the country:

> In the year of the emergency, in the year 1957, when financial stringency decrees that 50,000 of our people must leave in order that our balance of payment be preserved, the Government allows the wilful destruction of forty thousand pounds of Irish public property which from a point of view of history and tradition is priceless. With a mounting toll of unemployed, without money for necessary rebuilding, with an average eighty thousand jobless, and with twenty thousand jobs less this year than there were last year, this 'poor' country now turns to destroy what it might live by.[24]

For MacEoin, the destruction of the houses exemplified the poor policy decisions which had been made by the government since independence, and was only another example—alongside emigration—of the destruction of the natural capital of the country in order to fulfil the ideological economics of independence. These links between the failure of the state and the destruction of the houses was frequently made, but criticism was cultural as well as economic. In relation to the destruction, Seamus Kelly (as Quidnunc) writing in the influential column *An Irishman's Diary* quoted Micheál MacLiammóir's parody of Yeats, 'All changed changed utterly/A terrible suburb is born.'[25] The architect, John Butler, in a letter to the *Irish Times*, called for the Kildare Place buildings' preservation on account of 'their inherent value as examples of civilized building, architectural character, and above all quality', and noted that, 'it is tragic, in an age when so much is shoddy and third-rate, that they should be destroyed by those entrusted with their care'.[26] Taking a similar view in 1956, Gerald Nicoll, president of the RIAI, compared the nineteenth-century houses of Herbert Street with Dublin Corporation's new residential estate in Ballyfermot, and contrasted the 'urbanity' of the former with the 'grim and

[24] *Irish Architect and Contractor*, June 1957, 23.

[25] *Irish Times*, 3 July 1957, 6; see Micheál MacLiammóir, *Put Money in Thy Purse* (London, 1950), 168.

[26] *Irish Times*, 20 June 1957, 7.

anonymous desolation' of the latter.[27] Unlike Montgomery and Scott, who looked forward to modernism to provide renewal, these commentators looked to the eighteenth-century city as a repository of a more vital and creative culture, and saw its preservation and rehabilitation as a way of restoring some of Ireland's seemingly lost vitality.

The dissent regarding Kildare Place was not widespread; indeed, the altercation would only have been known to have even taken place by a small section of Dublin's population. The controversy regarding the houses was reported solely in the news and letters pages of the *Irish Times*, the former newspaper of the southern Protestant and Unionist population which, by the 1950s, was moving to be the paper of the cultural, administrative, and financial elites. Following on from this, the petition organized by Terence de Vere White was signed by only a handful of people. These were, however, some of the country's most important and best-known cultural figures; they included the head of the Guinness dynasty Lord Moyne, the writer Seán Ó'Faoláin, the actor and owner of the Gate theatre Micheál MacLiammóir, the artist E. Richards Orpen, the senator George O'Brien, the artist Norah McGuinness, and the architects John Butler, Uinseann MacEoin, Niall Montgomery, Eleanor Butler, and Desmond FitzGerald (who signed with the caveat that he only agreed if there were no plans for the site).[28] In limiting the signatories in this way, the campaign did not seek legitimacy through showing weight of numbers in support of the preservation of the houses, but rather aimed to show the weight of an informed cultural and intellectual opinion against demolition.

Kildare Place was situated in the heart of prosperous Dublin; it was located near the governmental and administrative district around Leinster House and Merrion Square, and was also adjacent to the expensive shopping area centred on Grafton Street. It was, therefore, an area of the city which would have been well known to the prosperous middle class. These combined physical and social geographies were essential to the form this controversy took, and subsequently to the formation of gradations of 'value' of the eighteenth-century city. Indeed, this reinscribed and reinforced pre-existing socio-spatial divisions; areas which had fallen into tenements during the nineteenth and early twentieth centuries, despite often having both rich plasterwork and historic associations, were rarely thought to be worth preserving. For example, at the same time as Kildare Place was being taken down, so too were most of the grand eighteenth-century

[27] *RIAI Yearbook*, 1956–7, 4.

[28] NAI S5004C, Letter from de Vere White et al. to de Valera, 19 June 1957.

terraces of Gardiner and Dominick Streets to the north of the Liffey. These streets had been in tenements since the mid-nineteenth century, and their demolition caused no discernible outcry. Middle-class commentators and activists had the political and cultural capital required to make a demolition a news story, and they defined the 'worth' of the city by sites and symbols they knew and understood. It was overwhelmingly the areas that were known, lived in, and walked past by Dublin's middle class that came to represent the heritage site of 'Georgian Dublin' as it emerged during the late 1950s and 1960s; this slowly coalesced as the south-east quadrant of the city surrounding Fitzwilliam and Merrion Square.

During the mild-mannered altercation over Kildare Place, there were frequent calls for a society to campaign for the preservation of Irish architecture.[29] Quidnunc recalled Micheál MacLiammóir's calls for a 'society of architects and cranks to see what could be rescued from destruction'.[30] Ailtire similarly stated that the country required a body to record Ireland's architectural heritage, and remarked that Ireland had fallen 'heavily between two stools in the matter of preserving our heritage', comparing the country's record unfavourably with both the English habit of preserving everything and the American habit of replacing everything every generation: Ireland was too poor to follow either of these routes.[31] Most importantly for the future of preservationism in Ireland, a letter appeared in the *Irish Times* from the Honourable Desmond Guinness asking:

> As the Georgian Society seems to have lapsed, has anyone any objection to my restarting it? Our aims are to bring the photographic records up to date, publish further volumes of the Georgian Society's books, and fight for the preservation of what is left of Georgian architecture in Ireland.[32]

Following on from this public announcement, the Irish Georgian Society (IGS) was set up by Desmond Guinness and his wife Mariga on 21 February 1958, as a refoundation of John Pentland Mahaffy's Georgian Society, which had been in existence from 1908 to 1913. In the first issue of its bulletin, the aims of the new society were listed:

> To awaken an interest in Ireland's Heritage of Georgian Architecture.
>
> To investigate reports from members on any Georgian buildings in danger of demolition or decay, and, where necessary, fight a campaign for their preservation.

[29] *Irish Times*, 24 June 1957, 5.
[30] *Irish Times*, 3 July 1957, 6.
[31] *Irish Architect and Contractor*, January 1958, 14.
[32] *Irish Times*, 23 June 1957, 5.

> To arrange expeditions to buildings of interest, which might eventually be made open to tourists.
>
> To continue the work of the old Georgian Society in recording Georgian Architectural features, and later to publish a book of houses as yet unknown to the public.
>
> To arrange lectures on Architecture, 18th Century decor, gardens, etc. Also discussions on repair and uses for problematical buildings.
>
> To publish a quarterly bulletin, of which this is the first Number.[33]

These goals reveal the society's notions of preservation and heritage. Their conception of architectural value was similar to that espoused by Summerson; they conceived of buildings as having an intrinsic architectural worth which could be understood by a knowledgeable elite.[34] As such, the group aimed to define and discover buildings from the eighteenth century which they deemed to be under threat. These were invariably individual buildings or architectural set pieces, designed by well-known architects and lived in by great men; vernacular idioms, the unified townscape, and the social functions of preservation were subsidiary considerations in the society's first years. They were also influenced by Ruskin's conception of the aura of the past as key to the practice of conservation; they neither 'over-restored' nor reconstructed or used retained-façades, except when forced into this position.[35] In so doing, they positioned themselves as a vanguard of taste, defending and fostering appreciation of an inheritance which was under threat from government and decay.

Even though the impetus for the foundation of the IGS had come through the destruction of Georgian buildings in Dublin, the society's principal focus in its first years tended to be on the preservation of country houses. This took the form of organizing working parties of volunteers to help with building work, attempting to find buyers for empty houses, and providing financial support for restoration. From the outset the organization was notable for its professional approach to campaigning and fundraising. For example, the first issue of the *Quarterly Bulletin* displayed the price in both pounds and dollars (8s. 6d. or $1.50 for four issues).[36] Indeed, this active courting of the American market became a cornerstone of IGS policy; American donors provided a large amount of money for preserving historic structures, while American public opinion was seen as a useful tool in lobbying government departments.[37] Furthermore,

[33] *Quarterly Bulletin of the Irish Georgian Society*, January–March 1958, 4.

[34] Pendlebury, *Conservation in the Age of Consensus*, 14–21.

[35] Jokilehto, *A History of Architectural Conservation* (Oxford, 1999), 174–81.

[36] *Quarterly Bulletin of the Irish Georgian Society*, January–March 1958, 1.

[37] NAI DT S5004E, Letter from Desmond Guinness to Edward Keelan, 25 September 1962.

the society aimed to be not only a pressure group but also a scholarly organization. The bulletin's first edition began with an outraged cry written by Desmond Guinness about the state of Georgian building stock in Ireland, but also contained two articles: on eighteenth-century industry in Kildare, and a piece on courthouses by Maurice Craig.[38] These campaigning and educational facets of the society's purpose were linked; the focus on scholarship also served an instrumental function. It was an attempt to save the Georgian past from destruction by awakening appreciation for it through education.

The society's founders and long-term driving force were the Honourable Desmond Guinness and his wife Mariga.[39] The couple were not only members of the Irish aristocracy but also part of a network of British elites, which straddled the Irish Sea and had links throughout Europe and America. Desmond Guinness was part of the eponymous brewing dynasty, the son of Bryan Guinness, second Lord Moyne and Diana Mitford, and thus grew up in the wilting, anomalous world of Ascendancy culture after independence. He met his wife Mariga—or Princess Henriette Marie-Gabrielle von Urach, daughter of Prince Albrecht von Urach—while they were both in Oxford during the 1950s. Their life at Leixlip Castle maintained a sense of glamour and distinction out of place in the austerity of 1950s Ireland, and notable during a period when country house culture was in a rapid period of decline in Britain. The long-standing *Country Life* journalist John Cornforth described the glamour and style of their home in his 1985 book on country house style in the twentieth century:

> Already it is clear that [Leixlip Castle] was the key country house in the British Isles in the late 1950s and 1960s . . . it was the conjunction of the look of the house, the Guinnesses' approach to life and the aims of the Society that made Leixlip such a stimulating place as well as a remarkable visual experience for the diverse circle of people who flowed in and out through the seemingly ever open doors.[40]

Similarly, in *Vogue's Book of Houses, Gardens, People* (1968), the couple were described as inhabiting an almost dreamlike world, moving between aristocratic refinement and Irish fairy story. Horst's illustrations of the good-looking and fashionable Guinnesses in hyper-real primary colours surrounded by the traditional symbols of Irishness (a pony and trap, a

[38] Maurice Craig, 'A note on Courthouses', *Quarterly Bulletin of the Irish Georgian Society*, January–March 1958, 8–16.

[39] *Quarterly Bulletin of the Irish Georgian Society*, January–March 1958, 3.

[40] John Cornforth, *The Inspiration of the Past: Country House Taste in the Twentieth Century* (Harmondsworth, 1985), 109.

harp, Mariga Guinness in a traditional Irish shawl) only reinforced their unsteady position between British aristocracy, historic Irish family, and self-designated protectorate of the eighteenth-century landscape.[41]

The IGS took its name from the society founded by Sir John Pentland Mahaffy, Provost of Trinity, in 1908. This first Georgian Society was dedicated to recording—rather than saving—Ireland's eighteenth-century architecture, and only remained in existence for five years, ceasing to exist after having completed a set of five volumes (four on Dublin and one on country houses) which recorded the architectural legacy of eighteenth-century Ireland. The emphasis of Mahaffy's society is displayed in the preface to the first volume of records, which urged its readers 'to induce those who live in houses still containing good and interesting work both to take care of it, and to have sketches and photographs taken from the Society's collection'.[42] These volumes were, however, not a systematic record of all of Ireland's eighteenth-century buildings, the scholarship being disordered and piecemeal in its focus. Nevertheless, they provided not only a beautifully illustrated record of the country on the eve of profound change but also an intervention into the struggles regarding the cultural positioning of the new Ireland emerging during this volatile time. The period of the first society's existence was a time of great political and cultural flux; by defining, listing, and celebrating the architectural achievements of eighteenth-century Ireland, the Georgian Society was also making a political statement regarding the parameters of national culture.

The Guinnesses made a conscious effort to link their society to the first Georgian Society. The original name was reused, and the new group was founded on the fiftieth anniversary of the foundation of the predecessor.[43] However, the new society took its place in a very different Ireland. The culture of the big house had almost entirely disappeared; by the time that the IGS was founded, the combined efforts of the IRA and the Office of Public Works had already cleared the rural landscape of a sizeable proportion of its eighteenth-century structures.[44] Indeed, the 1950s had witnessed the widespread destruction of many of Ireland's finest country houses, including John Nash's Rockingham and Stradbally.[45] Moreover, this change in the landscape was symptomatic of broader political forces. The society that had populated these houses had now almost entirely gone, having lost wealth and influence throughout the nineteenth century

[41] Valentine Lawford, *Vogue's Book of Houses, Gardens, People: Photographed by Horst* (London, 1968), 71–83.

[42] *The Georgian Society Records* 1, xi.

[43] *Quarterly Bulletin of the Irish Georgian Society*, January–March 1958, 3.

[44] Randal MacDonnell, *The Lost Houses of Ireland* (London, 2002), 6–10.

[45] *Irish Times*, 3 October 1957, 7.

and emigrated in large numbers in the years immediately after independence; indeed, many of the houses had stood empty for long years before their destruction. Ascendancy culture now lived on only in small enclaves that coalesced around the Church of Ireland, the Horse Show, and Trinity College.[46] The IGS was a new force in this small world. The majority of those who joined the group in its first years were the owners of big houses, who were helped by the society to restore and maintain their homes. At a time when Ascendancy culture appeared to be in terminal decline, the society attempted to restore the 'big house', its primary symbol, and foster interest in its culture. Therefore, despite how much the country had changed, the new society had much in common with the old. Indeed, if Mahaffy's Georgian Society had been a participant in a culture clash regarding the parameters by which 'national' culture would be defined, the IGS also posed similar questions after almost forty years of independence.

In May 1958 the new society held its first big event, the Irish Eighteenth Century Georgian Convention. This gathering was attended by a delegation from the London Georgian Group, led by Lord Rosse.[47] The group was received at Áras an Uachtaráin, given a tour of Georgian Dublin, and visited some of the great houses in the vicinity of the city, including Russborough and Castletown.[48] This event precipitated a certain amount of activity on the theme of Irish Georgian architecture: there were two exhibitions, by the IGS and by the RIAI, of prints of eighteenth-century buildings; while Córas Iompair Éireann (the state-owned transport company) arranged special bus tours; the Photographic Dealer's Association held an international open photographic competition on the subject of eighteenth-century Ireland; and Irish Shell and Bord Fáilte jointly published a pamphlet on Georgian buildings.[49] The *Irish Builder and Engineer* remarked that the event 'instigated a considerable amount of activity towards reviving a public interest in the architecture of a period of gracious living'.[50] Indeed, perhaps wooed by the glamour of the Georgian Group's visit, the IGS grew quickly, by the end of its first year having 400 members.[51]

[46] Jack White, *Minority Report: The Protestant Community in the Irish Republic* (Dublin, 1975), 96; Kurt Bowen, *Protestants in a Catholic State: Ireland's Privileged Minority* (Dublin, 1983), 66; J. C. Beckett, *The Anglo-Irish Tradition* (London, 1976), 167; R. McDowell, *Crisis and Decline: The Fate of Southern Unionists* (Dublin, 1997), 194.

[47] *Irish Times*, 5 May 1958, 5.

[48] *Irish Times*, 5 May 1958, 4.

[49] *Irish Builder and Engineer*, 17 May 1958, 351.

[50] *Irish Builder and Engineer*, 17 May 1958, 351.

[51] *Quarterly Bulletin of the Irish Georgian Society*, October–December 1958, 45.

The response to the new society and the upsurge in interest in Georgian architecture was not universally positive. In August 1958, Caroline Mitchell derided the 'taste birds' who had joined 'this dreary Georgian cult' in her fashion column in the *Irish Times*.[52] Ailtire was also sceptical about the new group. He scorned the 'vulgar Georgian craze' he saw manifesting itself in the shop windows of Grafton Street, and characterized the IGS as retrogressive and elitist, stating that 'belief in the superiority of the past over the present is the hallmark of good breeding. Thus runs the argument—"these buildings were erected by our ancestors (or by the ancestors of our betters)".'[53] On a similar note, Niall Montgomery wrote a sardonic piece on the arrival of the London Georgian Group for the *Architects' Journal*: 'The Georgian Group, lords to a man, had come to appraise the quality of the Free-Stately homes of Ireland. A week later, following detailed inspection of Irelandshire, complete including hunting boxes, belvederes and ha-has, the georgeous guests were complaining that they had seen it all before.'[54] In this period, preservation of existing structures was frequently condemned—across Europe as in Ireland—for being elitist. As modern architecture was understood to reformulate social patterns, then inversely, to preserve the buildings of a former era was seen as preserving not only material remains but also the social hierarchies which they embodied.[55] However, as shown by Montgomery, these social tensions also held nationalist overtones in Ireland. In his description of the 'Free-Stately homes' of 'Irelandshire', he used a surreal lexicon to associate preservationism with unionism, and so mock the society as an aristocratic collective, as a group which was out of place in the independent republic, and was nostalgic for British rule. These combined social and national critiques undermined their attempts to preserve the architecture of the eighteenth century; they were battles which would continue to dog the IGS throughout its existence.

During the 1950s, there was a pervasive culture of blindness in relation to the architectural remains of the eighteenth century. There was no desire to preserve the city, and the city had little cultural worth as a heritage site. It was seen as a place of old, dirty buildings that had outlived their age and usefulness, rather than as a place which was worthy of, or requiring, preservation. This apathy towards the buildings of the eighteenth century may have been pervasive, but it was not universal. The end of the 1950s

52 *Irish Times*, 4 June 1958, 6; *Irish Architect and Contractor*, August 1958, 12.

53 *Irish Architect and Contractor*, May 1958, 12.

54 *Architects' Journal*, 12 June 1958, 885.

55 Robert Hewison, *The Heritage Industry: Britain in a Climate of Decline* (London, 1987), 9–11; *New Statesman*, 12 April 1963, 529.

also witnessed the birth of an incipient preservation movement, as individuals came together to attempt to ensure the survival of the Royal Hospital and Kildare Place, and to found the IGS. In this period it was restricted to an alliance of elites; it was a coalition of senators, architects, artists, and members of the Ascendancy. Although it had very different aims to the architects who called for Dublin's reconstruction, in many ways the two groups had much in common; both were reacting against the seeming decay and stasis of the city—and the state—in the 1950s, and looking to the built environment to provide a better future.

In many ways these first efforts at preservation were reactionary; they were characterized by a warm glow of nostalgia that looked to a distant era as a repository of a better Ireland. But their attitude to the past was more complex—even radical—than this, as they looked to a past which had been debarred from the status of 'tradition' and 'heritage' in the cultural codes of the new state, and in so doing both interrogated and revealed how these codes were constituted. However, it is notable that the preservationists, while defending the preservation of Ireland's eighteenth-century structures, also partook in the creation and reinforcement of these cultural definitions. In choosing to name themselves the Irish *Georgian* Society, and limiting their remit solely to protecting the buildings of the eighteenth century, they were also part of a process of cultural entrenchment which defined the built legacies of the eighteenth century as separate from the principal narrative of Irish history. However, it is notable that the debates regarding the built environment during the 1950s were neither as vituperative, nor were attitudes as polarized, as they became a decade later; as land prices increased, the scale of buildings projects advanced, opinions solidified, and apathy often became antipathy.

4

Modernization and Preservation, 1958–65

From the late 1940s until the mid-1960s the Dublin correspondent to the *Architects' Journal* was the architect and Joyce scholar Niall Montgomery. He wrote his pieces for the *Journal* as stylized literary nonsense, a distinct Irish mode made popular by his contemporaries Flann O'Brien and Seán Ó'Faoláin. However, the flippancy of Montgomery's prose belied the seriousness of the subjects he addressed. On 11 April 1962 he began his article by describing how a friend had given him a beautiful old briefcase, 'compartmented and designed to carry the literature of the earth-moving characters for whom, briefly "worked" my friend'. The briefcase represented Dublin: 'made originally for other fellows, used for other purposes, taken from them by other fellows, given to other fellows, used for other purposes, taken back again, repaired, restitched, turned inside out, and still in mint condition, best hide in the world, good for another hundred years'. However, Montgomery did not consider his view of the city to be widely shared:

> For centuries the Irish have hated the city. They're always trying to burn it. Now they actually live in it and think they own it, because they've bought everyone. The architects say the place is just a building site and when the Irish say to them 'we want to blow up the Four Courts again' the architects say, 'for that site you want an aluminium changidarhage with paraboloid hyperboles, and a podium; why not have a competition and build Raymond Casson and Sir Hugh McGrath into the conditions?'[1]

Montgomery's reflections on Ireland's problematic relationship to its own capital had been inspired by the most famous planning battle of the 1960s. One of the famous sights of Dublin was the long line of Georgian houses made up by Merrion Square East, Fitzwilliam Street, and Fitzwilliam Place; the earliest built in the 1760s by the property developer, Lord

[1] *Architects' Journal* 135, 11 April 1962, 101. Montgomery is parodying the names of the two Fitzwilliam Street architectural assessors, Sir Hugh Casson and Raymond McGrath.

Fitzwilliam, with the last being finished in the 1830s (Fig. 4.1).[2] This straight road, three-fifths of a mile in length, was the longest continuous eighteenth-century street in Europe. However, the vista was not immune from development. In the early 1960s, the state-owned Electricity Supply Board (ESB) proposed to demolish a central terrace to erect a new headquarters (Map 4.1). The fate of the street was undecided for five years; during this time, it attracted a huge deal of popular protest and professional attention; indeed, it was described in an editorial in the *Architects' Journal* as a 'monumental row'.[3] However stylized, Montgomery's article can be read as a perceptive summary of the factors which made the fate of Fitzwilliam Street such a high-profile media event. The themes he referred to included Dublin's ambivalent position within Ireland as the former site of British governance, the colonial symbolisms of Ireland's built environment, and modernist theories of town planning.

The controversy regarding Fitzwilliam Street coincided almost exactly with the period of Lemass's premiership, and Ireland's first sustained period of growth. Although it occurred only a few years later, the timbre of the debate was very different to that which had surrounded the future of Kildare Place and the Royal Hospital Kilmainham; while ideas of stasis

Fig. 4.1. Fitzwilliam Street in the early 1960s. Image courtesy of John Donat.

[2] Craig, *Dublin 1660–1880*, 191; Casey, *Dublin*, 573.
[3] *Architects' Journal*, 11 April 1962, 102.

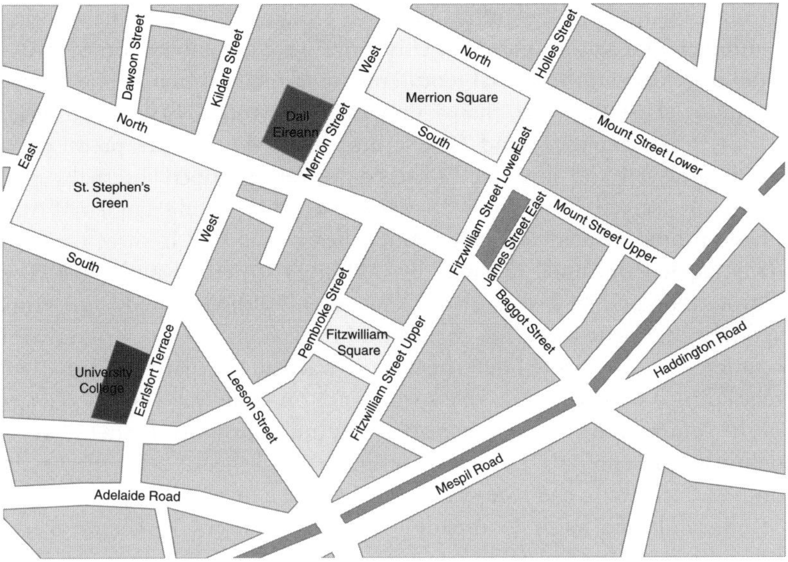

Map 4.1. Map of the Fitzwilliam Street area.

and failure had characterized discussions of the city in the 1950s, at Fitzwilliam Street a sense of optimism and ideals of national modernization were key to discourse and fundamental to how the planning battle developed. A consideration of the story of Fitzwilliam Street provides a way of exploring the cultural politics of Irish modernization during the early 1960s; through an examination of how architectural modernism interacted with longer-standing notions of nationalism and colonialism in the campaigns for preservation and reconstruction, the controversy offers a way of considering the links between Irish culture and architectural theory during a period of rapid cultural change.

The ESB had begun its operation in a drawing room flat in No. 28 in 1927, and over the next thirty years had expanded into neighbouring houses until it was the lessee of all property on the extensive site bounded by Lower Fitzwilliam Street, Upper Mount Street, and James Street East.[4] This dominance of a large portion of the area was entrenched with the completion of two new office blocks behind Fitzwilliam Street in 1951 and 1956.[5] From this point, and more actively from 1961, the ESB began

[4] NAI DT S17096 A/2, Memorandum for Government on the Proposed Demolition of 13/28 Fitzwilliam Street by the ESB, 27 June 1963.

[5] NAI DT S17096 A/2, Memorandum, 27 June 1963.

to make plans for a new office block to replace their Fitzwilliam Street buildings. The reasons given for this move were a combination of structural degradation, the spatial requirements of modern management, and commercial prestige. The Chairman of the ESB wrote to Erskine Childers, Minister for Transport and Power, describing the Board's premises as 'badly decayed and unstable houses, massively propped internally and externally, stayed from front to back, providing inefficient sized and placed rooms'.[6] An advertisement published by the ESB in three national daily papers continued to press the building's structural problems: 'The Corporation's Chief Inspector of Dangerous Buildings stated some years ago that the entire block was in a critical condition . . . recent professional opinions have confirmed that there is no practical alternative to complete rebuilding.'[7] Moreover, the ESB's insistence on retaining its headquarters in the centre of the city can be read as stemming from its desire to have a definitive presence in Dublin's landscape to equal that of other semi-state bodies: Bord Fáilte had recently commissioned a new building on Baggot Street, while the Sugar Company's new headquarters on Leeson Street had been completed in 1959.[8]

Seán Lemass took an early and active interest in the ESB's development plans; indeed, his reputation for decisive leadership and focus on economic and cultural modernity can be witnessed in practice in his intervention in the Fitzwilliam Street controversy. In November 1961, before any official planning application had been lodged, and even before the ESB had formalized its plans, he received a letter from one of his closest friends, David McIlvenna, chairman of the Guild of Master Builders.[9] McIlvenna was scathing of Childers's conciliatory approach to the problem of the street; he accused him of being 'unduly influenced by the Georgian Society', and stated that 'these particular houses are not true specimens . . . they were built by cheap speculative builders copying a few of the features of the time, and may not have had Architects engaged at all'.[10] He went on to say that 'these buildings are rotten throughout due to Dry Rot, and through the nature of their poor construction. I state emphatically that the façade or buildings could not be preserved' and deemed the whole affair 'damaging

[6] NAI DT S17096/A/1/63, Letter from Tom Murray, Chairman of the ESB to Erskine Childers, 29 June 1961.

[7] *Irish Press*, 7 December 1961, 6; *Irish Times*, 7 December 1961, 8; *Irish Independent*, 7 December 1961, 7.

[8] These are both state organizations. See *Irish Architect and Contractor*, April 1957, 14; *Irish Architect and Contractor*, May 1959, 12.

[9] Horgan, *Sean Lemass*, 162.

[10] NAI DT S17096/A/1/63, Letter from David McIlvenna to Sean Lemass, 16 November 1961.

to the [Fianna Fáil] Party'.[11] Although decisions on planning matters lay with Dublin Corporation, with final appeal to the Minister for Local Government, Lemass seems to have been won over by McIlvenna's views, and attempted to pre-emptively circumnavigate established channels to ensure that the building would be constructed. Although there is no record of his reply to McIlvenna, he put a note on the file dated 1 December 1961 stating, 'Allow ESB to go ahead'.[12]

Three days later, after a great deal of public speculation regarding the future of the street, the ESB finally made a formal application for permission to proceed with their plans.[13] During the long months of speculation regarding the future of the buildings, the Irish Georgian Society had formed the ESB Fitzwilliam Street Protest Group as a dedicated committee to campaign against any alteration to the street. In response to the planning application, the protest group organized a meeting in the Round Room of the Mansion House to rally opposition to the scheme. Posters announcing the meeting were posted all over Dublin, in particular outside the two universities, and, audaciously, about one hundred were posted on the doors and railings of the sixteen ESB houses listed for demolition.[14] The meeting, held on 12 January 1962, was filled to capacity; approximately eight hundred people were in attendance while another two hundred failed to gain admittance.[15] The IGS enlisted its own expert and celebrity architect to lead the discussion. Sir Albert Richardson, former professor of architecture at the Bartlett School and a fierce and high-profile opponent of modernism, rubbished the ESB's claims of structural degradation, stating that the houses could be returned to residential use for £6,000 each, and that the ESB could build in the space behind the terrace.[16] The other speakers were high-profile names from the Irish arts, many of whom had already campaigned against the destruction of Kildare Place. They included Norah McGuinness, Micheál MacLiammóir, Desmond Guinness, Eleanor Wicklow, and the artist Seán Keating. This spectacle was sufficiently interesting to attract comment from not only the *Irish Times* but also the *Irish Press* and *Irish Independent*.[17] However, the *Irish Independent* was cynical about the crowds and attention the meeting drew, and speculated that the average Dubliner attended with

[11] NAI DT S17096/A/1/63 Letter from McIlvenna to Lemass, 16 November 1961.

[12] NAI DT S17096/A/1/63, Memorandum on file, 1 December 1961.

[13] *Irish Times*, 7 December 1961, 11; *Irish Press*, 7 December 1961, 4.

[14] *Irish Times*, 10 January 1962, 1.

[15] *Irish Times*, 10 January 1962, 1.

[16] *Irish Times*, 10 January 1962, 1. The other speakers were Desmond Moore of the Old Dublin Society, Desmond Guinness, and Richie Ryan.

[17] *Irish Press*, 13 January 1962, 5; *Irish Independent*, 13 January 1962, 5.

the attitude that there was 'such a woeful famine of a bit of gas in this city that a fella has to make the most of every opportunity'.[18]

Despite the Mansion House meeting and a petition signed by over four hundred residents of the Pembroke Estate, on 17 January 1962 Dublin Corporation made an order, under the Town and Regional Planning Acts 1934 and 1939, granting the ESB permission to demolish 13 to 28 Fitzwilliam Street.[19] The permission granted was subject to the condition that the ESB should submit detailed plans to the Corporation illustrating their proposals before beginning any constructional work.[20] This was crucial to the argument that dragged on over the next three years about the buildings—in essence, Dublin Corporation had given the ESB permission to demolish but not to rebuild.[21] Indeed, the ESB was privately criticized by Lemass for not simply proceeding with the demolition after the initial planning permission was obtained, and therefore 'facilitating a re-opening of the issues involved'.[22]

At this time, the planning laws allowed only those 'directly aggrieved' to appeal against planning decisions, so there was little that those who desired the retention of the street but were not directly affected by the development could do but collect signatures. In January 1962, about four hundred residents of Merrion Square, Fitzwilliam Square, Fitzwilliam Street, and Fitzwilliam Place signed a petition addressed to Lord Pembroke, the ground landlord. The petition pointed out that his tenants had done all they could to preserve his property and to maintain it in accordance with his instructions; if the Georgian houses were pulled down by the ESB and a modern building was substituted, the value of his property in other parts of the estate would be diminished.[23] The Old Dublin Society launched a petition addressed to the Minister for Transport and Power, the Minister for Local Government, the Lord Mayor, and the aldermen and councillors of Dublin. The list of signatories was headed by Seán T. O'Kelly, former President of Ireland, who had received the Georgian Group at Áras an Uachtaráin on their visit to Ireland in 1958.[24] The IGS

[18] *Irish Independent*, 17 January 1963, 9.

[19] Dublin Corporation, 'Report of An Coisde Sraideanna: Breviate for January 1962', *Reports of Dublin Corporation 1962* (Dublin, 1963), 94; *Irish Times*, 29 January 1962, 1; NAI DT S17096 A/2, Memorandum for Government on the Proposed Demolition of 13/28 Fitzwilliam Street by the ESB, 27 June 1963; *Irish Times*, 18 January 1962, 9.

[20] *Irish Times*, 18 January 1962, 9.

[21] This was remarked on at the time as peculiar: see NAI DT S17096/95B, Memorandum on file, 22 June 1964.

[22] NAI DT S17096/95B, Memorandum Department of the Taoiseach, 22 June 1964; also NAI DT S17096/95B, Letter from Seán Lemass to Neil Blaney, 22 June 1964.

[23] *Irish Times*, 29 January 1962, 1.

[24] *Irish Times*, 14 November 1962, 11.

also collected three thousand signatures to their own petition, and devoted an entire issue of their bulletin to interviews with the main protagonists involved in the decision (see below).[25] Meanwhile, the Marquis of Sligo organized a petition on behalf of the ESB Fitzwilliam Street Protest Group, which was signed by a diverse—and surprising—collection of international stars, including Sir Basil Spence, Lord Harewood, Elizabeth Bowen, Charles Chaplin, Charles Forte, Lord Longford, Sir Gilbert Laithwaite, Compton Mackenzie, and Princess Grace of Monaco.[26] In May 1964, the preservationists made their final attempt at epistolary protest with a letter-writing campaign to the Taoiseach: forty-three prominent personages from Irish cultural life wrote asking for a commission to be set up to examine the fate of the houses.[27]

The value of foreign opinion, not only for the benefit of the tourist trade but also for Ireland's prestige as a nation, was also considered a vital tool in the battle for the preservation of Fitzwilliam Street. Eoin O'Mahony, the genealogist, raconteur, and public personality, toured America and Canada for six weeks on a mission to raise awareness of the controversy, and through this put pressure on the government to reverse its decision. He presented a lecture on Irish architecture across the continent, and had interviews with over one hundred leading Irish Americans, including Robert and Edward Kennedy.[28] Edward Keelan, an Irish émigré, also set up the Society for the Protection of Historic Ireland, Inc. to collect money for the campaign in America, and to use American opinion to petition the government.[29]

Although the group's minimum requirement was the retention of the façades, their desired goals were much more ambitious than this. On several occasions the group proposed schemes to the ESB which involved taking the entire Fitzwilliam Street site from them, providing them with alternative office accommodation, and restoring the terrace of houses as domestic accommodation; but despite the variety of suggestions for new offices in lieu of the Fitzwilliam Street terrace, the ESB remained intractable.[30] First, the IGS were involved in a proposal put to the ESB in February 1963, which offered the organization a modern multi-storey

[25] *Quarterly Bulletin of the Irish Georgian Society*, July–December 1961; NAI DT S17096 A/2, Memorandum for Government on the Proposed Demolition of 13/28 Fitzwilliam Street by the ESB, 27 June 1963.

[26] NAI DT S17096/95B, Memorandum on file, 22 June 1964.

[27] NAI DT S17096/95B, Memorandum on file, 22 June 1964.

[28] *Irish Times*, 15 April 1963, 6.

[29] NAI DT S5004E/62, Correspondence relating to the Society for the Preservation of Historic Ireland Inc.

[30] NAI DT S17096 A/2, Memorandum on the Proposed Demolition, 27 June 1963.

office block on a 5-acre site at Donnybrook in exchange for their Fitzwilliam Street site.[31] This was rejected, however, on the grounds of the expense involved in moving from their existing buildings, and to the organization's opposition to leaving the city centre.[32] Next, Lord Pembroke also attempted to negotiate the preservation of the property on his land. In March 1963, his land agent wrote to Neil Blaney to inform him that a developer had applied for permission to redevelop a site on East James Street, a few hundred yards away from the ESB's current location, as a multi-storey office building, and that permission for this development had been obtained from Dublin Corporation. The estate had agreed to the proposed development on the condition that they offered to the ESB a lease of the entire new building. This suggestion, however, was also rejected.[33] Finally, the Arts Council suggested to the Minister for Local Government that the houses could be converted into flats, while the ESB's extra accommodation needs could be met by building in the back gardens on the opposite side of East James Street, with a connecting bridge over the street to the existing modern ESB blocks. Although the council advised that a purchaser was available to undertake the conversion, this proposal was rejected by the ESB as impracticable and the council apparently accepted their view.[34]

While these efforts were taking place, two appeals by those 'directly aggrieved' were lodged with the Minister for Local Government, the highest arbiter of planning decisions, against Dublin Corporation's permission of January 1962. The first was from the Countess of Wicklow and five other residents of houses in Merrion Square, and the second was from Lord Pembroke.[35] Blaney waited until he saw the winning design before he adjudicated on these appeals. Indeed, his sluggishness in producing his report became the subject of comment: Childers wrote to Lemass exhorting him to put pressure on Blaney to come to a decision, making it clear that if he did not make the right decision, namely a positive answer, he would have to introduce remedial legislation in the Dáil.[36]

On 27 June 1963, Blaney finally submitted a report on the Fitzwilliam Street houses, laying out both sides of the debate on their future.[37] He began by questioning the ESB's emphasis on the building's unsafe

31 NAI DT S17096 A/2, Memorandum on the Proposed Demolition, 27 June 1963.
32 NAI DT S17096 A/2, Memorandum on the Proposed Demolition, 27 June 1963.
33 NAI DT S17096 A/2, Memorandum on the Proposed Demolition, 27 June 1963.
34 NAI DT S17096 A/2, Memorandum on the Proposed Demolition, 27 June 1963.
35 NAI DT S17096 A/2, Memorandum on the Proposed Demolition, 27 June 1963.
36 NAI DT S17096 A/2, Letter from Childers to Lemass, 24 April 1963.
37 NAI DT S17096 A/2, Memorandum on the Proposed Demolition, 27 June 1963.

structural condition. He had received a report from an officer of the Dangerous Buildings Section of Dublin Corporation, dated 8 January 1963 and endorsed by the City Architect, which stated that in carrying out the works needed to remedy the structural defects brought to their notice in 1955, the ESB had rendered the buildings safe. The report stated: 'the floors were shored, roofs made good and the back walls were tied with tie bars and plates to the front walls, which were then, and are now in a safe structural condition. The most recent inspection carried out on these premises took place on 15 January 1962 on which occasion no danger was found in any part of the structures.'[38] Blaney then went on to question the ESB's claim that the organization was being compromised in achieving work efficiency by not being able to provide suitable accommodation for its staff. He pointed out that from the ESB's own figures it was clear that 76 per cent of its 950 staff were housed in the East James Street and Mount Street offices, and the maximum number of additional staff to be provided for by the new buildings was 150.[39] A report from an architect in his department had stated that rebuilding behind the original façade was possible, although it would probably cost more than the target figure of £675,000; however, less comprehensive alterations which would retain the existing façade could be achieved for a total of £70,000.[40] Thus, he concluded that reconditioning the houses was practicable, would cost considerably less than an entirely new building, and, with the upper floors brought back into full usage, it would also cater for a large proportion of the envisaged staff increases.[41] He then posed two questions: 'Would the demolition of these houses and their replacement by a modern office block cause grave damage to the architectural unity of the area?' And, 'Is the present condition of the houses as dangerous and decayed as it is claimed by the ESB or would it be practicable to recondition them at a supportable cost?' He summed up his decision:

> Having carefully considered all the facts put before him, he has come to the conclusion that the demolition of these houses would cause irreparable damage to the character of the area, that the ESB have greatly exaggerated the position about the allegedly dangerous condition of the houses and that it would be practicable to recondition them at reasonable cost. He accordingly proposes that the appeals should be allowed and that the general permission granted to the ESB by Dublin Corporation should be revoked.[42]

[38] NAI DT S17096 A/2, Memorandum on the Proposed Demolition, 27 June 1963.
[39] NAI DT S17096 A/2, Memorandum on the Proposed Demolition, 27 June 1963.
[40] NAI DT S17096 A/2, Memorandum on the Proposed Demolition, 27 June 1963.
[41] NAI DT S17096 A/2, Memorandum on the Proposed Demolition, 27 June 1963.
[42] NAI DT S17096 A/2, Memorandum on the Proposed Demolition, 27 June 1963.

Blaney cited the reasons for preservation to be national prestige, good planning, and tourism, and stated that one of the reasons for his decision was that the Development Plan that would be introduced under the new Local Government (Planning and Development) Act would have protected these houses. The fact that the destruction of Fitzwilliam Street would go against the spirit of the new, but not yet enacted, legislation was also a major concern. He therefore proposed to allow the appeals, and to revoke the general permission granted to the ESB by Dublin Corporation.[43]

On receipt of this memorandum, Lemass arranged to meet Blaney after Dáil business to discuss the issue, and the item was subsequently withdrawn from the Cabinet agenda.[44] There was, however, a note on the Department of the Taoiseach file stating that, 'General feeling was that Minister should not allow the appeals and should permit the buildings therefore to be demolished.'[45] Despite Blaney's reasoned and careful opposition to the construction of the new ESB headquarters at this site—his report ran to eighteen pages—it seems that he was overruled by Lemass. Yet it was he who took the responsibility for the decision in the media. Only days later, the *Irish Times* ran a story entitled 'Blaney's "Yes" to ESB new office plans.'[46]

On 26 March 1964, detailed plans were finally lodged with Dublin Corporation by the architects, Stephenson Gibney and Associates, for the construction of their design in Fitzwilliam Street.[47] Despite the fact that the Corporation had given initial planning permission for a new building for the site, on 13 May the Streets Committee refused the designs for the new structure.[48] A report in the *Irish Press* revealed that the committee wished for a building which showed respect to the extant landscape, and had decisively rejected the proposals for a range of reasons relating to the colour, form, and scale of the proposed new structures. It stated that the Committee considered 'the window heights, lack of parapet and coping in the proposed building' to be 'out of harmony with the existing Georgian area'.[49] The ground-level concrete beam, instead of the railings normal to the area, was also considered 'out of harmony', and the colour was thought to be 'dull and monotonous'. Moreover, the buildings would be

[43] NAI DT S17096 A/2, Memorandum on the Proposed Demolition, 27 June 1963.
[44] NAI DT S17096/95B, Memorandum on file, 22 June 1964.
[45] NAI DT S17096 A/2, Memorandum on file, 2 July 1963.
[46] NAI DT S17096 A/2, press cutting *Irish Times*, 13 July 1963.
[47] *Irish Press*, 13 May 1964, 3.
[48] Dublin Corporation, 'Report of An Coisde Sraideanna: Breviate for Month of May 1964', *Reports of Dublin Corporation 1964* (Dublin, 1965), 335.
[49] *Irish Press*, 13 May 1964, 3.

'out of scale' with existing buildings. The planning officer suggested a considerable number of headings under which any future proposal should be examined for integration into the Georgian area. They included an 'examination of whether the proposed façade continued the main plane of the existing façade', whether it was 'unbalanced, disrupt[ed] the skyline, over-emphasize[d] the building', or made use of 'unsympathetic' materials'. The plans submitted, the Planning Officer pointed out, 'had not passed these tests'.[50]

This ruling was appealed against by the ESB, and so the decision once again reverted to Blaney. But the law regarding planning decisions was about to change: the Local Government (Planning and Development) Act 1963 would come into force on 1 October 1964, replacing the existing 1930s legislation.[51] As the new Act made provision to facilitate involvement by the public in the planning of their environment, it would have a considerable impact on the journey of the new ESB headquarters through the planning system. This public involvement had three forms: in the right of a person to object to an application of planning permission and to appeal against a decision of the planning authority; in the public display of draft development plans and the right of a person to make representations; and in the designation of Prescribed Bodies in the Act.[52] The existing planning laws did not give groups like the IGS a right to object, as they were not directly 'aggrieved' by the proposal.[53] The position of such groups would be stronger under the new law, which made provision for an oral hearing where requested by any party.[54] This was noted, however, in a memorandum of the Department of the Taoiseach dated 22 June 1964, and therefore so too was the need to push through the decision on Fitzwilliam Street before the enactment of the new legislation.[55] A note on file dated 30 September 1964 stated, 'I spoke to Mr Lawless, Department of Local Government, who said that everything possible was being done to get a decision today.'[56] This time Blaney did not put up any opposition to the ESB's plans: hours before the old legislation was replaced, he made an order overriding the decision of Dublin

[50] *Irish Press*, 13 May 1964, 3.

[51] *Irish Times*, 7 October 1964, 1.

[52] Prescribed Bodies: Four organizations were designated—Bord Fáilte, the Office of Public Works, the Arts Council, and An Taisce—to be sent details of every planning application, with the statutory right to comment. Mawhinney, 'Environmental Conservation, Concern and Action 1920–70', in Bannon (ed.), *Planning*, 99.

[53] NAI DT S17096/95B, Memorandum for Taoiseach, 22 June 1964.

[54] NAI DT S17096/95B, Memorandum for Taoiseach, 22 June 1964; see also Kevin Nowlan, 'The Evolution of Irish Planning 1934–64', in Bannon (ed.), *Planning*, 84.

[55] NAI DT S17096/95B, Memorandum for Taoiseach, 22 June 1964.

[56] NAI DT S17096/95B, Memorandum on file, 30 September 1964.

Corporation, giving permission for the Stephenson Gibney building to be constructed on Fitzwilliam Street.[57]

There was one final attempt to save the houses. This was the Electricity Supply (No. 2) Bill, entered into the Dáil by Seán Dunne, Independent Labour TD for Dublin County and a long-standing opponent of plans for the destruction of the houses on Fitzwilliam Street.[58] The fundamental point of the bill was that:

> The Board shall not, in the exercise of their powers and functions, demolish Georgian houses in the city of Dublin unless authorised in writing by the Minister [for Transport and Power] to do so, after a resolution so authorising the Minister has been passed by each house of the Oireachtas.[59]

The legislation was introduced because the ESB had used their powers of compulsory acquisition to purchase the freehold of the houses on Fitzwilliam Street from Lord Pembroke. The ESB had been granted these powers in order to allow them to purchase land for such electrical equipment as substations and transformer stations; it had never been foreseen that the legislation would allow them to bypass planning laws for their head office.[60] The bill was debated over four sessions in November 1964, and revealed explicitly many of the tensions inherent in the issue. The motion was defeated sixty-seven to thirty, dividing clearly along party lines. Labour, Fine Gael, and independents supported the bill, while Fianna Fáil opposed it, a split which prefigured the explicit politicization of Dublin's built environment which would be such a feature of the later 1960s. The nationalist and modernizing wings of the Fianna Fáil party combined to oppose the bill, differing in motivation and rhetoric but united in aim. This was the end of the preservationists' cause. The protest group explored every legal avenue to prevent the destruction of Fitzwilliam Street, but one by one these moves were rebuffed.

Demolition began in March 1965. An examination of the process which led to the building's destruction is revealing of the complex nature of Irish urban governance in this period, and the state's lack of a coherent response to the city. The ESB and the Department of the Taoiseach supported reconstruction, while Dublin Corporation and the Department of Local Government vacillated, and the Arts Council campaigned against it. Dominating the scene was Lemass, who was firm in his desire for

[57] NAI DT S17096/95B, Letter from Blaney to Lemass, 3 October 1964.

[58] He had raised questions in the Dáil regarding Fitzwilliam Street on 16 November 1961, 12 November 1963, and 2 November 1965.

[59] PDDÉ 212, 3 November 1964, col. 128.

[60] This was under the Electricity (Supply) Act 1927, Section 45, subsection 1. *Irish Times*, 7 October 1964, 1.

reconstruction and easily able to override the formal mechanisms of government in order to achieve this.[61] Thus the emerging bureaucratic and technocratic mechanisms of governance coexisted alongside an entrenched clientelism, where social networks and informal influence still continued to play a fundamental role in determining political decisions. Furthermore, the profile and tactics of the preservationist campaign were determined by this fractured decision-making process and the very limited provisions for protest defined in the planning legislation.

During the long-running planning processes which led to the construction of the new office block, the ESB also conducted a vigorous and high-profile campaign for the reconstruction of Fitzwilliam Street, which involved many well-known names from the transnational world of architecture, and drew upon long-standing debates regarding aesthetics, the social function of the built environment, and ideas of modernity in the creation of Europe's post-war cities. The first expert to report on Fitzwilliam Street was Sir John Summerson, Britain's foremost authority on eighteenth-century architecture as curator of the Soane Museum and author of a range of books, including the well-known *Georgian London*. He was, however, also a leading proponent of modernism in Britain, having been a founding member of the Modern Architecture Research (MARS) Group in 1933, and despite his historical writing had an ambivalent relationship with the developing preservationist movement.[62] In September 1961, he was commissioned by Erskine Childers, the Minister for Transport and Power, to examine the Fitzwilliam Street houses and give his opinion on proposals for a new edifice for the site. Summerson's support for reconstruction, and his views on the options available for the future of the street, had an important impact on the development of the controversy. His report was widely disseminated by the ESB; the Board took out half-page advertisements in the three major national newspapers on 7 December 1961, displaying Summerson's commentary in full.[63] As such, his report served as academic validation for reconstruction, and

[61] Brian Farrell, *Chairman or Chief?: The Role of Taoiseach in Irish Government* (London, 1971), 55–74 on Lemass's leadership style.

[62] Elizabeth McKellar, 'Populism versus Professionalism: John Summerson and the Twentieth Century Creation of the "Georgian"', in Barbara Arciszewska and Elizabeth McKellar (eds.), *Articulating British Classicism: New Approaches to Eighteenth Century Architecture* (Aldershot, 2004), 35–56; Peter Mandler, 'John Summerson (1904–92): The Architectural Critic and the Search for the Modern', in Susan Pederson and Peter Mandler (eds.), *After the Victorians: Private Conscience and Public Duty in Modern England* (London, 1994), 229–46.

[63] *Irish Times*, 7 December 1961, 3; *Irish Press*, 7 December 1961, 5; *Irish Independent*, 7 December 1961, 5.

played an instrumental role in shaping the terms of the debate regarding the future of the houses.[64]

Despite the ESB's emphasis on the structural problems of their buildings, Summerson's approach to the future of Fitzwilliam Street disregarded these considerations. As he told the *Bulletin of the Irish Georgian Society*, 'I was conducted round all the houses and given full information about their condition. But the condition of the houses, although pretty bad, did not worry me. You can preserve anything if it is worth preserving.'[65] Rather, his reasoning for supporting the plans for rebuilding was based on his understanding of the 'worth' of the eighteenth-century terrace that the ESB owned, and followed his ideas of urban preservation as set out in 'The Past in the Future'.[66] In his report for the Department of Transport and Power, Summerson described the buildings as of 'very slight architectural distinction… their value is almost entirely in the contribution made by the façades to the long vista of Fitzwilliam Street. Individually they are meagre enough and alterations in recent years have rendered the interior of negligible historic or architectural value.'[67] In the *Bulletin of the Irish Georgian Society* he reiterated this position, but was much more explicit in his conception of the architectural value of the site, stating that, 'It is nearly always wrong to preserve rubbish, and by Georgian standards these houses are rubbish.'[68] To Summerson, Dublin's eighteenth-century architecture was flawed, as it lacked either unity or uniformity throughout its streets. In contradistinction to London's Nash terraces, each of the plots along Fitzwilliam Street had been developed individually, and thus there was considerable variation in levels and detailing from house to house. This variation was seen by Summerson to compromise the street's architectural value; indeed, he derided any comparison between Fitzwilliam Street and the Place Vendôme or Regent's Park.[69] His conception of the worth of eighteenth-century architecture was created within a matrix of colonial and elite hierarchies which mapped onto scales of taste and value. As such, his understanding of Irish architecture was underpinned by transnational comparisons which denied the validity of local variations of Irish architecture. In this schema, the buildings of London designed by well-known architects for the city's social elites were positioned at the pinnacle

[64] NAI DT S17096 A/2, Memorandum for Government on the Proposed Demolition, 27 June 1963.

[65] *Quarterly Bulletin of the Irish Georgian Society*, January–March 1962, 3–5.

[66] Summerson, 'The Past in the Future', in *Heavenly Mansions*, 219–42.

[67] NAI DT S17096/A/63, Letter from Sir John Summerson to Tom Inglis, 26 September 1961.

[68] *Quarterly Bulletin of the Irish Georgian Society*, January–March 1962, 3.

[69] *Quarterly Bulletin of the Irish Georgian Society*, January–March 1962, 3.

of eighteenth-century design. Within this reading of architectural worth, in a restatement of enduring colonial hierarchies, speculative Irish buildings were socially, nationally, and aesthetically inferior.

While Summerson dismissed the buildings' architectural value as providing reason for preservation, he also went beyond this, to discuss the mooted 'compromise' of constructing modern offices behind the original façades. For Summerson, as for most of the architects of his generation, notions of authenticity and functionalism were fundamental to the rationale of urban planning and the construction of architectural worth. These values had been a central part of the development of the Modern Movement in the inter-war period, and were reasserted with renewed vigour in the years after the Second World War owing to the Brutalists' vocal adherence to Sartrean principles. These discourses also played a central role in debates regarding the future of Fitzwilliam Street. In his advice to Childers on the future of the houses, Summerson dismissed the option of rebuilding behind the façades. He stated that the the fronts of these houses 'dis-associated from the idea of individual domestic use' would not 'retain sufficient historic character and power of evocation to make their preservation and great sacrifice of space and convenience, worthwhile'.[70] Similarly, constructing a replica street front 'would preserve nothing and create nothing. Historically it would be a falsification.'[71] For Summerson, it was imperative that the external expression of the houses should relate directly to their function. Moreover, he conceived of a direct link between the epoch and aesthetic, which made building in the 'style' of a 'previous age' 'false'. Indeed, he believed that to retain the original façades or their design with a new interior would 'satisfy nobody and probably become an object of contempt'.[72] This emphasis on the 'integrity' of design made any form of compromise between preservation and reconstruction unworkable.

Central to Summerson's conception of the problem of Fitzwilliam Street was the need for architectural modernity. Not only did the ESB's new building have to suit and express its function, but it was implicit in their readings of the streetscape that this function was something uniquely new which could and should be fully embraced. This position had other high-profile adherents. Walter Gropius, pioneer of the Modern Movement and founder of the Bauhaus, wrote to Raymond McGrath, Principal Architect of Dublin's Office of Public Works and assessor of the ESB's competition, to endorse the proposals to rebuild. His letter, which was

[70] NAI DT S17096/A/63, Letter from Summerson to Inglis, 26 September 1961.
[71] NAI DT S17096/A/63, Letter from Summerson to Inglis, 26 September 1961.
[72] NAI DT S17096/A/63, Letter from Summerson to Inglis, 26 September 1961.

circulated by the ESB and published widely in the press, stated, 'Life in a city cannot be cased in. Though the beauty of the street attracts everybody, it would be a sign of unfortunate weakness if it should be impossible to find a contemporary solution... Living cities cannot be handled as a museum.'[73] For Gropius, the city was a site that constantly transformed itself, and a place of constant destruction and recreation, and he believed that these qualities should be expressed through the aesthetic and function of architecture. The views of Reyner Banham, the architectural historian and staunch supporter of modernism, were also enlisted to reinforce this view.[74] Although there is no record of Banham making any personal intervention in the Fitzwilliam Street case, in June 1962 the ESB also issued as a press statement an article by him from the *New Statesman*, which looked to a wholly new future for the city, and railed against the perceived snobbery and social retrogression of preservationism:

> There is no reason in sense or sensibility to make us carry our gratitude for its occasional elegance to the extent of preserving the boring, ill built and inhumanely planned rest of it just because the knights and barts of Establishment culture happen to live in it... The reappraisal of city living in all its modes and with all its skills is getting under way in a disorderly manner. And the disorder does at least promise an open minded attitude—an attitude capable of saying: 'Maybe we don't have a better alternative to the Georgian terrace, and the Regency square as yet, but we never shall if we don't get some practice in.'[75]

Banham's argument against preservation did not rest on structural concerns, but rather on the social obsolescence of buildings constructed for an elite which was diminishing in wealth, power, and influence. The preservation of the landscape of British cities, he suggested, was a highly exclusionary project which privileged elite forms of culture; in contrast, the reconstruction of the cities would provide an opportunity for rethinking the very meaning of society. Indeed, his *Theory and Design in the First Machine Age*, published in 1960, was written with the expectation that the 1960s would be a 'Second Machine Age', where technological developments would wholly reshape the structure of social intercourse and the hierarchy of the family.[76] In allying itself with the ideals of the international architectural elite embodied by Gropius, Banham, and Summerson, the ESB was able to position its building plans as not merely the

[73] NAI DT S17096A/2, press cutting *Irish Press*, 4 March 1963.

[74] See Reyner Banham, *Theory and Design in the First Machine Age* (London, 1972).

[75] Irish Architectural Archive (henceforth IAA) RW.D.99, press cutting *Irish Press*, 4 June 1962; *New Statesman*, 12 April 1963, 529.

[76] Banham, *Theory and Design in the First Machine Age*, 9–10.

reconstruction of its headquarters but as part of an international social modernity, in which the city and social relations would be reconfigured.

The way in which these architects conceived of the problem of the street was reflected in how the controversy was reported in the mainstream media, indicating the extent to which one-time avant-garde architectural theory had disseminated into popular culture. On 8 December 1961, the day the ESB published notices of its plans for reconstruction in all the major daily newspapers, the *Irish Independent* published an editorial in support of their decision. It described retaining the façades as a 'fraud', and stated that 'Public architecture should not be a matter of stage sets... building and shell alike suffer and nothing of genuine worth is left', stating that 'truth' was 'the basis of all aesthetics'.[77] Ventriloquizing the language of Banham and Gropius, the editorial argued that:

> Once the past begins to dominate the present, however, progress comes to a halt—and not least artistic progress. An urban vista which cannot accommodate the modern with the old is a museum piece; one might as well require the executives of the ESB to come to work in sedan chairs, for their motor cars are surely out of place parked beneath fan lights and wrought iron balconies.[78]

Another editorial on 24 October 1964 rearticulated these sentiments, describing 'propp[ing] up' the façades as 'a stage set to fill a gap, a pretty trick in short a deception. And when the architecture has to depend on deception it forfeits all claim to consequence... the Georgians have only the fraud to offer us.'[79] Echoing this position, when those in favour of the preservation of Fitzwilliam Street held its meeting at the Mansion House, it was picketed by architectural students chanting 'Don't make Dublin a museum.'[80]

The ESB's public relations campaign to raise support for its new Fitzwilliam Street building drew on architectural ideals of progress, modernity, and authenticity. These ideals received widespread support not only because they engaged with a transnational architectural discourse but also because they elided with a broader shift in national mood. It was not only architecture which was conceived in these terms; the language of modernity was part of a fundamental change in national discourse which had taken place since the economic revival of the late 1950s. Lemass conceived of a new Ireland where industrialization would provide a conduit to the realization of the goals of independence, and this political vision

[77] *Irish Independent*, 8 December 1961, 9.
[78] *Irish Independent*, 8 December 1961, 9.
[79] NAI DT S17096/95B, press cutting *Irish Independent*, 12 October 1964.
[80] *Irish Times*, 13 January 1962, 5.

played heavily on a similar vocabulary to that espoused by the founders of modernism: the values of efficiency, progress, and hygiene were central tenets of both discourses. But the link between the built environment and national transformation went further than rhetorical similarities. As shown in Chapter Two, the city's new buildings were understood not only to represent but also to bring into being Lemass's new society: through constructing the modern office blocks in which the new urban middle class would be employed, and creating the spatial forms of a modern, egalitarian, Irish nation. Lemass's only statement in the Dáil on the subject of Fitzwilliam Street followed this interpretation of environment and society. When, on 3 November 1964, he was asked for his opinion on the controversy, he stated that: 'I am completely a modernist. I think modern architects are capable of achievements the Georgians never thought of...We have enough museum pieces without looking for more.'[81] The importance of this position cannot be understated. In a country which had justified its search for independence on the claims of tradition, and had spent much of the early years of its independence in a search for this elusive past, Lemass's drive for cultural and economic modernity heralded a radical change in political rhetoric and national image.[82]

In contrast to the Board and its supporters' emphasis on modernity and functionality as providing justification for a new building, the ESB Fitzwilliam Street Protest Group invested a very different meaning in the street. That meaning was rooted in an alternative framework for the assessment of architectural worth, in which the value of the buildings was derived not only from the individual edifices but also from their contribution to the area—a criteria of assessment that Summerson dismissed. In a letter to the *Irish Times*, the Protest Group described the Fitzwilliam Square–Merrion Square area of Dublin as 'the finest townscape of this kind in Europe', and stated: 'The ESB stretch in Fitzwilliam Street is an essential element in the *unity* of the whole. This unity must not be lost. We appeal to the ESB and to the Government department concerned, at all costs to preserve this façade.'[83] Unlike the group in favour of reconstruction, the preservationists based much of their campaign on ideas of an emotional attachment to the city and the importance of the beauty—as opposed to the modernity—of the urban environment. Sir Albert Richardson told a meeting in the Mansion House that: 'The main issue in this controversy is the interest of the general public in a heritage of beauty. Dublin, like Venice, has a charm denied to most capital cities; the mountains, the sea, the

[81] PDDÉ 212, 3 November 1964, cols 153–4.

[82] Brown, *Ireland*, 255; O'Mahony and Delanty, *Rethinking Irish History*, 168–9.

[83] *Irish Times*, 21 July 1961, 9.

moist atmosphere blend the conventions of architecture and scenery in a way which is indescribable.'[84] An *Irish Times* editorial on the buildings continued this Venetian theme, emphasizing the beauty of the vista as the main reason for preservation: 'Standing outside Holles Street Hospital on a fine summer's evening and looking up towards the Dublin Mountains: what would Canaletto have made of that view?'[85]

But even more important to the preservationist case than the aesthetics of the vista was the past embodied in the street. The *Irish Times,* which consistently argued for preservation, saw in the Fitzwilliam Street buildings a repository of the culture of the eighteenth century. The street was described as having been 'built at a time when genius flourished in Ireland as never since, when the voice of Burke spoke to the world, and Grattan and Flood to an Irish parliament, when Charlemont united North and South in the Volunteers... and Curran and Sheridan made Dublin the second capital of Europe for intelligence and liberality and architectural beauty'.[86] Paradoxically, however, many of those who desired the preservation of the buildings believed that it was this link to eighteenth-century Anglo-Irish culture that was the reason for their destruction. In an article first published in the *Guardian* and reprinted in the *Bulletin of the Irish Georgian Society*, Jack White set out confrontationally why he believed that the buildings were being knocked down: 'They stand for an alien tradition. They stand for a Dublin which was an Anglo-Irish city. They stand for money and privilege and for the society that produced Sheridan and Oscar Wilde, the society that attended Castle levées and sent loyal addresses to the Sovereign. They stand for an urban, cosmopolitan culture, and not for the culture of the plain people.'[87] Like Banham, White admitted preservation's association with elite culture, however, in contradistinction to British divisions, this was a culture which was not only socially privileged but also distinct in national and confessional terms. Taking a similar position, an *Irish Times* editorial stated that in supporting the preservation of Fitzwilliam Street, 'we know that we lay ourselves open to a charge of unpatriotic behaviour. We are prepared to run the gauntlet. For some reason, the sudden intense interest in 18th century architecture and its preservation has aroused in many quarters hostility all the more intense because its motives are vague, confused and inspired by unlovely hate.'[88] In his paper, Uinseann MacEoin claimed that the

[84] *Quarterly Bulletin of the Irish Georgian Society*, January–March 1962, 3.
[85] *Irish Times*, 12 January 1962, 7.
[86] *Irish Times*, 31 January 1962, 7.
[87] *Quarterly Bulletin of the Irish Georgian Society*, July–December 1961, 29–30.
[88] *Irish Times*, 26 January 1965, 9.

destruction 'appealed to a number of pseudo-patriotic sentiments. People who forget that the Bolsheviks preserved the Czar palaces and churches are foolish enough to recommend the destruction of buildings simply because they were built during the period of English conquest.'[89] Despite the protestations to the contrary by the ESB, the preservationist group believed that the Fitzwilliam Street houses were being knocked down because Irish state and society had no understanding of the worth of cultural production which was not 'Gaelic' or 'republican' in origin. In its most extreme form this was articulated as the belief that the houses were being knocked down almost as an act of post-colonial iconoclasm.

In addressing these themes, much of the preservationist campaign coalesced around an attempt to prove that the buildings of Fitzwilliam Street were authentically Irish, and as such worth preserving. The fundamental point of much of the campaign was an attempt to set the buildings within the context of the history of Irish independence. When Seán Dunne, Independent TD for Dublin County, introduced legislation into the Dáil to try to block the destruction of Fitzwilliam Street, he claimed 'that you are looking at the city, not of George II or George I—if they were ever here, I do not know—but at the city of Grattan, of Napper Tandy, of Theobald Wolfe Tone and Robert Emmet'.[90] Similarly, Dr Edward Keelan described the destruction as a 'desecration to the memory of Grattan, in whose lifetime the houses were built'.[91] On 1 December 1962, Eoin O'Mahony and members of the Dublin Society of University College Dublin marched from Newman House on St Stephen's Green to Lower Fitzwilliam Street. 'For old decency's sake, rather than for protection', O'Mahony was accompanied by an Irish wolfhound.[92] As a symbolic baptism of the terrace into the history of the nation, wreaths were laid at the doors of Nos. 16 and 22, No. 16 having been the town residence of Sir Edward Tierney, second baronet, crown solicitor for Connacht, and No. 22 of Charles McCauley, a soldier in the War of Independence.[93] Thus, Dunne, Keelan, and O'Mahony attempted to reposition the buildings, not as a product of the 'society that attended Castle levees' but within broader histories of Irish nationalism. They engaged with long-standing narratives of Irish history when arguing for the buildings' retention, but reworked them to bring a set of Dublin-based motifs to the fore. Thus they attempted to reinterpret the buildings as 'Irish', and so worth preserving, because they were the cultural production of an Irish nationalist world.

[89] *Irish Architect and Contractor*, October 1964, 9.
[90] PDDÉ 212, 3 November 1964, col. 130.
[91] *Irish Times*, 9 October 1962, 10; also see NAI DT S5004E/62.
[92] *Irish Times*, 1 December 1962, 14.
[93] *Irish Times*, 22 November 1962, 9; *Irish Times*, 1 December 1962, 14.

This was not the only way in which ideas of Irishness were manipulated to make a case for the buildings' preservation. Maurice Dockrell, a Dublin TD, gave a speech in support of Dunne's legislation, which claimed the street's national pedigree not through its links to eighteenth-century nationalism but through its links to a middle-class, Catholic, Dublin culture. He stated that 'these buildings, as Deputy Dunne pointed out, had nothing to do with the different Georges, I, II, III and IV. They were built during the reign of one of them but they were designed by Irishmen and they were carried into effect by Irish workmen and generations have paid tribute to the work of those Irishmen.'[94] In so doing, he imbued the houses with a solid working-class history in which they were not the legacy of the people who owned them but rather the material production of the people who built them. For Dockrell, the Irishness of the builders was unquestioned; the Irishness of the owners was passed over. This sentiment was echoed in many letters to the *Irish Times*.[95] But he also went further than this, and argued that not only was the 'Irishness' of the houses solid because they were built by Irish workmen but also because they were occupied by Irishmen:

> These houses in Lower Fitzwilliam Street, far from being the homes of an unwanted and unwelcome aristocracy, were in fact the habitations of Dublin professional people … in the 1830s … the houses were occupied by families named Hughes, Darley, Daly, O'Hagan, Murphy and Driscoll. Another was Alderman Tom Makinney, Lord Mayor of Dublin … Did you ever hear of aristocrats with names like that? These were Irish names of Irish people at that time … There is no reason to think it is in any way perpetuating a part of Irish life which now, in a new state, some people wish to forget.[96]

For Dockrell, the 'Irishness' of the buildings was located not just in their architectural style but also through the community that resided there. However, his rhetorical positioning was also implicitly predicated on the notion that if the inhabitants of the houses had had particular surnames, this seemingly would have justified the destruction of the terrace. His argument rested on the assumption that these houses were worth preserving because their owners were the Catholic middle class rather than a Protestant upper class. As such, Dockrell was not using this planning controversy to debate the boundaries and limitations of contemporary ideas of national belonging. He was instead working with a definition of national identity rooted in Catholicism, but seeking to ensure the preservation of the buildings by moving their cultural interpretation within these boundaries.

94 PDDÉ 212, 3 November 1964, col. 150.
95 See for example *Irish Times*, 8 September 1961, 7; *Irish Times*, 19 February 1962, 10.
96 PDDÉ 212, 4 November 1964, col. 308.

However, it was not the case that those who favoured reconstruction looked to the future while the preservationists argued over the past. When the Fitzwilliam Street issue was debated in the Dáil, there were frequent instances when the buildings' colonial provenance was cited as reason for their demolition. Joseph Lenehan, Fianna Fáil TD for Mayo North, called not just for a new ESB headquarters but also for the reconstruction of the city: 'Anything the British built should be knocked down as far as it can be if the last big storm did not knock it down. I make no apology to any Irishman for saying that. We are now our own bosses and it is time we showed them we are not afraid to take down the buildings they put up with the blood of Irishmen.'[97] Patrick Cummins, Fianna Fáil TD for Dublin South-Central, described the houses' retention as 'cultural and artistic sabotage', stultifying efforts to build a 'city worthy of our native genius'.[98] However, the argument against preservation often went even further than this: not only were the buildings not worth preserving because of their foreign pedigree, but the attempt to preserve them was an attack on Ireland's authentic culture. The *Irish Independent* labelled the Georgian Society 'a major menace to true cultural appreciation in the country today'.[99] Similarly, Kevin Boland accused those who wished to preserve the houses of trying to destroy the repository of national identity, the Irish language. At the opening of the Oireachtas exhibition of books and manuscripts at the Royal Irish Academy, he described those 'so earnestly working to save the Georgian heritage of Dublin' as 'urging us to save something that is already dead and ready to fall and kill something that is alive and vigorous'.[100]

The newspapers, architects, and TDs who promoted the rebuilding of Lower Fitzwilliam Street were motivated by two seemingly contradictory images of Ireland; one stemming from a desire to create a new Ireland based on technology and the ideal of progress, and the other derived from a traditional position which sought to protect a unique indigenous culture. However, these two discourses were by no means mutually exclusive. Cummins, like Ailtire and Gibney, linked the project of modernization with the rekindling of a Gaelic culture when he stated in reference to Fitzwilliam Street, 'We are charged with the responsibility of assisting our people to create for themselves a tradition in the realms of the arts which will not only be in keeping with a heritage which is almost

[97] PDDÉ 205, 29 October 1963, col. 496.
[98] PDDÉ 212, 10 November 1964, col. 560.
[99] NAI DT S17096/95B, press cutting *Irish Independent,* 12 October 1964.
[100] *Irish Times*, 19 October 1964, 1.

lost but which will be representative of every worthy modern trend.'[101] He went on:

> What we need now are blocks of new flats containing every amenity demanded by ever-rising standards. Our architects and craftsmen can supply these if they are given the opportunity to do so and thereby help to re-create some of our own culture and artistic heritage which was bludgeoned into unconsciousness many centuries ago.[102]

Cummins linked a rhetoric of technology, modernism, and progress with a simultaneous emphasis on the protection of an essentialized Irish culture from continued British influences. In the post-war years, Europe had experienced a revolution in affluence for which industrialization was the conduit of progress, prosperity, and equality. But the Lemassian idea of progress, which on one level seems to echo Harold Wilson's exultation of a new Britain born in the 'white heat' of technology, had a particular national resonance, which was epitomized by the ESB. In its celebrated scheme to provide electricity to the entirety of rural Ireland, which was still ongoing during the 1960s, the organization used indigenous technology and manpower to bring electricity to the small farmers of the west and islands. In so doing, it contributed to preserving a traditional way of life, deeply inscribed in the political vocabulary of the nation, through the introduction of modern conveniences; in the words of Joe Cleary, a 'quasi-religious redemption from an inchoate primeval darkness'.[103] That this reciprocal and mutually constituted relationship between modernity and tradition was articulated in the simultaneous deployment of contradictory vocabularies is fundamental to understanding the Ireland of the early 1960s. Although there was a new-found quantification of national success through the appraisal of economic performance, Terence Brown goes too far in suggesting that this replaced a lexicon of Gaelic protectionism.[104] While any specific project to recuperate a Gaelic civilization may have been cast aside, imprints of this cultural project remained in rhetorical adherence to these values, and a distinct antipathy to cultural forms that had been defined antithetically as 'British' or 'Anglo-Irish'. This tension was reified in the new head office building in Fitzwilliam Street. While modern architecture had made its break with the nineteenth century through its emphasis on an international design and ethos, in Ireland the modern design campaigned for at

[101] PDDÉ 212, 10 November 1964, col. 561.
[102] PDDÉ 212, 10 November 1964, col. 561.
[103] Joe Cleary, *Outrageous Fortune: Capital and Culture in Modern Ireland* (Dublin, 2007), 158.
[104] Brown, *Ireland*, 232.

Fitzwilliam Street was imbued not only with a national symbolism but also with a very particular form of nationalism, which allied progress and technology with a post-colonial agenda.

These debates regarding the parameters of 'Irish' culture had been a key feature of Irish life since the cultural revival of the late nineteenth century. They were constituted around ideas of cultural authenticity, which was usually derived from Gaelic, Catholic, and rural associations. However, during the early 1960s, these local concerns were animated and invigorated with a particular reference to architecture, owing to the interaction and overlapping of post-colonial and architectural discourses. Ideas of Irish cultural authenticity were reinforced by an architectural professional and conservation movement which both emphasized authenticity as the fundamental criterion upon which architecture was judged. Therefore, the buildings of eighteenth-century Dublin, which had gradually changed since their construction, were now conceived as the relict remains of this era, and as such symbolic of colonial rule. These views had a profound impact on the shape of the developing conservation movement. For the preservationists, the proposed destruction of Fitzwilliam Street came to symbolize broader tendencies within the state: of the partition of culture, the sectarianization of form, and the quantification of the 'worth' of culture through explicitly national criteria.

Despite the enormous amount of space given to the Fitzwilliam Street controversy in the Irish media during the early 1960s, perhaps thanks to the uncompromising standpoints of both sides, an aspect which received relatively little coverage was the actual appearance of the new building. However, the form it took arose from the particularities of the case: from Summerson's report, from the pressure put on the ESB from preservationists, and from international trends in architecture. The replacement for the terrace was chosen through an architectural competition judged by Raymond McGrath, Principal Architect of the Office of Public Works, Tom Inglis, Chief Architect of the ESB, and Sir Hugh Casson, one-time architectural director of the Festival of Britain.[105] There were forty-five entries to the competition, with the twelve best as chosen by the assessors published in the *Architects' Journal*. The assessors of the competition came under considerable pressure from the preservationist lobby to withdraw support from the scheme or, failing this, to choose a sensitive design for the site.[106] They took notice of their critics; the competition conditions for the new building stated that the new design should preserve the

[105] *Irish Architect and Contractor*, March 1962, 27.

[106] See correspondence between Niall Montgomery and Sheila Wheeler in Niall Montgomery papers.

parapet height, colour, and plane of the existing façade.[107] Moreover, their report stated that they were quite firm in their resolve to choose a building which would respect the streetscape; those that 'broke up the street line by kicking it to pieces with very powerful modelling', used a 'very strong horizontal emphasis', or chose 'very light colour or over smooth materials' were all rejected.[108]

The three commended entries all followed a similar pattern, using vertically articulated concrete, steel, and plate glass to create a distinctly modern office within eighteenth-century proportions.[109] The winning entry was designed by the young Irish architects Sam Stephenson and Arthur Gibney, and superficially attempted an architecturally sensitive treatment for the site (Fig. 4.2). The design was described as 'divided into fourteen bays with a set back ground floor. In these bays the dominant Georgian window proportions have been used for groups of five windows on the first, second, and third floors. On the ground floor, solid brick

Fig. 4.2. Exterior of ESB headquarters, Fitzwilliam Street. Image courtesy of Norman McGrath.

[107] *Architects' Journal,* 21 November 1962, 1161.
[108] *Architects' Journal,* 21 November 1962, 1162.
[109] *Architects' Journal,* 21 November 1962, 1161–8.

walling is introduced. Precast facing units of suitable colour and texture are proposed for the upper floors.'[110] The assessors' report stated that the design had 'considerable elegance and dignity', and that the building fitted 'politely but not too self-effacingly into the general street picture'. While the building's external features were largely dictated by its place in the landscape, the interior expressed the commercial status of the organization (Fig. 4.3). The floor and walls of the double-height entrance hall were clad in Wicklow granite, as were the cantilevered stairs. Uinseann MacEoin described the entrance: 'the revolving doors in black metal and glass, exposing a dramatic foyer of polished granite and stainless steel is evocative of power, deliberately so, one assumes; the power of a power station'.[111] This stark modern design continued throughout the interior. The photographs released to the press revealed a headquarters consisting of leather seats, feature lighting, coffee bars, bright colours, and specially designed furniture: a world of American-style work and management in the centre of the eighteenth-century city.[112]

Fig. 4.3. Entrance hall of ESB headquarters. Image courtesy of Norman McGrath.

[110] *Architects' Journal*, 21 November 1962, 1164.
[111] *Plan*, December 1970, 20.
[112] *Building*, 3 March 1972, 48–53; IAA RW.D.98, *Our New Head Office*, pamphlet issued by the ESB on the opening of its new building.

As this discussion suggests, notwithstanding the strident debates surrounding its conceptualization and development, the completed ESB headquarters did not create a strong new presence on Fitzwilliam Street. Despite the emphasis on functionalism and honesty by Summerson, Gropius, and their supporters in the media, the building could not meet the needs of the ESB on the site. The 'long thin building with extended central corridor' was described by the *Architects' Journal* as 'inefficient and wasteful, besides being difficult to adapt to current trends in office organization, particularly as regards mechanization and the use of electronic calculating machines'.[113] Critics also questioned the logic of constructing a new building that blended in so well with the older streetscape. Echoing Walker's plan for the eighteenth-century city, Niall Montgomery, in a characteristically outspoken letter to the *Irish Times*, stated that the only route to a satisfactory solution would come through 'demolishing all the old buildings on the island block and by building free of fancy dress obsessions a new block set well back from the existing building lines'.[114] Similarly, while supporting the preservation of the terrace, Neil Downes, former professor of architecture at UCD, was unimpressed by the solution proposed for the site; he pointed out the foolishness of the policy of erecting something 'not necessarily Georgian in character which is not in conflict with its neighbours' as a policy for building in Dublin, so that the end-product would be 'a street where every building had to rhyme in with something which no longer exists... Only Swift might have taken a savage amusement at such a display of stupidity.'[115]

This gap between the way that the Fitzwilliam Street stand-off was debated and the final form of the building indicates the paradox of the ESB's new headquarters project. While justifying their need for a new building based on ideas of architectural modernity, the ESB could never fulfil their own criteria while remaining on their city centre site. Indeed, the ESB's desire for a visible location in the city centre demonstrated that it was much more important for the organization to be *seen* to adhere to notions of functionalism and modernity than any more substantive engagement with these values. Despite being constructed as 'rational', these values were deployed in a highly politicized fashion by government, media, and ESB alike. This contradiction was symptomatic of the highly subjective way in which modern architects handled their own theory. Sarah Goldhagen has definitively challenged much of the posturing of the modernists; she has shown how, 'despite the claims to modernity of the modern movement's chroniclers and practitioners, a profound engagement with

[113] *Architects' Journal*, 21 November 1962, 1165.
[114] *Irish Press*, 12 November 1962, 9.
[115] IAA RW D.99, press cutting *Irish Independent* (n.d.).

the past was a formative element of the style', and 'the assertions of Corb, Gropius or Mies notwithstanding, the employment for new technologies and a "rational" approach to structure' never determined the look of the new architecture. Moreover, the concept of 'functionalism' 'was so vague that it offered few directives for actual design—if it was even a value to which the early modernist architects attended at all'.[116] At Fitzwilliam Street, the language of modernism was instrumentalized as part of a broader political project; indeed, this discourse was central to a reimagined national project in the early 1960s. Not only was the reconstruction of Dublin a central motif of the narrative of national renewal, but this also took the form of a project of post-colonial repudiation.

However, this project contained an inherent contradiction. The replacement of eighteenth-century architecture with a building in the corporate vernacular of the international service economy was, if anything, more of a 'British' landscape than that which preceded it. Indeed, as Niall Montgomery and Downes noted, the forms, colours, and proportions of the new building echoed those of the old. This outcome was the result of adjudicators reluctant to make a more decisive visual statement, and an international architectural vocabulary which tended towards Palladian proportions for office constructions. Most importantly, the new building reflected a domestic architectural community which had defined itself in opposition to the island's extant built environment, but was yet to theorize how this antithetical positioning could be reconciled with an adherence to international modernism. This was, of course, not confined to the new ESB building on Fitzwilliam Street. During this period many of the eighteenth-century buildings of the city were replaced piecemeal by speculative offices, which replicated the street pattern and proportions of the eighteenth-century city, 'preserv[ing] nothing and creat[ing] nothing'.[117]

The Fitzwilliam Street altercation in many ways was exceptional. The period of Lemass's premiership was characterized by a palpable optimism regarding the future of the nation, which also manifested itself as general enthusiasm regarding modernization of the capital. However, this consensus would alter significantly as the decade progressed: the rate of change increased, private developers—as opposed to the state—took the lead in urban development, and issues of housing increasingly complicated notions of heritage.

[116] Sarah Williams Goldhagen, 'Coda: Reconceptualizing the Modern', in Sarah Williams Goldhagen and Réjean Legault (eds.), *Anxious Modernisms: Experimentation in Postwar Architectural Culture* (Canadian Centre for Architecture and MIT, 2000), 301.

[117] NAI DT S17096/A/63, Letter from Summerson to Inglis, 26 September 1961.

5

Housing, Community, and Preservation, 1963–70

In 1967 Liam O'Cuanaigh revisited the house he grew up in. He retraced the path he had taken out of the area to adulthood and employment, walking back slowly through Ballybough, Summerhill, Charles Street, Fitzgibbon Lane, and Gardiner Street, on the way to his old home. He eventually arrived at Rutland Street, and stood for a while outside the house in which he had spent his childhood. He cast his eye over the eighteenth-century building unsentimentally, describing it as 'a musty green building containing a dozen or more dark rooms, broken down woodwork and staircases, chipped plaster, a few attempts at wallpaper, and quite a reasonable cross section of humanity... decaying doors and damp halls, black railings with half their teeth missing, grass spreading across the steps, basements fouled with cigarette cartons, and ice pop wrappers carpeting the gutter'.[1] He juxtaposed this image with the modern, prosperous city President Kennedy had been shown: 'civil servants and shorthand typists are rushing up and down to catch the 15A to Rathgar, or the number 10 to Donnybrook; places where each man has his own house and each house has its own garden and wouldn't that be lovely'.[2] O'Cuanaigh dramatically contrasted the squalor of the city with the prim domesticity of the suburbs. His personal testimony regarding his childhood home was not a nostalgic piece; rather, he inverted this traditional form to create a political statement regarding the state's failure to solve Dublin's housing problems.

As O'Cuanaigh's memoir indicates, the government was faced with a severe housing problem during the 1960s, which grew worse as the decade progressed and—despite economic growth—compared unfavourably with earlier periods of independence. For example, while the numbers of people living at a density of two or more to a room had declined from 688,000 to 478,000 between 1946 and 1961 (an average of 14,000

[1] *Evening Herald*, 3 March 1967, 10.
[2] *Evening Herald*, 3 March 1967, 10.

yearly), between 1961 and 1966 this number fell only to 464,000—or on average less than 3,000 a year.[3] In Dublin, these problems were particularly severe. Since the deflationary drive of the late 1950s, Dublin Corporation and the Department for Local Government had made serious cutbacks in the provision of housing; in 1951, the Corporation in Dublin had built 2,600 new homes, but that figure had shrunk to 279 by 1961.[4] While numbers of houses built had nose-dived, other factors, including office construction in the city centre, dangerous buildings operations, zoning, and internal migration, were also putting additional pressure on the housing stock. Thus, during the period 1961 to 1966, the number of households with an average of three or more people per room increased in Dublin by 10 per cent, whereas in the rest of the country the number of these severely overcrowded households fell by 10 per cent.[5] However, the housing solutions offered often caused their own problems; the necessity for the swift provision of housing in the wake of the dangerous buildings scare led directly to the construction of Ballymun, a high-rise housing development of 3,000 units 4 miles to the north of the city centre, which was soon recognized as one of Europe's worst town planning disasters.[6] This shortfall in housing, and in particular in city centre housing, would prove to be highly significant during the 1960s in causing discontent and challenging ideas of prosperity.

The history of housing is a crucial part of the story of Ireland. It has played a central role in determining standards of living, shaping patterns of gender, and moreover in driving political change. The 1960s in Dublin are no different; protests against housing shortages combined social issues, nostalgia for city life, republican politics, and a global vocabulary of protest to create an explosive territorial battle for possession of the spaces of capital. In particular, there were two moments during the decade when housing protest came to prominence. The first was in 1963, when the collapse of two eighteenth-century tenements precipitated the sudden clearance of many similar houses in the city centre, which led to profound housing shortages; the second was at the end of the decade, when pickets, marches, and squats of the Dublin Housing Action Committee played a fundamental role in

[3] NAI DT 2001/6/262, Department of Local Government Memorandum, 8 April 1970. For census purposes, a 'household' is a group of persons jointly occupying a private dwelling and sharing the principal meals; a 'family' is a man and wife, a man and wife with one or more single children or one parent with one or more children.

[4] Lee, *Ireland*, 1912–85, 364; Dublin Corporation, 'Report of An Coisde Teaghlachais: With reference to the corporation's building programme under the housing of the working classes acts,' *Reports of Dublin Corporation 1961* (Dublin, 1962), 407.

[5] *Plan*, March 1970, 5.

[6] Anne Power, *Estates on the Edge: The Social Consequences of Mass Housing in Northern Europe* (Basingstoke, 1997), 241–2.

bringing housing conditions and shortages to light. This chapter explores how these protests resulting from housing shortages were incorporated into a broader discourse regarding the future of the city. Although housing protest and activism had a very different character and emphasis to the preservationist campaigns witnessed in Kildare Place and Fitzwilliam Street, their emphasis on social conservation elided in many aspects with ideas of architectural preservation; and there was considerable overlap in terms of their vision for the city, and their conception of the threats facing the urban environment. However, the housing campaigns brought a wider cohort to conservation than would ever have been interested in architectural preservation. They could not be dismissed as irrelevant or elitist; they rested on the testimony of working-class people against the bureaucratic strength of state and machinery of the speculator; and they could draw upon long-standing narratives of nationalist struggle. As such, they were crucial to the creation of both a broad-based opposition to urban modernization and a constituency of support for a more widely defined preservationist movement.

The most significant moment in the evolution of housing in Dublin in the 1960s was the dangerous buildings scare of 1963–4. Shortly before 5 a.m. on the night of 2 June 1963, an 84-year-old man and his 83-year-old wife were 'hurled to their deaths from their beds' and seven other people were trapped as their tenement collapsed in Bolton Street, in the former Gardiner Estate area of the city.[7] In the week that followed, many were evicted from similar buildings in the locality by panicked dangerous buildings inspectors. On the night of 4 June, eight terrified families, including eleven adults and nine children, were given a moment's notice to evacuate a dangerous four-storey tenement building in Upper Buckingham Street, while at Bolton Street a Dublin Corporation building inspector summoned by the tenants took one look at a 30ft long crack which had appeared in a gable, and ordered everyone out.[8] The next day, sixteen people were ordered from 20 Upper Dominick Street, the occupants being rehoused in Coolock, Cabra, and the Fatima Mansion flats, and Corporation officials were also called as rubble fell in 3 Henrietta Street, where sixteen families were living.[9] However, the timbre of media coverage of events and the rate of removals changed fundamentally when, on 12 June, another tenement collapsed on the other side of the city, causing the deaths of two young girls.[10]

[7] NAI DT S17486/63, *Local Inquiry at City Hall Dublin*, 24 June 1963 to 5 July 1963, 3; *Irish Press*, 3 June 1963, 5; *Irish Times*, 3 June 1963, 1.

[8] *Irish Press*, 5 June 1963, 7.

[9] *Irish Press*, 6 June 1963, 5.

[10] *Irish Press*, 13 June 1963, 1; *Irish Times*, 13 June 1963, 1.

The residents of these tenement areas immediately responded with anger at their poor housing conditions, and made demands for new houses. As demolition gangs tore down the remains of the two collapsed houses in Fenian Street, extra Gardaí had to be brought in to keep order as an angry crowd clamoured for faster provision of new homes.[11] On 13 June, about forty women, many of whom were pushing prams, and a large number of children, from the Fenian Street, Hogan Place, Macken Street, Lincoln Place, and Brunswick Place areas of the city marched to the City Hall with the intention of making a protest to the City Manager. They carried banners bearing the slogans 'Clear the Slums' and 'Don't wait for the Houses to Fall'.[12] They failed to see the City Manager, so then marched through College Green and Nassau Street to the Mansion House in Dawson Street, where a deputation was received by the Lord Mayor, Alderman J. J. O'Keefe TD.[13] When the Lord Mayor visited Fenian Street later that afternoon, he was mobbed by the crowd; in spite of his assurances that everything possible would be done to find accommodation for the homeless, the protest continued, and Gardaí had to ensure his safe departure.[14]

After the second collapse, the already panicky responses of the dangerous buildings division now ascended in key. On 13 June, while Neil Blaney ordered a public inquiry into the collapses, inspectors 'dealt with' about fifty houses as an emergency measure in the Fenian Street, Grattan Street, Hogan Place, Holles Street, Kevin Street, Upper Dorset Street, and Coleraine Street areas. Notices were nailed on doorways informing the residents that the buildings were condemned and they had to leave within seven days.[15] In the three weeks following the first collapse, the Corporation received over 1,500 phone calls regarding unstable buildings, and 156 houses were evacuated because of their condition.[16] This necessitated the displacement of 520 families. However, owing to the housing shortage, the Corporation was only able to offer 200 of these families new accommodation.[17] At an emergency meeting to discuss the housing crisis, Dublin City Council voted unanimously that the City Manager, Tom O'Mahony, and the Lord Mayor should approach the Minister for Defence, the school authorities, and the Red Cross to seek accommodation. It was decided that if this was not successful, authority should be

[11] *Irish Press*, 14 June 1963, 1.
[12] *Irish Times*, 14 June 1963, 1; *Irish Press*, 14 June 1963, 1.
[13] *Irish Times*, 14 June 1963, 1; *Irish Press*, 14 June 1963, 1.
[14] *Irish Press*, 14 June 1963, 1.
[15] *Irish Press*, 14 June 1963, 1.
[16] *Irish Times*, 22 June 1963, 15.
[17] *Irish Times*, 22 June 1963, 15.

given for the use of the Mansion House for housing those evicted by the dangerous buildings operations.[18]

When the inquiry reported back, it revealed how years of poverty and neglect of the city, combined with the recent wave of structural modernization, was putting increased pressure on the built stock. While the exceptional weather conditions which had preceded the two collapses were noted—a long period of heat, accompanied by drying winds, and followed by one of the worst thunderstorms within living memory—the report also made frequent reference to the cumulative stress placed on the Georgian city by new constructions and new materials.[19] In the case of Bolton Street, the collapse occurred because the house next door was being demolished to be replaced by a petrol station on the same site.[20] Its chimney had already lost much of its structural strength because long-term use had resulted in the burn-out of its mid-feathers (the chimney's interior structural supports); thus when the next-door demolition removed lateral support a heavy rainstorm was enough to make the house collapse.[21] At Fenian Street, the long winter of rainfall had completely saturated the brickwork, so when the moisture quickly evaporated in the hot weather 'nothing was left of the bricks except powder'. The heat had also caused the timbers in the house to become swollen and to push the walls outwards as they expanded. Mr Culliton, head of the dangerous buildings section of Dublin Corporation, added that this process had been exacerbated by the introduction of reinforced concrete roads, producing a greater transference of traffic vibration than from cobbled streets.[22]

As the inquiry blamed the weather, the degrading yet unseen structural condition of chimneys, and the modernization of the capital's infrastructure, it suddenly became clear that any house in the city of a similar construction could have been equally affected.[23] The crisis of confidence in the structural viability of Dublin's extant built stock precipitated what has become known as the dangerous buildings crisis of 1963–4. During the eighteen months which followed the Fenian Street collapse, around 1,200 of Dublin's Georgian terrace houses and mews were destroyed, mainly in the north and east of the city.[24] This process was ultimately accelerated by the latterly notorious Exempted Development regulations of the Local Government (Sanitary Services) Act 1964, which, in an attempt to speed

[18] *Irish Times*, 18 June 1963, 1; *Irish Times*, 17 June 1963, 1.
[19] *Hibernia*, July 1963, 16.
[20] NAI DT S17486/63, *Local Inquiry*, 3.
[21] NAI DT S17486/63, *Local Inquiry*, 6–7.
[22] *Irish Times*, 4 July 1963, 6.
[23] NAI DT S17486/95, Letter from Seán Moore to the Taoiseach, 20 August 1963.
[24] *Build*, January 1966, 12–13; *Build*, January 1967, 31.

up the process, exempted demolition from construction work which required planning permission.[25] The crisis had a sudden impact on the housing situation and land-use patterns within the city. Indeed, the housing problem was so severe that by February 1965, Dublin Corporation could only offer accommodation to families where seven or more were inhabiting one room, while in 1966, Uinseann MacEoin estimated that in the three previous years the dangerous buildings clearances alone had been responsible for the loss of 10,000 people from the central area.[26]

This operational work by the Corporation was reinforced by a moral panic in the press regarding the condition of the city. Ailtire warned in the aftermath of the collapses that 'only the most determined drive by the authorities can clear up the mess of the dangerous and largely insanitary slums forming the major portion of our glorious Georgian heritage', while G. K. Ingram, writing in *Hibernia*, took a similar position:

> We have been recently and dramatically reminded that old buildings can kill. As a result we can never again look at them with quite the clear starry eyes of the preservationist, for whom the past is always to be preferred to the present. The question of what we may put in their stead is a separate issue; but let no one deceive himself but that the present situation is extremely grave and perilous.[27]

Sam Stephenson also took the opportunity to further his own cause in Fitzwilliam Street, writing to the *Irish Times* to speculate about the full-scale reconstruction of the city, and wishing 'a plague—bubonic or other approved—on the preservationists'.[28]

Despite the almost frenzied condemnation of the extant city as dangerous and the amply documented poverty and overcrowding of city centre housing, there was a significant minority of city centre residents who resisted Dublin Corporation's attempts to remove them from their homes. In late July 1963, for example, a group of sixty adults and eighteen children refused to leave their condemned Georgian houses in Jervis and Wolfe Tone Street, located to the west of O'Connell Street.[29] During this time, beds, sofas, and chairs were piled up on the pavements beside the houses, and the evicted slept under temporary shelters on the pavement.[30] This stand-off between Corporation and residents took place because they had been offered either no accommodation or unsuitable accommodation by Dublin Corporation. Of the group, six single people were given no

[25] *Build*, January 1967, 31.
[26] PDDÉ 214, 11 February 1965, col. 251–6; *Build*, January 1966, 12–13.
[27] *Hibernia*, July 1963, 16; *Irish Architect and Contractor*, June 1963, 10.
[28] *Irish Times*,17 June 1963, 10.
[29] *Irish Times*, 29 July 1963, 1.
[30] *Irish Times*, 29 July 1963, 1.

accommodation, but were informed that they could find shelter in the Mendicity Institute on Kevin Street; six couples were also not rehoused, but were similarly told they could be sheltered individually in the institute. Several of the families were only offered accommodation in Griffith Barracks, which was considered unsuitable and insanitary.[31] These institutions were considered to be the modern equivalent of the workhouse; newspapers reported that they were surrounded by barbed wire, that men and women were separated, and that residents were only allowed in the accommodation to sleep.[32] Indeed, there was a mass breakout from Griffith Barracks in 1965, with its inhabitants camping on a derelict site beside Mountjoy Square rather than returning to the Corporation housing.[33] The spokesman for the Jervis Street group, Francis Fitzgerald, set the condition that they would only leave their homes if they could receive assurances that they would be housed in the flats in Bridgefort Street or the North Strand, which were both new developments.[34] However, the group finally dispersed with their demands unmet; some going into the Corporation flats that they had initially rejected, while others found accommodation with their families.

This was not the only group to contest the state's actions. A group from George's Place also refused to leave their tenements; Danny Madden, the leader of the group, wrote to Lemass to protest about their situation.[35] In vivid terms he described how 'hordes of inspectors can now be seen haunting the tenements of Dublin', and condemned them for presiding over a situation where the old and infirm were being forced:

> on to the streets of Dublin by the Garda who are employed in the role of bailiffs. Where is our constitution now? Such tactics as was employed by the British when in control who with their batter and ram aided by police did similar to our peoples in the years now gone. The British government gave them a shy. As God knows where and when local workhouses and such like became overcrowded; but today the Dublin Corporation gave us the street to face death when we are loath to go to an Institution which degrades and stigmas the Paupers.[36]

[31] NAI DT S17486/63, Letter from Declan Costello to the Taoiseach, 18 July 1963; *Irish Times*, 6 August 1963, 7.

[32] NAI S17486/63 press cutting, *Sunday Independent*, 15 December 1963.

[33] *Irish Times*, 14 September 1965, 6; *United Irishman*, September 1965, 2–3; *United Irishman*, October 1965, 1.

[34] NAI DT S17486/63, Letter from Declan Costello to the Taoiseach, 18 July 1963.

[35] *Build*, January 1966, 12.

[36] NAI DT S17486/63, Letter from Danny Madden to the Taoiseach, 18 August 1963.

Madden described how the disciplinary arm of the Irish state had now stepped into the role of bailiff, a figure demonized as a personification of the iniquities of British rule. However, he looked to Lemass to provide for the people of Dublin accommodation based on national values of Christianity and the rights inscribed in the constitution. Like Fitzgerald, he was pragmatic in his requests, evoking the totems which defined the state to demand finally, 'in the name of Christian Charity and of Ireland's dead to take over flats at North Strand, Botanic Avenue and Bridgefoot Street'.[37] In Hendrick Street, James Farrell also refused to leave his flat. He told an *Irish Times* reporter that he had lived in the street since 1919, and although he had been offered accommodation at Crumlin, an estate to the south-west of the city centre, he would not take it as it meant his losing his status as tenant and 'becoming a lodger'. This he was not prepared to do as his wife, Mary, had only recently returned from hospital, and he was anxious to be housed near his neighbours, who were going to the Dolphin's Barn area. He decided not to leave until his wishes were met.[38]

These cases of resistance to removal only provide a small snapshot of a much wider phenomenon. Of the 466 families evicted during the summer of 1963, 120 refused at least one offer of alternative accommodation in Corporation houses and flats.[39] In particular, evictees refused to be rehoused in Keogh Square, Benburb Street, Mount Pleasant buildings, and Corporation Buildings, which were all known for the substandard quality of accommodation provided and social problems.[40] While many of those affected secured alternative accommodation outside Corporation provision, many others insisted—against all advice—on remaining in their condemned homes.[41] Indeed, a survey made during a few nights at the end of August 1963 showed that of 262 buildings waiting for demolition, 138 were vacated but 124 continued to be occupied by a total of 260 families and 107 single people. As it was deemed to be necessary to secure the clearance of these occupied dwellings as quickly as possible, vacation was frequently forced through Court Removal Orders executed by the Gardaí.[42]

The recurring demand from those evicted for housing in Bridgefoot Street and North Strand indicated an attachment to the city within the

[37] NAI DT S17486/63, Letter from Danny Madden to the Taoiseach, 18 August 1963.

[38] *Irish Times*, 18 June 1963, 9.

[39] NAI DT S17486/95, Letter from Seán Moore to the Taoiseach, 20 August 1963.

[40] *Build*, May 1966, 28.

[41] NAI DT S17486/63, Memorandum from Department of Local Government to the Taoiseach, 29 July 1963.

[42] NAI DT S17486/63, Report of An Coisde Teachlachais, 16 August 1963.

canals, where little of the Corporation housing stock was situated. Indeed, even during the period of the dangerous buildings scare, applications to return to the city centre greatly exceeded supply. As a Department of Local Government civil servant noted in July 1963, Corporation procedure was to extend to all families of three and over 'two offers of accommodation in Corporation areas on the outskirts of the city', while couples without children and single people were offered accommodation in flats in the city centre. It was 'the policy of the Corporation . . . to give [city centre] flats, as far as possible, to persons moved from central city houses'. However, as the number of available flats was smaller than the numbers evacuated, it was 'not possible to satisfy demands'. Indeed, this new pressure on the city centre housing stock was merely adding to an already existing waiting list; there was already a considerable list of 'people in outlying areas, who went reluctantly from the centre of the city and who [had] applied to get back to flats in the city'.[43]

However, proximity to the centre of the city was not the only concern of those evicted during the summer of 1963; the demands of these individuals and families were based on requirements for modern, clean facilities, 'good' neighbourhoods, and a greater sense of control in relation to the seemingly arbitrary evictions and arbitrary housing allocations. During the same period, the debate which surrounded Fitzwilliam Street, located within the bureaucratic and symbolic core of the capital, revolved around conceptions of the nation and the role of modern architecture. However, those who lived in Georgian tenements in less esteemed parts of the city had an attachment to place which had little to do with the ideological imagery created by their streetscape; rather the tenements which they were loath to leave were sites of community and places of residence which, however dilapidated, fulfilled their requirements for housing better than the alternatives provided by the state.

The concerns and experiences of those displaced from the city centre animated a variety of responses from artists and writers, who sought to record and eulogize city culture as evictions and office construction seemed to herald its rapid decline. In 1965, the journalist Elizabeth Leslie published 'A Northsider's Lament' in the *Irish Times*, describing how the city which had in her youth seemed 'solid, immutable, and there for all time' was now disappearing so fast that few of the streets bore any similarity to the city of her memory: 'Gardiner Street, Temple Street and Summerhill were the first to change and now Mountjoy Square is going too. Then Dominick Street disappeared completely and is still waiting to be

[43] NAI DT S17486/63, Memorandum on file from Department of Local Government to Taoiseach, 29 July 1963.

completely rebuilt. Between Parnell Street and Henry Street there's a desolation of open space.'[44] However, Leslie asserted that this was not only the loss of the physical fabric of the city, but also the loss of an identity:

> When you went around on a bicycle you knew all the back streets and all the short cuts and had a superior sense of knowing your city much better than other people. Now that knowledge is useless because all the back streets have either gone or are no longer back streets... It's quite irrational but you do get the feeling of being dispossessed. In that warren of streets behind the quays you were safe from the world, but now traffic signs are everywhere, someone else has found Cuckoo Lane and has made it into a one-way street, and that's the last straw.[45]

Stating that the streets 'were part of what I knew and because of that I regret the changes', Leslie's journalism played on a conception of the city as a repository of memory and identity, as explored in works by an earlier generation of writers, including Walter Benjamin.[46] In this piece she explored how signs, one-way streets, and traffic lights constituted the visible manifestation of the bureaucratization of city space and indicated the encroachment of urban modernity on the city, and how this clashed with her own view of the same neighbourhoods as a foreign, uncharted space: a 'warren... safe from the world'.

Taking a similar position, Elinor Wiltshire took many photographs of Dublin life during the 1960s, focusing in particular on street life in the city. She was a professional photographer who, alongside her husband, ran Green Studios in central Dublin. She has cited Henri Cartier-Bresson as a strong influence on her work and, indeed, she used the style of inter-war urban photography in her portrayal of Dublin at this time. In her photograph reproduced here, she captured a family in York Street in 1964 after they had been evicted because of dangerous buildings operations (Fig. 5.1).[47] This street, which was on the west side of St Stephen's Green, had originally been cleared in October 1962, with all the families who had been living there being rehoused by the Corporation. However, the premises were subsequently reoccupied by squatter families, who were then removed by the Gardaí in July 1964.[48] Like those in Jervis Street, they refused to leave, and instead constructed makeshift accommodation out of furniture and boards.[49] Their pram, scattered possessions, and ad hoc camp fire, surrounded by

[44] *Irish Times*, 13 December 1965, 10.
[45] *Irish Times*, 13 December 1965, 10.
[46] *Irish Times*, 13 December 1965, 10.
[47] NAI DT S17486/95, Memorandum on file, 24 July 1964.
[48] NAI DT S17486/95, Memorandum on file, 24 July 1964.
[49] NAI DT S17486/95, Memorandum on file, 24 July 1964.

Fig. 5.1. Family resisting eviction, York Street, July 1964, by Elinor Wiltshire. Image courtesy of Elinor Wiltshire/National Library of Ireland.

notices protesting at their removal, created a striking image of parents and children at odds with Catholic notions of family life, and evoked a domesticity disrupted and dispossessed by the intervention of the state.[50]

Leslie and Wiltshire both shared a fascination with Dublin life, and sought to record it during the 1960s in the face of physical disruption and declining population. Their writing and photography both responded to and helped to create a sense that the city was at the end of an era, and that traditional customs, trades, and communities were in decline. David Ley has described urban culture as having rhythms, repetitive activity patterns, and routines which are often taken for granted and are apparently

[50] Elinor Wiltshire and Orla Fitzpatrick, *If You Ever Go to Dublin Town* (Dublin, 1999), 5.

inconsequential, yet in cumulative form define much of the meaning of the city to its residents.[51] Leslie's melancholy description seemed to evoke the loss of these ephemeral events, and points to an unquantifiable sense of identity bound up in urban space which those resisting eviction from their tenements, or on Corporation waiting lists to return to the city centre, would have shared. However, neither Leslie nor Wiltshire, both from wealthy backgrounds, would have experienced these emotions first hand. Rather, their nostalgia at the destruction of city communities can be likened to a different generation's search at another period of profound change. Just as Yeats and Synge travelled to the west of Ireland in search of a purer, more 'authentic' version of Irishness, so too were the spatial, social, and economic changes to the capital in the 1960s responded to by Dublin's artistic elite though the discovery and valorization of a working-class Dublin culture. Indeed, Terence de Vere White made this link when he speculated on the loss of a distinct Dublin dialect in 1969: 'there is every reason to fear that this wonderful Dublin quality is as fated to die as the Irish language has been. The language will be kept by scholars; Dublinese is only a mode of talking English. Future generations will have to guess what Joxer Daly sounded like when he talked with Captain Boyle.'[52]

But it was not only artists and writers who were exploring the meaning of the city anew during this period. Arising from the same concerns regarding the evolution of the city and changes to community life, the demands and desires of working-class residents for their accommodation also began to be more widely appraised by sociologists. From the late 1950s there was a growing concern that modernist housing schemes were destroying traditional, functioning communities, and creating environments of isolation and social malaise. The first pioneering study to articulate this position was Michael Young and Peter Wilmott's *Family and Kinship in East London*, published in 1957. It described the residents of Bethnal Green as a homogenous working-class group, embedded in a dense network of family and employment rooted in the locality.[53] This was followed, in 1961, by Jane Jacobs's highly influential *The Death and Life of Great American Cities*, which studied her neighbourhood in New York, and emphasized the role played by the physical fabric of older districts in building community cohesion, through the creation of close interaction between people and multiple-use environments of residence, work, and socialization.[54]

[51] David Ley, *A Social Geography of the City* (London, 1983), 99.

[52] Terence de Vere White, *Ireland* (London, 1968), 11.

[53] Michael Young and Peter Wilmott, *Family and Kinship in East London* (Harmondsworth, 1962).

[54] Jane Jacobs, *The Death and Life of Great American Cities* (Harmondsworth, 1994).

These studies had their Irish counterparts. Connor Ward's *New Homes for Old* of 1969 interviewed 249 housewives from a Dublin Corporation estate approximately 4 miles north of the city centre, over half of whom had moved from the city centre in the previous four years. Although he concluded that conditions in suburban estates were good overall, he highlighted loneliness, reduced contact with family members, and distance from amenities as problems.[55] Father Liam Ryan's article 'Social Dynamite', which appeared in the journal *Christus Rex* in 1967, was far less positive, pointing to the lack of amenities and lack of involvement of the community in the planning of a suburban estate, which he named 'Parkland', as central factors in creating social failure among early school leavers.[56] These studies were united by a methodology that linked societal formation and urban space; their approaches—like those of Leslie and Wiltshire—were framed by a nostalgia for a 'golden age' of working-class city life, and, tautologically, these publications went on to provide a scientific basis for these ephemeral emotions. Ultimately, they contributed to a wider backlash against modernist architecture and town planning, fracturing the consensus which looked to the dispersal of urban concentrations of population as essential for a peaceful and respectable society.[57] Just as the communities at Jervis Street and George's Place had lost faith in the state's ability to rehouse them in better conditions than they had created for themselves, these sociological studies were part of a process which questioned planners' ability to provide model surroundings for working-class residents and also the full-scale remodelling of city centre areas as providing the solution to the problem of the slums.

The dangerous buildings scare brings to light the differential experiences of Lemass's Ireland. Poverty was worsening for a certain sector of Dublin's residents, who were badly hit by increasing housing shortages, and remained outside the new-found affluence that came with economic growth. In the period 1960 to 1972, of the eighty speculative office developments completed in the city of Dublin, only two were north of the river: the Phibsboro Centre on Phibsborough Road, and Raven House in Finglas.[58] Furthermore, while there was no office construction in the north city, this was the area where the dangerous buildings inspectors

[55] Conor Ward, Mary Galligan, Margaret Glynn, Katherine Hodkinson, *New Homes for Old: Report* (Dublin, 1969).

[56] Liam Ryan, '"Social Dynamite": A Study of Early School Leavers', *Christus Rex* 21/1 (1967), 1–54; Fanning, *The Quest for Modern Ireland*, 127.

[57] This reflected a move away from the Catholic urban theory as articulated by Humphreys in ch. 1.

[58] Malone, *Office Development in Dublin 1960–80*, 54–8 for a complete list of office development in Co. Dublin in the period.

concentrated their work. Indeed, in 1965, MacEoin described the area as 'a wasteland of dereliction stretch[ing] from the North Wall to Phibsboro'.[59] Thus in the mid-1960s, many of the buildings in this area were demolished, much of the long-standing residential population was removed, and there was little in terms of 'renewal'. Indeed, the collapses in Bolton and Fenian Street took place only two weeks before John F. Kennedy's celebrated visit to Ireland. Thus, during his time in the country, many in Dublin were experiencing homelessness and hardship. This juxtaposition between the Ireland presented to the young Irish-American president and the homelessness and uncertainty facing much of the city was indicative that although the economic upturn of the early 1960s may have decreased the rate of emigration and brought a new language of optimism into public discourse, Ireland still faced problems resulting from long-standing poverty and infrastructural decay: the celebrated prosperity of the era was both limited and socially circumscribed.

The collapses which occurred in June 1963 had a profound impact on the lives of thousands of inhabitants of Dublin: many were forcibly rehoused, while many more were evicted from their tenements without the provision of any Corporation housing. There was some resistance to the clearance of the tenements, led by three disparate groups: residents resisting eviction; sociologists studying working-class culture; and writers and artists, who witnessed events in the city and reflected on their meaning. Readings of the city provided by these different groups worked together to generate considerable opposition to local government policy, to foster the idea that working-class Dublin culture was something which was becoming extinct and required protection, and to create a culture of nostalgia regarding city life. Indeed, this sensation of nostalgia, alongside the feeling of dislocation from the prosperity of the period and the severe housing shortage, would play a vital role in creating a constituency of support for a more radical breed of housing activism during the later 1960s—the Dublin Housing Action Committee (DHAC).

DUBLIN HOUSING ACTION COMMITTEE

The DHAC was active in Dublin for approximately three years from the middle of 1967. It was, of course, not the first organized housing activism in Dublin in the 1960s. As discussed above, many resisted eviction during the 1963 housing clearances, and there had been some efforts at coordinated

[59] *Build*, December 1965, 10.

responses, including the Griffith Barracks break-out. However, the DHAC's campaign was more organized, systematic, and sustained than these earlier incarnations of housing activism. Indeed, it was part of an island-wide growth of housing protest during the later 1960s. In Northern Ireland this activism played a crucial role in the politicization of the Catholic community, and the escalation of violence at the end of the decade. However, the formation of the DHAC preceded the foundation of many of the Northern groups, including the better-remembered and more fully documented Derry Housing Action Committee.[60] Although the DHAC's origins lay in the housing shortages which were affecting the city at this time, it had a much broader political platform, capitalizing upon this issue to draw support for an extensive radical agenda.

On 13 May 1967 the *Irish Independent* reported that 'a new group, the Dublin Housing Action Committee, at its first meeting in Dublin last night, called on Dublin Corporation to appreciate the plight of thousands of Dublin homeless families'.[61] The group had emerged from a variety of sources. During the mid-1960s, Sinn Féin began to actively campaign on housing issues, and to run housing advice sessions through their Citizens' Advice Bureau.[62] Mairin de Burca, secretary of Sinn Féin, Proinsias de Rossa and Seán Ó Cionnaith, chairman and secretary respectively of Dublin Comhairle Ceantair, and John McDonnell and Seán Dunne all played leading roles in the movement. However, although Sinn Féin dominated the group it did not control it; in March 1967, Denis and Mary Dennehy, members of the Irish Communist Organization (ICO) living in a caravan in Cherry Orchard, had begun to campaign for homeless people to organize independent representation for themselves in that year's local elections. They were also founding members of the DHAC, and played high-profile roles as activists and squatters.[63] During this period the Communist Party (CPI) was simultaneously developing an increasing membership and campaigning on issues of housing and land ownership, bringing many of its members into the movement, and leading to Bernard Browne becoming chairman of the DHAC.[64]

60 Niall Ó Dochartaigh, 'Housing and Conflict: Social Change and Collective Action in Derry in the 1960s', in Gerald O'Brien (ed.), *Derry and Londonderry: History and Society: Interdisciplinary Essays on the History of an Irish County* (Dublin, 1999), 635.

61 *Irish Independent*, 13 May 1967, 3.

62 Richard English, *Armed Struggle: The History of the IRA* (Oxford, 2003), 85–96; Tobin, *The Best of Decades*, 181; Keogh and McCarthy, *Twentieth Century Ireland*, 279.

63 *Evening Herald*, 1 March 1967, 6.

64 Roy Johnston, *Century of Endeavour: A Biographical and Autobiographical View of the Twentieth Century in Ireland* (Dublin, 2006), 175, 270–1; *Irish Times*, 17 June 1968, 8.

The group had a natural constituency of supports among the long-term homeless and those living in over-crowded conditions, who were unable to get on Corporation housing lists and unable to find accommodation at an affordable price; indeed, these problems affected women particularly severely, and women frequently dominated DHAC's picket lines. The fate of this urban underclass was followed closely by a newly critical and investigative media; this included journalists with an interest in social issues and poverty from journals such as *Hibernia* and the *Irish Times*, and factual television programmes including *Outlook* and *7 Days.* For example, Nell McCafferty documented squatting by Jimmy, Lilly, and their two children, who had been sharing Lilly's mother's house with her five brothers and sisters until a family argument led to them spending a night on a park bench, and followed their progress subsequently between squats in Pembroke Road and the Fiat Cottages.[65] In 1968, Mary Maher profiled the lives of a group of squatters in the Gardiner area of the city. This included John Byrne, a docker, and his wife Bernadette, who had lived in five furnished flats in 18 months of marriage before becoming illegal squatters in private property in Mountjoy Square. Similarly, Francis and Marie Smith and their 11-month-old baby, Sandra, had stayed with Marie's mother in a one-room Corporation flat before squatting in Rutland Street; while John and Catherine Waters lived with his family of six in a flat on North Great George's Street, before they forced their way into a two-roomed Corporation flat on Sean McDermott Street.[66]

By the summer of 1967, DHAC had already compiled the list of demands that would define its campaign for the next two years. This five-point programme, which was published both in national papers and in the socialist press, called for:

> 1—the declaration of a housing emergency and the adoption of emergency measures to provide adequate temporary family accommodation, making all vacant accommodation available as living accommodation; 2—the introduction of bye laws to prohibit the demolition and conversion to other uses of sound living accommodation; 3—the repair of dwellings by Dublin Corporation where landlords refuse to do so; 4—an immediate halt to the building of prestige office blocks and the redirection of the capital and labour involved to the construction of family accommodation; 5—house loans of 100% to low income citizens at low interest rates.[67]

[65] *Fortnight*, 20 November 1970, 8–9.
[66] *Irish Times*, 18 September 1968, 6.
[67] *Irish Times*, 17 June 1967, 8.

This programme interrogated the state's plan for the city. As discussed in Chapter 1, local government policy placed the onus of responsibility for urban renewal on to private developers; in contradistinction, the DHAC called for much more active intervention from the state in managing patterns of land use and directing the allocation of finance. Not only did the group demand an immediate solution to the housing situation, but in petitioning for the prohibition of change of use of residential property and the halt of prestige office accommodation it also linked this shortage of housing to the increase of office space in the city. In many ways these links were tenuous; in no sense were the 'capital and labour' of office construction taking men or money away from building houses, and the majority of new office blocks were not removing tenants from their accommodation. The critical mass of new office blocks in this period were located between St Stephen's Green and Ballsbridge, an area of the city which had been in commercial use throughout the twentieth century. However, in arguing that there was a causal link between increasing overcrowding and rising office blocks, the DHAC engaged their campaign for more housing to a broader unease regarding the changes of modernization.

This agenda was often presented in terms which appealed to the conservative, Catholic values of Irish society. For example, the *Irish Socialist* declared that the DHAC was fighting for:

> families that are split and forced to live apart by the lack of a house; married couples living in accommodation where children are not allowed; families forced to live with their in-laws; the homeless in corporation centres like Griffith Barracks; families who are compelled to pay excessive rents; fatherless families; families forced to live in overcrowded conditions; most caravan dwelling families; and families who are forced to squat because they cannot get any accommodation.[68]

Similarly, when Dennehy appeared in court for squatting (discussed below), he used the platform to point to the contradictions inherent in the constitution between the centrality of the family and the rights to private property which, in their 1960s guise, were seen to be making so many homeless. As the *United Irishman* summarized: 'the overall conclusion from [the case] is that despite the grand language of the Sacred 1937 constitution, a working-class family counts for nothing against the might and majesty of Landlordism in Ireland'.[69] After independence, the family was the organizing unit of Irish life, and was fundamental to notions of

[68] *Irish Socialist*, March 1969, 1.
[69] *United Irishman*, January 1969, 10.

citizenship; DHAC positioned itself as the guardians of the sanctity of the family through its campaign for housing, and in so doing was able to present its radical politics as a defence of the constitution and traditional values, which were under threat from economic and social modernization.

This emphasis on the family drew members of the clergy to DHAC's campaign, in particular a group dubbed the 'militant priests' by *Hibernia* magazine, which went on to declare, 'we are perhaps on the threshold of a new era—that of the priest as activist'.[70] This group included figures such as Michael Sweetman, Liam Ryan, and Austin Flannery, the presenter of the controversial *Outlook* programme on RTÉ. They were characterized by their elision of Catholicism and social theory, and shared an interest in the condition of city-centre housing as both symptom and cause of societal failures. More than any other, the vocal support of Father Michael Sweetman SJ of St Francis Xavier's in Gardiner Street was instrumental in raising awareness of the committee's demands. He repeatedly addressed DHAC meetings with a particular form of Christian socialism which was very much out of step with views expressed from the archdiocese. On 18 January 1968, he spoke at a meeting on O'Connell Street, a speech which he began by shouting, 'We are told that the family is the hub of Christianity... how the hell can a family start without a home?' He went on, 'I speak in the knowledge that a great number of priests are in close contact with this housing problem. We know of young people who cannot get married because they have no home, and of people married who cannot have children because they have no home for them. They are afraid to start their life in fear and squalor and that should come to an end.'[71] On one well-known occasion, he suggested that church land should be sold for low-income accommodation.[72]

The DHAC's campaign for more housing in Dublin often used emotive rhetoric to describe in extreme terms the conditions still in existence in central Dublin, presenting housing in the city as insanitary and improper for bringing up a family. Father Michael Sweetman took an *Evening Herald* reporter on a tour of this area of the city to show him the 'grim facts of Dublin's housing conditions', commenting that 'These places where it is impossible to lead a decent human life—they are a horror!'[73] In a similar vein, members of the DHAC hijacked the Congress of the International Federation for Housing and Planning schedule, to

[70] *Hibernia*, April 1968, 5.
[71] *Irish Times*, 19 January 1968, 1; *Irish Independent*, 19 January 1968, 11.
[72] *United Irishman*, November 1968, 10.
[73] *Irish Independent*, 23 January 1968, 3; *Evening Herald*, 23 January 1968, 5.

take about twenty American and Swedish delegates on a tour of locations in the north city to bring international attention to the poor conditions in existence in Dublin, visiting Mountjoy Square, Gardiner Street, Corporation Buildings, and Sean McDermott Street. 'We took them', a spokesman said, 'to see parts of the city that they would be unlikely to see.'[74] These journeys characterized the city centre as a *Heart of Darkness*, an uncharted, unknown world of poverty and degradation which existed only yards away from the lights and statues which demarked the ceremonial capital of the city. In tracing paths and leading tours around the city, the DHAC actively reconfigured urban geographies; they participated in a modern slumming which reconnected seemingly distant areas of the city to the ceremonial capital.

This visualization of hidden poverty was also a key part of the DHAC's monthly protests at City Hall. The committee first drew the attention of the national newspapers through their placing of noisy pickets on meetings of Dublin City Council at City Hall to demand the implementation of their five-point programme.[75] The first of these demonstrations was on 12 June 1967, when an estimated fifty members of the DHAC held a meeting at the GPO and then marched to City Hall. A representative then handed in the committee's list of demands, which included the declaration of a housing emergency.[76] The pattern of marches and pickets continued throughout the autumn and winter of 1967, with demonstrations becoming increasingly organized, violent, and embittered.[77] For example, on 2 October, one hundred people marched from the GPO to City Hall, carrying banners which expressed the crowd's distance from modernization, contrasting government-financed industrial projects with the lack of housing. The banner at the front of the procession declared that the Government should 'use Taca to build houses', while the crowd also carried other banners which provided sardonic reposts to the glorification of Irish achievement: 'Mise Éire 1967: 10,000 homeless'; 'Memorial Hall but no Houses'; 'Potez, Avoca, Electra, or 2,500 dwellings which?'; 'Grants for foreigners but no houses for Irish'; 'Condemned to live in condemned houses'.[78] When the City Council meeting commenced, Dennehy interrupted with a speech from the public gallery,

[74] *Irish Times*, 22 May 1969, 10; *United Irishman*, June 1969, 10.

[75] *Hibernia*, 1–14 November 1968, 9.

[76] *Irish Times*, 12 June 1967, 11; *Irish Times,* 13 June 1967, 8.

[77] *Irish Times*, 2 October 1967, 1; *Irish Times*, 7 November 1967, 11; *Irish Times*, 5 December 1967, 14; *Irish Independent*, 19 October 1967, 14; *Evening Herald*, 3 October 1967, 3.

[78] *Mise Éire* was the title of a poem by Patrick Pearse, written in 1912. It gave its name to a 1959 documentary, directed by George Morrison, on the 1916 Rising.

declaring that there were people living in conditions in Dublin 'which would bring tears to the eyes of Rachman'. He and another member of the committee were then removed by ushers.[79] After the next meeting on 16 October, Mary Dennehy dramatically brought the poor conditions faced by many residents of the city to the notice of the councillors when she struck the Labour deputy Seán Dunne in the face with a dead rat, which she was reported to have caught in her caravan.[80]

In 1968, the monthly meetings at City Hall continued to be interrupted by DHAC protests. In January, the group held a 'torch-light poster picket' outside the building; meanwhile the meeting inside was interrupted for forty minutes by protestors.[81] The *Irish Times* described the scene:

> A bearded member of the DHAC began to read a statement while Mr Sean Dunne TD was addressing the council and other members of the public gallery began to chant: 'houses for the people'. The Lord Mayor, Mr Tom Stafford left the chamber and the Gardaí were called. Leaflets calling on the government to stop the building of office blocks and to declare a national housing emergency were thrown in the air and littered the council chamber. The demonstrators accused the police of brutality while several of their comrades were being carried from the gallery. Garda caps were knocked to the ground. 'Is there one councillor who will stand up and say he agrees with the homeless?' asked one of the demonstrators.[82]

These aggressive exchanges brought Dublin's bureaucratic governing class into dramatic confrontation with a group of the city's radicalized, impoverished citizens. The cycle of meetings at the GPO, followed by torch-lit marches, pickets, and scuffles in the visitors' gallery continued throughout the first nine months of 1968, interrupted by spikes in violence. A large force of Gardaí were in place for the February meeting of Dublin City Council when 250 people marched to City Hall, shouting 'We want houses' and 'Evict the landlords'. In May 1968, as barricades were being thrown up across Paris, batons were drawn on the placard-waving crowd as the councillors left the Dublin City Council meeting, leading to two women and a man needing treatment in Jervis Street hospital.[83]

Although DHAC did much to publicize the insanitary conditions in much of the city, most of their efforts were based on helping families resist

[79] *Irish Times*, 3 October 1967, 1.
[80] *Irish Times*, 17 October 1967, 1.
[81] *Irish Times*, 6 January 1968, 1; *Irish Independent*, 30 December 1967, 11; *Irish Independent*, 9 January 1968, 1.
[82] *Irish Times*, 9 January 1968, 8.
[83] *Irish Times*, 7 May 1968, 1; *Irish Times*, 14 May 1968, 9.

eviction from very similar eighteenth-century homes. Beginning with a protest in Mount Street in October 1967, the DHAC was active at many locations around the city, helping tenants resist eviction through pickets and violent confrontations with Gardaí and bailiffs.[84] Over the succeeding three years the group was involved in organizing campaigns to prevent the eviction of tenants in East James Street, Sarah Place, Gardiner Street, and the Christchurch area among others.[85] These evictions all resulted from the gradual redesignation of the city centre as a place of commerce rather than residence; in the case of the East James Street and Mount Street residents their accommodation had been purchased by developers for the site to be used as offices, while evictions at Sarah Place and Gardiner Street resulted from dangerous buildings work by the Corporation.[86] These urban conflicts were refracted through hundred-year-old tropes of Fenian struggle, but with the role of rich and poor, Irish and British, bureaucrat and peasant recast. The police and bailiffs' antagonistic exchanges with the poor were visualized strikingly in the press as nineteenth-century Land League agitation brought from a rural to an urban setting, providing a damning—and very potent—visual criticism of the nature of the government.

This emphasis on defending local communities against Dublin Corporation and private finance was part of a shift in direction for the DHAC. In September 1968, it announced that it would no longer be placing pickets on Dublin City Council meetings as its activity during the past year had exposed the 'uselessness of the Corporation'.[87] Instead, the DHAC urged homeless people to occupy empty houses. The resolution, passed at a meeting on 29 September 1968, stated:

> Since there are many homeless families in Dublin, while hundreds of empty houses are scattered throughout the city, we state that homeless families are justified in squatting in these empty houses and in militantly defending their right to a house against a system which is both inhuman and corrupt. We state that since this system gives virtually no protection from eviction to the majority of working class people, we are morally justified in militantly opposing every attempt to evict us. We state, since the system uses violence against the family when affecting an eviction, the family in turn is justified in using

[84] *Irish Independent*, 11 January 1968, 10; *United Irishman*, February 1968, 4; *Irish Times*, 23 January 1968, 13; *United Irishman*, February 1968, 1; *Build*, November 1967, 16–17.

[85] *Irish Independent*, 16 January 1968, 1; *Irish Independent*, 9 November 1967, 11; *Evening Herald*, 21 October 1967, 3; *Evening Herald*, 9 January 1968, 3; *Evening Herald*, 15 January 1968, 1.

[86] *Irish Times*, 23 October 1967, 1.

[87] *Irish Times*, 2 September 1968, 11.

> physical force, if need be in order to defend its right to a home. Finally, we pledge ourselves to support each other in our struggle for one of the most basic rights of all—the right to decent homes at fair rents of our families.[88]

This was a move to a new militancy for the DHAC, and indeed the group achieved success in organising squats by homeless people. By July 1969, the *United Irishman* reported that families were squatting in various locations in the prosperous south-east of the city: '146 Pembroke Road Ballsbridge Dublin 4, occupied by five families since the month of March 1969; 12 Estate Cottages off Mount Street Bridge Dublin 4, occupied by two families since May; 17 and 19 Waterloo Road, Dublin 4, occupied by six families, three in each since early June.'[89] Throughout 1969, the DHAC grew more militant in the squatting tactics used; indeed, it organized squats of prominent locations in Dublin such as the Carlton Hotel and the Hume Street buildings (see Chapter 7).[90] It also sent a warning through the *United Irishman* to those who opposed it, drawing on forms of non-statist policing as practised by the IRA in the revolutionary period. 'We give public warning to all landlords and their agents that the DHAC will hold them personally responsible for any attempted eviction or for the jailing of any homeless person. All such persons will be justly rewarded.'[91] In so doing, DHAC also took on roles usually assigned to the state in order to both subvert the state's power and draw attention to its failures in social policy.

This new emphasis on the politicization of Dublin's homeless led to the DHAC producing its own newspaper, *The Squatter*, to promote and enable squatting. Printed in telegraph typescript and surrounded by a border of barbed wire, it acted almost as an estate agent's brochure of potential properties, presenting the city in an easily understandable register as a territorial and ideological war zone between property developer and long-time resident. The paper contained letters from squatters, stories of successfully resisted evictions, news of housing figures and even ended with 'STOP PRESS: TWO EMPTY HOUSES TAKEN OVER NUMBERS 17 & 19 WATERLOO ROAD LATE LAST NIGHT SOME ROOMS STILL VACANT PANORAMIC VIEW JOIN THE DHAC NOW.'[92] The news-sheet also forcefully propounded a Marxist analysis of the housing problem and its solution. The first edition made the link between homelessness and anti-capitalism:

[88] *Irish Times*, 30 September 1968, 15.
[89] *United Irishman*, July 1969, 11.
[90] *United Irishman*, August 1969, 2.
[91] *Irish Socialist*, September 1969, 6.
[92] *The Squatter*, 15 June 1969, 4.

> We say that the housing problem in Dublin wouldn't be half as bad if the thousands of families with a housing problem organised themselves and squatted in some of the empty, surplus property owned by foreign and native parasites. We admit that there cannot be a solution—that is a final solution—until the capitalist system in the 26 counties is destroyed by force. But there is more than adequate accommodation lying empty at this moment while thousands of families desperately need shelter. So we say to the homeless and all working class families with a housing problem: organise now and if possible SQUAT under the banner of the DHAC. The DHAC would like to see people squatting in some of the empty, surplus property owned by the foreign bums and parasites who have come in here to tear our city to shreds in order to build gaudy office blocks and expensive hotels. We say that the idle, surplus property of any big speculating landlord should be squatted in. People come before profits, and the worker's natural right to proper accommodation comes before the legal rights of landlords.[93]

As the quotation reveals, in this newspaper the DHAC went far beyond its original five-point programme in its demands. Unlike in its press releases to the national newspapers, in its own publication the group was forthright in arguing that the cause of the housing problem was capitalism, and that its only solution was the destruction of this system. While contemporaneous architectural debate regarding the future of the city tended to revolve around binaries of Irish and British styles, in the DHAC's analysis the division was between the city as a place with an essential character, and the 'foreign parasites' who threatened it with destruction.[94] In many ways the DHAC's conception of authentic and inauthentic in Dublin's environment and culture mapped on to pre-existing divisions, but in this schema post-colonial legacies had little importance in the face of neo-colonial threats. In calling for the active involvement of homeless people in squatting, it aimed to politicize a broader section of Dublin's working class. Members of the DHAC had repeatedly spoken out against the lack of political consciousness among Dublin's homeless population; however, in bringing homeless people into the centre of activism and campaigning, squatting blurred the boundaries between mode of implementation and aims of protest, serving to radicalize this unpoliticized constituency.[95] Moreover, the promotion of very visible locations in the centre of the city for families to squat served to bring the iniquities of the Irish economic system to the attention of the wider public.

93 *The Squatter*, 15 June 1969, 1.

94 Doreen Massey, 'Places and their Pasts', *History Workshop Journal* 39 (1995), 183.

95 *Irish Times*, 1 February 1969, 10.

While much of DHAC's campaigning and protesting outside City Hall focused on ideas of the insanitary nature of the city centre, their parallel campaign to help families resist eviction was predicated on the idea of the city centre as a place which the working class had an almost territorial right to inhabit. This view had held power from the time the middle class had left the city within the canals in the nineteenth century, and had been expressed in Dublin with greater intensity and frequency since the concerted slum clearances of the 1940s and 1950s. However, in the 1960s, the idea of working-class entitlement to city spaces gained increasing politicization and urgency as the area became the site of exponentially increasing land values and home to a new growth: the large, inevitably modernist, purpose-built office block. Across Europe in the 1960s, the city became a site of conflict between older patterns of life and new capital, and thus the spaces of the city became a locus for the political activity of the new left, a movement which DHAC was part of. This left-wing mobilization built on the valorization and nostalgia for the communal life of these areas, which was given a scientific validity through research and publications such as *Family and Kinship in East London*. In Dublin these broader European tendencies played out in a local register. As the *Irish Socialist* stated, urban preservation became social politics:

> The protests about the closing of the Grand Canal, or the demolition of Georgian houses may seem to many workers to have nothing to do with them. Many of those who are protesting probably think it has very little to do with the workers either. In fact these acts of vandalism are part of the whole problem of providing houses for people, of giving accommodation to workers in areas where transport costs won't cripple them, of providing a proper environment for our people to live in.[96]

The piece went on to cite Lewis Mumford's depiction of the nineteenth-century British industrial city, describing the poor physical conditions which subjected environment to profit, 'not because it better expressed the vital social needs of the new day, but because it offered some callous philistine the opportunity for speculative gain'.[97] The author saw the same pattern of land acquisition and transference of property from public amenity to private profit taking place in 1960s Dublin. He asked: 'Why are people being housed miles from their work in Ballymun and Finglas? Because private greed demands that sites in the city centre should be used for unproductive monstrosities of office blocks. Why are the canals being filled?' He answered his own question: 'So that speculative builders can

[96] *Irish Socialist*, December 1967, 3.
[97] *Irish Socialist*, December 1967, 3.

throw up another concrete jungle and further foul Dublin Bay with sewage which is being treated in a more primitive fashion than in mediaeval times.'[98] While DHAC had little interest in saving the fabric of the city of Dublin, and, indeed, campaigned for an improvement of housing conditions in the ageing built stock, it waged a territorial war for the spaces of the city in order to oppose the new strain of capitalism embodied in the industry of office construction. Uinseann MacEoin described the situation that allowed property speculation to continue during the housing shortage as 'political nitro-glycerine', and stated that housing activists 'have a common interest with the conservationists, but there is dynamite, political dynamite in their weight of numbers'.[99] Thus—in an unlikely alliance—the DHAC's housing activism led them into an often uneasy coalition with the Dublin Civic Group and the Irish Georgian Society for the preservation of the city.

In Dublin this Europe-wide phenomenon battle over the centre of the city took on particular significance, as it was enlisted into a longer running struggle regarding the nature of independence and nationalism post-partition. The failure of the state to protect the city and thus provide for its working class population was held up by the DHAC as axiomatic of the failure of the inheritors of the Republic to fulfil the promises of those who fought for its creation. As Bernard Browne wrote in the *Irish Socialist*:

> The housing agitations are part (perhaps a small part) of the revolutionary struggle of the Irish people to build the kind of Irish republic that great men like Wolfe Tone, Fintan Lalor and James Connolly lived, fought and died for. An Irish Republic that is not only free from British Imperialism but free too from an alien social, political, economic and cultural system that was foisted on this country by Britain—a system whereby property rights supersede human rights—a system that puts profit before the welfare of people—a system of power and privilege for the few at the expense of the many. In short a system that is not only alien but is the direct opposite of everything Irishmen and Irish women fought and died for many generations ...[100]

For Browne, the provision of a decent standard of housing for all was a key part of fulfilling the vision of previous generations of nationalists in achieving an independent Ireland, which would be both politically free and have an economic system which was geared towards providing for the well-being of its citizens rather than moving capital to the metropole. He also utilized Connolly's argument—that capitalism was an alien imposition

[98] *Irish Socialist*, December 1967, 3.
[99] *Build*, April 1967, 13.
[100] *Irish Socialist*, October 1969, 4; *Irish Socialist*, February 1968, 1.

brought to Ireland as part of British imperialism, and that for Ireland to truly regain independence this British economic system had to be jettisoned alongside British administration—to link these housing issues to the wider ideological project of the Irish left, and to link contemporary leftist politics with nationalist themes.

The symbols of Irish history were frequently enlisted to reinforce this elision of republicanism and anti-capitalism. For example, the group's campaign against new offices in East James Street led to a 'torchlit picket' outside Castleknock Lodge, the home of the developer. The twenty-four person picket carried such posters as 'Penal days are here again', 'Mansions for lords and the streets of the people', and 'End needless cruelty, save East James's street houses', creating a successful link between the nineteenth-century land wars and twentieth-century anti-capitalism.[101] Similarly, on Easter weekend 1968 five men and a woman squatted in an eighteenth-century house on Mount Street, newly acquired for redevelopment by the Duncairn group, and went on hunger strike to campaign against the demolition of the houses, flying a tricolour and the Starry Plough, the flag of Connolly's Citizen Army, over the building. A spokesman for the group said: 'It is fitting that we should make this protest at Easter. Fifty years ago a big battle was fought for Irish freedom only a few yards from here. Is this freedom? We will make the protest and the public can take whatever action they think fit then.'[102]

Squatting therefore became a political act for DHAC, which drew attention to fundamental national questions. The most high-profile and best remembered of these political squats was that by Dennis Dennehy in Mountjoy Square. Born in Kerry in 1938, Dennehy emigrated to England when he was eighteen, working there for eight years and becoming involved in a variety of socialist and republican groups.[103] He returned to Dublin in 1964, where he became involved in the Irish Communist Organization, a small hard-left organization led by Brendan Clifford.[104] During this time he lived in a caravan park in Cherry Orchard, and campaigned on many issues, including itinerant rights and birth control, before becoming a leading member of DHAC. However, Dennehy subsequently became frustrated with Sinn Féin's dominance over the group, and decided to act on his own to raise awareness of housing shortages in the city. To this end, he squatted at 20 Mountjoy Square.

[101] *Irish Times*, 4 January 1968, 6.

[102] *Irish Times*, 16 April 1968, 13; *United Irishman*, May 1968, 2.

[103] Brendan Clifford, *The Dubliner: The Lives, Times and Writings of James Clarence Mangan* (Belfast, 1988), ch. 1; Brian McCamley, *Dennis Dennehy: Socialist Agitator* (Labour History Workshop, 1985).

[104] *Hibernia*, 31 January–13 February 1969, 4.

His choice of Mountjoy Square was significant. Indeed, the square had symbolic resonances not only as an eighteenth-century site of Protestant culture (explored in Chapter 6) but also as a long-standing area of working-class accommodation, enshrined as the tenement setting of Seán O'Casey's famous Dublin trilogy. Furthermore, in 1968 the house was the property of Ivor Underwood. Underwood had inherited many houses in the north city, and in the early 1960s had bought many more, with reports on his death stating that he owned seventy houses in Dublin, most of which dated from the eighteenth century.[105] However, Underwood was not a straightforward 'slum landlord'. Although he did little to restore his property, and rented the large eighteenth-century rooms out as small flats, he also refused to sell the buildings or knock them down, even during the property boom of the late 1960s. Indeed, Underwood was an active member of both the Irish Georgian Society and Dublin Civic Group, and a leading figure in the conservation of Mountjoy Square. The DHAC, however, viewed Underwood simply as one of the wealthiest property owners in Dublin. During 1969, the group had painted slogans on the wall of his Dalkey home and damaged his Austin Cambridge with a bomb.[106]

Dennehy's aim was to get himself imprisoned, and indeed in January 1969 he was, not for squatting but for breaking undertakings made to the court; a subtlety which was lost in the reporting of the case. Using the symbols of Irish history to full effect, Dennehy went on hunger strike upon imprisonment, leading to a wave of violent protests across the city. Briefly, Dublin resembled Derry, as chaotic protests filled the streets and violent conflicts with Gardaí ensued.[107] The city was dominated by the protests of his supporters; there were nightly marches from the GPO to Mountjoy prison during his incarceration, and pickets were placed on Mountjoy Jail, the Department of Justice, and the Department of Local Government.[108] Moreover, these protests were designed to cause maximum disruption to the running of the city. At a meeting at the GPO on 15 January, 160 members and supporters of the DHAC sat down in the street for half an hour, blocking traffic in O'Connell Street. On Saturday 20 January, 400 people staged a sit-down protest on O'Connell Street Bridge which was violently broken up by Gardaí.[109] Six people were hurt,

105 *Sunday Independent*, 10 December 2006, 8.

106 *Irish Times*, 22 October 1968, 5.

107 *Irish Times*, 14 January 1969, 13; *Irish Independent*, 14 January 1969, 1; *Irish Independent*, 15 January 1969, 1.

108 *Irish Times*, 16 January 1969, 1.

109 *Hibernia*, 31 January 1969–13 February 1969, 4; *Irish Times*, 20 January 1969, 4; *Irish Independent*, 20 January 1969, 1.

and six were arrested in fighting which lasted over an hour.[110] In response to this, on the following Monday, over 1,200 people marched from Abbey Street, via the GPO to Mountjoy Jail, as the Gardaí stepped up their presence around the key sites of the city.[111] In tracing a path between the principal nodes of the capital, they reappropriated, redesignated, and reanimated the landmarks of national struggle. It is of particular note that they assembled at the GPO. Indeed, engaging with a common tactic in Irish history, the DHAC protestors utilized the sacred places and symbols of the Irish independence struggle to position themselves as a 'purer' incarnation of the national forefathers' wishes for the state than those now in government. In beginning their marches at the location where Patrick Pearse assumed the leadership of advanced nationalism, and ensured the eventual supersession of Redmondism, the housing protestors could also dramatically enact their loss of faith in the intentions of their middle-class leaders.

The fiftieth anniversary of the first Dáil fell in January 1969, during Dennehy's incarceration. On the first day of the First Dáil in 1919, the Democratic Programme had been adopted; a document which had outlined a socialist policy including the public ownership of the means of production, natural resources, and 'wealth'; state provision of education for children and care for the elderly; a commitment that all children be fed; promotion of industrial development; and the exploitation of natural resources. However, in the succeeding fifty years, little had been done to secure these commitments. Thus the commemoration of the First Dáil was a politically charged moment, which revealed the gap between the aspirations of the generation which fought for independence and the achievements of the state. The Labour Lord Mayor of Dublin, Frank Cluskey TD, urged the Taoiseach, Jack Lynch, to free Dennehy as a mark of the day's significance. The Lord Mayor's telegram to the Taoiseach said: 'As Lord Mayor of Dublin I appeal to you, as leader of the Government, to secure the release from prison of Denis Dennehy to his wife and children on humanitarian grounds, as a tangible token of our acceptance on the great occasion we will commemorate tomorrow, and of the principles espoused on that occasion.'[112] However, Dennehy was not released, and the day was used by Dennehy's supporters to call attention to his ongoing incarceration. There were protests at the GPO, the Pro-Cathedral, and the Custom House, while a reported 2,000 students marched across

[110] *Irish Times*, 20 January 1969, 1.

[111] *Irish Times*, 20 January 1969, 1.

[112] NAI DT 2000/6/423, Letter from Frank Cluskey to Taoiseach, 22 January 1969; *Irish Times*, 21 January 1969, 1.

Dublin under the banner of the Students for Democratic Action.[113] Outside the celebrations in the Mansion House, students in support of Dennehy carried banners proclaiming 'Evictions: English landlords, 1868; Irish landlords, 1968–69', '50th anniversary of homeless families and enforced divorce (emigration)', and 'Classless society? Ballyfermot, Foxrock!' Protests also took place inside. The ceremony, conducted in stilted Irish, was interrupted by Joseph Clarke, a veteran of the 1916 Battle of Mount Street Bridge, protesting at the arrest of Dennehy. 'This is a mockery', shouted the old man, who had been present at the original ceremony, as he was carried out by security guards. These housing protests only compounded Dermot Keogh's description of the commemoration as an 'object lesson for the historically conscious of the vast difference between the revolutionary aspirations of the founders of the state and the political and social achievement of their successors'.[114] The shambolic nature of commemorations received widespread coverage in the press, in marked contrast to the relative success of the fiftieth anniversary celebrations of the Easter Rising only two and a half years before.[115] Indeed, Joseph Clarke was not the only ghost of revolution to arise in support of Dennehy. Muriel MacSwiney, widow of Terence MacSwiney, the Lord Mayor of Cork who died on hunger strike in 1920, wrote to Dennehy's wife. The letter, which was widely reproduced in the press, stated:

> It is nearly sixty years since my husband was on hunger strike. He often said and wrote that although we could certainly gain independence, would we be worthy? It is an anxious time for you: but you and your husband and some others have at last resurrected the old glory of Éire which was almost dead since the end of 1922 and the beginning of 1923. I cannot express to you how very grateful I am to you, your husband and the children. I had been living in despair for years.[116]

This letter made a striking claim for the importance of Dennehy's protest; to MacSwiney it was a glimmer of hope for a different Ireland as visualized by much of the revolutionary generation, unseen since the triumph of the Free State government in the civil war.

But the DHAC did not only use imagery from the independence movement to draw links between Ireland's social and political failure. The

[113] *Irish Times*, 22 January 1969, 10; *Irish Times*, 21 January 1969, 23; *Irish Independent*, 22 January 1969, 11; *Evening Herald*, 18 January 1969, 1; *Evening Herald*, 21 January 1969, 1; *Evening Herald*, 21 January 1969, 3.

[114] Keogh, *Twentieth-Century Ireland*, 306.

[115] Daly, 'Less a Commemoration of the Actual Achievements and More a Commemoration of the Hopes of the Men of 1916', in Daly and O'Callaghan, *1916 in 1966*, 18–85.

[116] *Irish Times*, 1 February 1969, 10.

DHAC's spokesmen used Dennehy's imprisonment to draw parallels with the housing protests in the North, drawing comparisons between the governments in the two states to present the southern administration as just as illegitimate as its northern counterpart. For example, a report in the *United Irishman* declared that 'Everyone who supports the Civil Rights struggle in the North must also give their support to the Dublin squatters', while the *Irish Socialist* declared that, 'the 26 Co. Government is as much opposed to the granting of basic civil rights as their counterparts—the Unionist Government—are in the north. They have merely been more successful in hiding the fact. Rather than conceding to the democratic demands of the people of Dublin for the provision of adequate housing, they chose to attack the victims of their own misrule.'[117] At the meeting at the GPO on 15 January, Seamus Ó Tuathail of Sinn Féin told the crowd that the people squatting in Derry Guildhall had telephoned their support to DHAC's meeting. They had also sent a telegram to Mr Dennehy in Mountjoy saying: 'The struggle is the same, North and South'. Shay Geraghty followed Ó Tuathail by saying that people should show their strength and bring Derry and Newry to the streets of Dublin.[118] Indeed, explicitly linking the two campaigns, the People's Democracy, on its march from Belfast to the GPO, held a meeting numbering 800 people outside 20 Mountjoy Square to protest about the housing situation in both parts of the island.[119]

A week after the fiftieth anniversary celebrations of the First Dáil, Dennehy was released from prison, having given another undertaking to find alternative accommodation. However, having not met this undertaking a second time, he was reimprisoned. After two months of wrangling, Dennehy was finally found accommodation in a caravan on Queen's Street by a supporter of the DHAC, and on 15 March finally appeared before Justice Butler to purge himself of his contempt of the court.[120] This was, however, one of the final high-profile acts of the DHAC. In November 1968 the ICO members of the DHAC had forced through the group's democratization; that is, reorganization to allow only homeless people, rather than professional activists, to vote in policy matters. *Communist Comment* declared that, 'The ICO regarded this democratization as a means of strengthening the committee both politically and physically. Squatting in private property would offer an immediate temporary solution to the problem of homeless families while at the same time exposing

[117] *Irish Socialist*, No. 89, September 1969, 6; *United Irishman*, September 1969, 2.
[118] *Irish Times*, 15 January 1969, 1; *Irish Press*, 15 January 1969, 4.
[119] *Irish Times*, 8 April 1969, 1; *Irish Times*, 20 January 1969, 4.
[120] *Irish Times*, 15 March 1969, 5.

the whole matter of property regulations in capitalist society.' This removal of decision-making from professional campaigners was controversial within the movement, and its contestation by the Sinn Féin and Irish Workers' Party members led to the eventual walk-out of the ICO—including Dennehy—from the DHAC in March 1970.[121] This fall-out led to exchanges of recriminations in the pages of the left-wing media, and from this point the movement fractured and began to lose momentum.[122] At the same time as these disputes were taking place, the situation in the north was also deteriorating; conflict between the nationalist and loyalist communities was increasingly frequent and violent throughout 1969, while the Republican movement split and the Provisional IRA formed in January 1970. In this context, the existence of a broad-left organization to campaign about housing in Dublin became less and less tenable, as the positions of the various groups that had made up the DHAC divided on northern issues, and as the attentions of many of the leading activists were increasingly drawn northward. Although housing activism continued, and a similar group was active during the mid-1970s under the name Sinn Féin Housing Action Committee, by the middle of 1970 the organization in its late-1960s guise had lost much of its momentum. In the words of Prionsias de Rossa, 'it faded out of existence, rather than a formal decision to dissolve it'.[123] However, even in its short life the organization had a long-term impact; the Housing Act of 1969 prevented the demolition or change of use of habitable accommodation, and fulfilled one of the DHAC's key demands.[124]

The housing protests during the 1960s had a striking impact. As the office boom refashioned the city's skyline, the poverty still existing in the streets below became all the more marked. Within the city centre, such beacons of modernity as Liberty Hall and O'Connell Bridge House rose in the same spaces as families were living six to a room, strikingly indicative of the differential effects of the economic reforms of the period. However, those residents who were not gaining from these changes did not passively accept them. In marching through Nassau and O'Connell Street, protesting at City Hall, and squatting in buildings in the centre of the city, protestors aimed to make themselves—and their poverty—visible. In

[121] *Communist Comment*, 14 March 1970, 4.

[122] *Communist Comment*, 14 March 1970, 4.

[123] *Communist Comment*, 14 March 1970, 4; also quoted in Bill McCamley, *Dennis Dennehy: Socialist Agitator*, 21.

[124] NAI DT 99–1–535 Housing Act 1969, Department of Local Government Memorandum for the Taoiseach, 18 January 1968. Legislation was introduced to prevent the demolition or change of use of habitable housing in 1948, but it was allowed to lapse at the end of 1962. It was reintroduced in 1969.

so doing, they rejected the description of the city as a 'heart of darkness', but rather aimed to show the reality, and proximity, of abject need to the ceremonial sites of the capital. These performative protests constructed narratives of the city not only as a place of commerce or national display but also as a site of extreme deprivation.

Housing activism brought the changes taking place to the built environment to a much larger sector of Dublin's population than the IGS ever could acting on their own. Protests against suburbanization and slum clearance by residents of the city were taken up by journalists, writers, and artists, who did much to promote a new interest in preservation of communities, trades, and customs of the city. This also fed into new explorations of the link between place, landscape, and people being conducted by sociologists. The retention of the city core therefore took on a new significance: its worth was derived not only from the intrinsic value of historic architecture but also from a desire to preserve the community that inhabited these spaces. This new interest in the life of city-centre Dublin represented a shifting conception of heritage from material artefacts to cultures and customs, being a formulation of heritage which sat much more comfortably with other forms of tradition which were being actively conserved at this time; indeed, it placed the customs of the city alongside the Gaelic traditions of the west of Ireland as another 'authentic' Irish culture that was disappearing and worthy of preservation.

While these approaches were suffused by nostalgia, another strand of housing activism was much more pessimistic about life in the city. In the later 1960s the DHAC took the lead in protesting against housing shortages. In revealing the poverty of much of the city, publicizing the evictions that resulted from office construction and dangerous buildings work, and campaigning around housing shortages, the DHAC graphically showed that the modernization of the city was not wholly benevolent. Rather, they created an image of the physical changes to the capital as unfair, enforced, and violent; images which were fundamental in changing responses to the physical evolution of the capital later in the decade. However, they also attempted to help the families who had been adversely affected by these changes; in organizing squats, helping families resist eviction, and campaigning for more housing they provided an alternative welfare mechanism for those without homes. In so doing, they not only appealed to conservative, Catholic sentiments regarding the primacy of the family to Irish life but also to notions of modern welfare provision. But their activism, rhetoric, and usage of the city had more important implications. In drawing attention to the failings of the state to provide housing for its citizens, they questioned the achievements of independence; in making explicit comparisons with the housing situation in the northern counties, they positioned the Republic of Ireland as a state which also lacked legitimacy; in campaigning at the GPO and at evictions, they expropriated the symbolic vocabulary of the state, to position themselves as the true inheritors of the Republican movement. This combination of republican symbolism, anti-capitalism, and territorial politics was a powerful mix—and provided a sustained challenge to the legitimacy of the government and the state.

6

Material Culture and Social Politics, 1964–73

> One of the morbid subhuman pretences adopted by keltured idiocated Dubliners is that Georgian Dublin simply must be preserved do you hear me, I mean these marvellous facades, exquisite squares, the foot and the cavalry were here then, and 500 Dublin people made a good living making military uniforms at sixty pounds a time, Fitzwilliam Square was a blaze of lights, the grand old Whig nobility, gracious way of living... Wide Streets Commissioners, mellow old brickwork, observe how a century's weathering has modulated the first bright plumflush to wan winehues incomparably nice... But what are the facts about this Georgian ramp? I'll tell you (they'll get me for this but my public comes first) I'll tell you the inside guts of it. Dublin is a slum. Dublin is a slum do you hear me. At its best (in Fitzwilliam Square), a well preserved flat ridden professional slum. At its worse (in Bride Street, the Liberties, Summerhill, Mountjoy Square), a sprawling dung-hill on stilts, giving off a constant odourless vapour of rancid unwashable profit rents. Ah yes, it is all real Dublin... old Dublin is so picturesque that you can smell its nostalgic charm when the mail boat is ten miles out coming in by Lambay (do you remember the time when we had a picnic there in the old days, poor George was alive then).
>
> Myles na gCopaleen, 1966.[1]

Dublin attracted a wide spectrum of jarring opinions. Myles na gCopaleen (a pseudonym of the novelist Flann O'Brien) derided what he saw as the 'keltured idiocated' Dubliners to whom the city was a repository of the memory of an elegant era, softened and improved by the mellowing impact of age. For Myles, this view could only be maintained at a distance. In his opinion, the ageing built stock was not gaining more character but only becoming more decrepit; the city was not a place of 'marvellous facades,

[1] *Irish Times*, 9 May 1966, 10.

exquisite squares' but a 'slum', a 'dunghill on stilts', a 'rancid' site of 'unwashable profit rents'. The tension between nostalgia and realism, between architectural values and social problems, was fundamental to shaping debate regarding the future of the city during the 1960s. More than any other location within the eighteenth-century city, the former Gardiner estate epitomized the problem of these juxtaposed readings of urban space. The area contained some of the city's finest architecture, but over one hundred years' occupancy as tenements had left the area structurally tired and decaying. This dereliction only accelerated as the city began to modernize; in the 1960s, the area was subject to the worst effects of road plans, the dangerous buildings scare, and site clearance for office construction.

After the failure to preserve Fitzwilliam Street, the Gardiner estate was the IGS's next focus. In response to the area's increasing decay, the group attempted to secure the preservation of the built stock and its plasterwork by orchestrating the return of the eighteenth-century buildings to middle-class residency. However, they faced considerable problems in fulfilling their goals owing to a combination of pressures which were common to areas labelled as 'blighted' across European and American cities: the conflicting aims of a property developer for the area; the very real structural decay of the built stock; competition for territory from housing activists; and the demands and aspirations of the extant population.[2] However, through locating to a socially deprived area, another outcome occurred. Away from the contemporary areas of middle-class occupancy in the south of the city, the collective action of restoration enabled the group to function outside social norms, and to use preservationism to spatialize and visualize dissent.

The Gardiner estate was an area of Dublin on the north side of the Liffey, sweeping across the north and east of O'Connell Street (Map 6.1). Developed by three generations of the Gardiner family throughout the eighteenth century, it contained some of the city's most impressive streetscapes, such as the 8,500 square foot mansions of Henrietta Street, built in the 1720s; the curved Hardwick Place; Mountjoy Square, Dublin's only square with four sides of equal length; and some of Dublin's finest architecture, including Francis Johnston's St George's Church, William Chambers's Charlemont House, and Richard Castle's Rotunda Hospital.[3]

Despite its illustrious beginnings, in the 1960s the area was one of Dublin's, indeed Ireland's, most deprived locations. In 1967, Mary Maher described a Mountjoy Square tenement:

[2] Klemek, *The Transatlantic Collapse of the Urban Renewal Order*, 148.
[3] Craig, *Dublin 1660–1880*, 187–201.

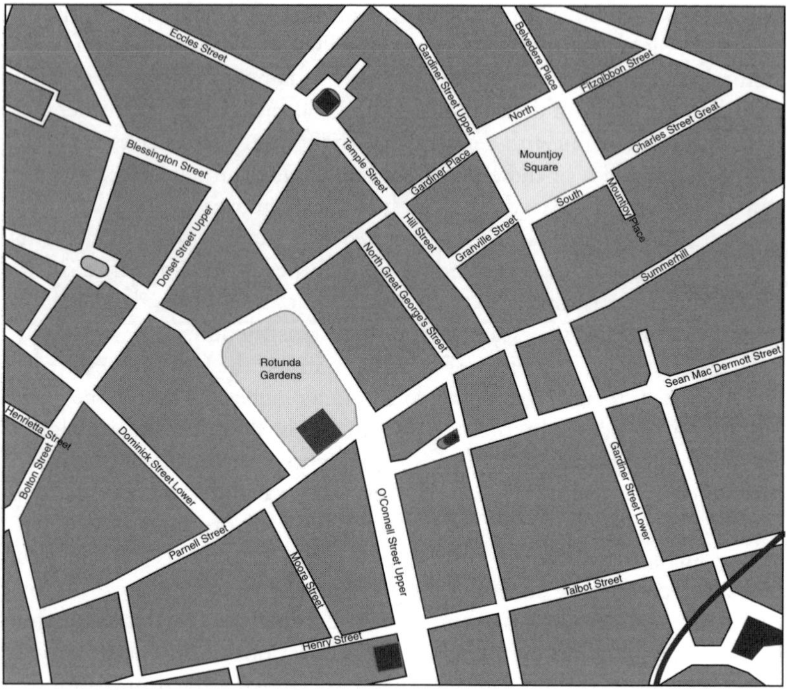

Map 6.1. Map of the Gardiner estate.

> Half way down the street No. 44 gapes blackly and odorously at the iron-fenced square. There is no sign of life in No. 44, and life remains largely unchanged. The passage to the cellar is six inches deep in refuse, and one section of the banister is missing altogether. There was a toilet in the basement, but the floor collapsed last summer and the cubicle is now stuffed with rubbish. Two more toilets and a trough are on the second floor landing, but at the moment they are used for dumping. 'Someone cleared them a while back now, but they won't work for very long. I don't think they were put in properly', one tenant said... Thirty four people live in No 44, ten of them children.[4]

Maher described Mountjoy Square using classic tropes evocative of a slum, focusing on the dirt and the lack of sanitation, and, despite the thirty-four people in residence, creating an image of a desolate and empty landscape. Indeed, the buildings were certainly not vacant; the 1971 census recorded Mountjoy electoral ward as the most overcrowded in the whole of Ireland, with 54.8 per cent of the population living in housing

[4] *Irish Times*, 5 May 1967, 12.

units containing two or more persons per room, being about four times the national average of 14.8 per cent.[5] In 1967, *Thom's Directory* listed thirteen of the houses as being occupied as tenements; twelve demolished; eleven in flats; eleven as small-scale industry, such as upholstery, electricians, and silk screen printers; and four religious institutions, including the Society for St Vincent de Paul, Legion of Mary, and St Francis Xavier's Pioneer club. Only three houses in the square were listed as being owner-occupied: No. 47 on the south side, and Nos. 65 and 67 on the west side.[6] Throughout the 1960s, Mountjoy Square's occupants, commercial and residential, changed from year to year.[7] The square, indeed the whole of the former Gardiner estate, was a shifting landscape characterized by urban decline and deprivation, conforming to the classic understanding of the inner city developed by the Chicago school early in the twentieth century. Although near to the centre of the city, it was benefiting little from economic progress. In fact, its condition had only deteriorated during the early 1960s, as the dangerous buildings scare and site clearance for potential redevelopment had resulted in demolished sites where there had previously been occupied buildings and unified frontages.[8]

In the mid-1960s, the IGS turned its attention to the maintenance of the area (Fig. 6.1).[9] This was a radical policy shift for a group which had, up to this point, not intervened directly in the preservation of eighteenth-century houses in Dublin. In 1964, Mariga Guinness began this broader move to save the area with the purchase of 50 Mountjoy Square for £550, and in that year the IGS also set up the Friends of Mountjoy Square to coordinate the purchase and restoration of houses in the locality.[10] The group also made a commitment protecting other important local structures; it provided funds for the maintenance of the Black Church, deconsecrated in 1962, until a use was found for it, and also paid for the repair the roof of 9 Henrietta Street, occupied by St Vincent de Paul.[11] As part of this new awareness of the decaying structures of Dublin city, the group also began the long process of restoring Tailor's Hall, Back Lane.

The foundation of the Friends of Mountjoy Square precipitated the involvement of a diverse range of interests in securing the Gardiner estate

[5] O'Connor, *Housing in Dublin's Inner City*, 25.

[6] Listing for Mountjoy Square in *Thom's Dublin Street Directory 1967*. No. 47 was listed as Kathleen O'Dwyer, occupant prior to John Molloy (see below p. 148).

[7] *Thom's Directories*, entries on Mountjoy Square.

[8] *Thom's Directories*, entries on Mountjoy Square.

[9] *Irish Times*, 3 February 1966, 11.

[10] *Quarterly Bulletin of the Irish Georgian Society*, April–December 1964, 45.

[11] *Quarterly Bulletin of the Irish Georgian Society*, April–June 1966, 57; *Quarterly Bulletin of the Irish Georgian Society*, October–December 1962, 37; Kearns, *Georgian Dublin*, 172–8.

Fig. 6.1. Mountjoy Square, 1981. Image courtesy of the Irish Architectural Archive.

area against further structural degradation. Early on, the campaign was given a considerable boost when the spirits distributor Edward Dillon and Co. purchased 25 and 26 Mountjoy Square, formerly occupied by the Church of Ireland Divinity School.[12] After restoration work costing £12,000, they moved into No. 25 in July 1964, and sold No. 26 to Grants of Ireland, bringing two well-known brands to the area. However, the scheme rested primarily on the involvement and commitment of private individuals. For example, Ivor Underwood, who already owned several houses in Mountjoy Square, began to restore these, alongside seven more which he purchased in the adjacent Belvedere Place; five houses in Mountjoy Square, along with three in Henrietta Street, were also purchased by Uinseann MacEoin; Harold Clarke, the managing director of Easons, Ireland's largest chain of bookshops, bought a vacant house in nearby North Great George's Street; while John and Ann Molloy moved into 47 Mountjoy Square in 1967.[13]

[12] IAA RW.D203 press cutting, *The Cellar*, November–December 1966.

[13] IAA RW.D203 Press Release (n.d); IAA RW.D203 press cutting, *Sunday Independent*, 11 September 1966; *Irish Independent*, 8 February 1968.

The efforts of the Georgian enthusiasts in Mountjoy Square also sparked interest from other residents; the six houses which were occupied by Dublin Corporation's architects department on the north side of the square were also restored during the late 1960s, while An Oige, which occupied No. 39, also committed itself to staying in its current location and maintaining its property.[14] In 1968, Ivor Underwood estimated that thirty-three houses in Mountjoy Square and seven in Belvedere Place were retained through the combined efforts of dedicated preservationists who had bought in the area and long-term residents who had given assurances to the IGS that they would keep up their property.[15]

However, the Georgian enthusiasts were not the only group to take an interest in the Gardiner area in the wake of the dangerous buildings scare. As Neil Smith has shown, in cities across Europe and North America the price of land became far higher than the value of the property occupying it during the 1960s, a phenomenon which he has called the 'rent gap'.[16] This attracted developers to the city centre, and heralded a dramatic shift in land occupation in these areas. Although the former Gardiner estate was yet to experience the boom in office developments that was affecting Dublin's south city, the area was not immune from these global trends. Matt Gallagher, the property developer and close friend of Charles Haughey's, known for a similarly extravagant lifestyle, began to acquire property in Mountjoy Square during 1963, like the preservationists taking advantage of the low selling prices for Georgian buildings in this part of the city.[17] Eamonn Walsh, the barrister for Gallagher's company Leinster Estates, revealed the extent of the company's ambitions for the area, telling the subsequent planning inquiry that 'there is room for controversy as to what form of development would be most suitable and there is probably a good deal to be said in favour of the argument that it would be desirable to have a comprehensive development of all four sides of Mountjoy Square in a modern idiom'.[18]

If comprehensive redevelopment had been Gallagher's aim, this ambition was stymied by the acquisition and refurbishment of property by the Georgian enthusiasts. But Gallagher was not easily dissuaded; he made a forthright attempt to force the preservationists out of the area by demolishing the two houses he owned on each side of the IGS's headquarters in

[14] *Build*, January 1966, 25.

[15] IAA A00495 98/7 Frederick Rogerson Papers Box 3, File 6717: Letter from Frederick Rogerson to Mr. Figgis, Solicitor for Ivor Underwood, 22 January 1968.

[16] Neil Smith, 'Blind Man's Buff, or Hamnett's Philosophical Individualism in Search of Gentrification', *Transactions of the Institute of British Geographers* 17/1 (1992), 110–15.

[17] For more about Charles Haughey (1925–2006) see pp. 184–5.

[18] *Irish Times*, 13 February 1968, 7.

an attempt to structurally weaken the Guinness's property. After a high-profile court battle in 1966, he was made to put back lateral support, leaving No. 50 looming gauntly over the square in a surreal fashion, a terrace house without any terrace.[19] Nevertheless, Leinster Estates had already acquired twenty-two properties on the square—nearly half the houses on the south side, five on the west side, and one on the north side—before their plans to acquire it in its entirety were renounced.[20] Instead, the company then lodged two planning permissions with Dublin Corporation for 34 to 45 Mountjoy Square, a sizeable quantity of the south side: the first application, which was for an office block in a modern design, was rejected, while the second, for a neo-Georgian block, was given planning permission.[21]

The Mountjoy Square preservationist group challenged Dublin Corporation's planning approval for the office block, and the appeal, held at the Custom House, opened on 7 February 1968.[22] During the inquiry, a range of conflicting interest groups articulated a spectrum of competing visions for the future of the square: as a historic site, a commercial area, and a place of residence. While the case for preservation was put forcefully by Kevin Nowlan and Mariga Guinness, the other groups with interests in the square had little interest in the value of its historical associations. Eamonn Walsh, the barrister for Leinster Estates, told the tribunal that the houses had 'reached the end of their useful lives', stating that 'there is no use in argument about the merits of the past if the Square is now obsolete and worn out'.[23] Dublin Corporation largely concurred with this view. Dermot Walsh, Law Agent to Dublin Corporation, while giving assurances that the Corporation had imposed conditions with the aim of making the proposed development fit in with the character of the area, stated that they did not believe that the buildings could be preserved at a 'reasonable' cost, and therefore it could not justify asking developers to restore the buildings as individual houses in the Georgian idiom. Indeed, he described it as a 'pipe dream' to suggest that the enormous amount of money required for restoring the square could be obtained by voluntary effort.[24] The encouragement of investment in the north side was a specified aim of the Draft Development Plan, and Mountjoy Square had been

[19] IAA RW.D203 press cutting, *Irish Independent*, 3 February 1966; *Quarterly Bulletin of the Irish Georgian Society*, April–June 1966, 55.

[20] *Build*, June 1966, 23.

[21] *Irish Independent*, 8 February 1968, 3.

[22] *Irish Independent*, 8 February 1968, 3; *Irish Times*, 13 February 1968, 7.

[23] *Irish Times*, 13 February 1968, 7; *Irish Independent*, 13 February 1968, 12.

[24] IAA RW.D203 press cutting, *Irish Press*, 16 February 1968.

zoned for office and residential development under these provisions.[25] In granting planning permission for this office development, Dublin Corporation had conceived of a process of renewal for Mountjoy Square through its redevelopment as a commercial area in partnership with private investors; Walsh described the office development as 'a genuine effort to salvage something of benefit to the square'.

However, the City Council's conception of the future for the area had undergone a decisive about-face since it had granted this planning permission. Instead of seeking renewal through offices and commercial prosperity, the onus of Corporation policy had now shifted to retaining the long-term population, and ameliorating their housing conditions. A resolution had been passed at the Planning Committee to the effect that they were 'desirous of seeing workers' dwellings erected on this site and that permission should not be granted for either offices or luxury flats'.[26] In contravention of the Corporation's previous decisions, Dermot Walsh told the court that if it decided against the Leinster Estates office development, it was now the Corporation's intention not to allow the IGS to preserve the buildings, but instead it would build workers' flats in the square.[27]

But the court never adjudicated on these competing urban visions. This was because Leinster Estates made a surprise offer to sell their twenty-two properties on the square at cost price, on condition that the buyers 'rebuild and restore them to their former state'.[28] On 15 February, five minutes before the end of the fourth day of the appeal, Eamon Walsh announced the offer, stating that Leinster Estate would sell to the IGS, or any other group, but only if they could produce a purchaser or purchasers for all twenty-two houses, and its complete interest in the square was bought out. If not, they 'would ask to be allowed to get on with the development'. This was very far from an act of goodwill on the part of Leinster Estates: Walsh told the planning tribunal that he had been instructed to make the offer only 'for the purpose of demonstrating our contention that the square cannot be restored by rebuilding and constructing individual houses. Mrs Desmond Guinness...made a plea that Leinster Estates should agree to sell their properties at cost to the purchasers, which, it has been contended by her and by Uinseann MacEoin and Professor Kevin Nowlan, are standing in the wings, ready and willing and anxious to take

[25] IAA RW.D203 press cutting, *Irish Press*, 16 February 1968.

[26] Dublin Corporation, 'Minutes of a Quarterly Meeting of the Dublin City Council held in the Council Chamber, City Hall, Cork Hill, 2 October 1967 at 6.45 p.m.,' *Reports and Printed Documents of the Corporation of Dublin*, 257.

[27] IAA RW.D203 press cutting, *Irish Press,* 16 February 1968.

[28] IAA RW.D203 press cutting, *Irish Press,* 16 February 1968.

up the burden of restoration. We are prepared to accept the challenge which we believe to be unreal and impractical.'[29] Walsh said that the offer would have to be taken up before the Minister for Local Government reached his decision on the appeal, a period estimated to be between two and three months.[30] The following day this was amended, so as to insist that all twenty-two houses would be bought, contracts signed, and deposits paid within thirty days, and the sale completed within two months.[31] It was also made known that the 'price without profit but including all expenses' being asked for by Leinster Estates was £68,000.[32]

The price at which Leinster Estates offered to sell their twenty-two properties represented £3,091 per house, a figure which was not only substantially more than the amount for which most of them were purchased in 1964, but was also considerably above their 1968 market value. After much vacillation, the IGS offered Leinster Estates £50,000 for the twenty-two houses, which was rejected, and then secured the purchase having found the full £68,000 in December 1969.[33] This was an enormous sum to raise for a small society with an average yearly revenue of about £5,000, but by July 1969 purchasers had been found for three houses, six ruins, and two cleared sites, representing about half the total price, while the rest of the money had been acquired through gifts and short-term loans. Thus it was possible to accept the offer.[34] After the monumental task of finding the financial means to secure the houses, the group was faced with the even bigger challenge of restoring its newly acquired collection of demolished, ruined, and decaying buildings.

INVALUABLE TO WHOM? THE SOCIAL POLITICS OF URBAN SPACE

The interaction between capital, material culture, and social politics created tensions in Mountjoy Square which were common to many urban preservation efforts.[35] In aiming to save the eighteenth-century plasterwork and fittings, the group came into conflict with the residents of the local area, who were less concerned with the restoration of original features than with staying in the area, and obtaining clean and comfortable

[29] IAA RW.D203 press cutting, *Irish Press,* 16 February 1968.
[30] *Irish Times*, 16 February 1968, 1.
[31] *Irish Times*, 17 February 1968, 13.
[32] *Build*, July 1968, 11.
[33] *Irish Times*, 10 December 1969, 1.
[34] *Country Life*, 23 October 1969, 1031.
[35] Klemek, *The Transatlantic Collapse of the Urban Renewal Order*, 149–52.

accommodation. This discontent was explicit and visible; a group of residents marched from Mountjoy Square, through Gardiner Street to the Custom House to deliver a petition to the Minister of Local Government against both the office development and restoration. The petition had been signed by over one hundred residents of Mountjoy Square, asking that priority should be given instead to rehousing residents in suitable houses in the locality.[36]

Seán McCarron SJ used his position as the high-profile Superior of St Francis Xavier's Church on Gardiner Street to champion the demands of the residents. He was emphatic that the people who currently resided in the square should be kept in this area, laying out his plans for the area at the planning tribunal:

> the area should be used for the provision of suitable housing for the lower income group and there should be no development of the site which entails further demolition until the many demolished sites in the vicinity have been rebuilt. Once these sites have been rebuilt, the present residents of Mountjoy can be rehoused in them. Only when all the present tenants in the square are suitably rehoused in the same locality should work on Mountjoy Square begin.'[37]

He put a profound emphasis on the importance of place; it was not enough that the current residents should be found housing nearby, but instead he stressed that the community in and around Mountjoy Square had to be retained and preserved. Although he acknowledged that the repair of the housing to a suitable, inhabitable standard would be costly, he speculated that if this was weighed against the cost of providing the many ancillary amenities necessary in newly developed areas, the option of reconstructing Mountjoy Square as low-income accommodation might be more economically efficient. In deference to the wishes of the IGS, he stated that it would not be beyond the power of the architects to design low-income housing which would preserve the character and architectural harmony of the square; however, this had to be secondary to the retention of the community in the locality.[38]

McCarron also used the situation in Mountjoy Square to put forward a broader critique of government policy towards the city within the canals. He told the planning tribunal that if the office block was allowed, it would be an unwelcome innovation in an area which had been a traditional location of low-income housing. Not only would it be wrong, in his opinion, to allow the development, owing to the dwindling amount of working-

[36] *Irish Times*, 24 February 1968, 9.
[37] *Irish Times*, 10 February 1968, 11.
[38] *Irish Independent*, 10 February 1968, 3.

class accommodation in the city, but it had to be stopped as it was contributing to a social crisis in the city:

> Bad housing, in the lower income groups, was a cause of widespread and serious mental illness…I would suggest that the position has now been reached, or at least is close to being reached, where this mental illness is not just the suffering of many individuals, but has become, or is fast becoming, a kind of social illness. There is unrest in the city, a smouldering resentment, a sense of frustration and anxiety among so many people in Dublin, that one might almost call it a social psychopathic condition. This is a dangerous condition—more dangerous and widespread than perhaps is realised. It may well have grave and destructive effects on the social well being of all the city. The symptoms are there for all to see. If office block development is authorised in Mountjoy Square, it will become the critical point in a very serious situation.[39]

McCarron gave an unsettled picture of city life, which linked individual alienation, social malaise, and spatial structure. He described the existence of an underclass in Dublin, suffering from a 'social psychopathic condition', who were disenfranchised and dispossessed by the modernization of the capital; the further loss of housing and further destruction of their environment would have a profoundly negative impact on this group, which would rebound on the whole of the city. However, he contrasted this chilling picture of the future dystopian city with an alternative vision of the area as functioning and harmonious, if in need of physical renewal. He described the Mountjoy Square area as 'readymade for housing', and detailed how it had an excellent provision of schools, hospitals, churches, and open space in the immediate vicinity.

However, the IGS was not in a position to fulfil the demands of McCarron or the local population. Having paid considerably above the market value for houses which had long been in tenements, located in one of the poorest areas of central Dublin, the group were required, as part of their agreement with Leinster Estates, to complete a considerable amount of expensive structural work. Mariga Guinness had told the planning tribunal that restoration would cost '£10,000 or £12,000 on each house', and '£30,000 to develop a vacant site'.[40] In order to recoup these costs of investment, it was necessary that the properties could be sold on for more than the purchase price and restoration price combined.[41] She also revealed the society's plans for its new properties, stating that some of those interested in investing in Mountjoy Square planned to restore the exteriors,

[39] *Irish Times*, 10 February 1968, 11.
[40] IAA RW.D203 press cutting, *Irish Press*, 21 May 1968.
[41] IAA RW.D203 press cutting, *Irish Press*, 21 May 1968.

and turn the interiors into flats without upsetting the plasterwork inside, as 'there was a perceived shortage of elegant flats in Dublin'.[42] Limited by the constraints of capital, and with the retention of original features their primary aim, the concerns of the extant population could only be a subsidiary consideration; in order for the scheme to be financially viable, it would necessitate a shift in the social profile of occupancy.

However, the IGS's need of capital for restoration to secure the future of the square's eighteenth-century character meant that the group soon looked beyond its strategy of persuading Irish families to occupy the houses, and instead sought the funding of its supporters abroad, in particular on the east coast of America. In so doing, it utilized an international network of wealthy and mobile supporters, locating the square's future within the transnational geography of an Anglo-American cultural elite. Indeed, in an effort to engage the financial capacity of these distant supporters, the society put together a 'package deal' which could be bought to cover the complete restoration of a property:

> For the convenience of potential purchasers who reside outside Ireland, the Company is willing to supply an all-in charge which would constitute a 'package deal' for the complete work required. This charge would include for the purchase of existing property, the legal, estate agency, architectural and other professional fees connected with the restoration, together with the entire reconstruction costs. All statutory building approvals will be obtained and any grants which are, or may be available will be applied for. Additional amenities such as extra bathrooms, central heating, completely cleaning down the decorative plaster work (where this exists in the existing property purchased), elaborate painting, etc, can be provided at extra cost.[43]

The scheme put forward a vision for the future of the square in marked contrast to tenets of community, place, and localism as propounded by McCarron and O'Leary. The IGS's package put a great emphasis on the gentility of the accommodation which would be provided: the restored plasterwork, elaborate painting, extra bathrooms, and central heating prospected revealed the emphasis on finding new, prosperous owners and inhabitants. Moreover, the package deal required a substantial financial commitment from those who signed up, but in so doing it abrogated their need to be based in Mountjoy Square, or to engage in the dirty physical work or restoration; the commitment of capital removed a commitment of time or a commitment to a place. The IGS looked not to preserving the extant community, or even repopulating the north city

[42] *Irish Independent*, 10 February 1968, 3.
[43] IAA RW.D203, Mountjoy Square pamphlet, 9.

with 'sweat equity' families from the south Dublin suburbs, but rather to creating prêt-à-porter investments for wealthy Irish-Americans in one of Dublin's poorest areas.

The social dynamics of preservation led many to oppose the IGS's efforts. Rosita Sweetman was forthright taking in this position against the IGS. In *On Our Knees*, she stated that 'If the Georgian Society actually succeed in saving original buildings they open them up as museums, or guest houses, and that doesn't help the families who've been evicted out of them. The Georgian Society claim that by saving us our Georgian architecture, they're saving an invaluable asset. Invaluable to whom?…the people of Dublin are still being pushed out in ever growing suburbs, and the Georgian Society is chasing its tail in pursuit of a dilettante's dream.'[44] Similarly, Colm O'Riordan, from the School of Architecture at UCD, wrote to the *Irish Times* to protest that while 'devout romantics gather in select social enclave to marvel at the exquisite patterns of their Georgian ceilings some distance away groups of destitute families cower under rotting ceilings'.[45]

This local tension between preservationists and residents came to national attention when Dennis Dennehy squatted the restored property of Ivor Underwood in Mountjoy Square. The media tended to gloss over, or to ignore, the fact that this house was in the process of preservation as part of a wider campaign to save Mountjoy Square. Rather, the Dennehy case was held up as emblematic of Dublin's housing problems, and Underwood was frequently vilified as a slum landlord.[46] The preservationists' attempts to contest this image had limited impact on the construction of the story in the press. Uinseann MacEoin condemned DHAC's actions in *Build*, for showing more interest in preserving 'the sanctity of the few slim Georgian houses still upon the north side, as Sean O'Casey left them, ten families to one tap, impossible sanitation and all' than in the housing situation in general.[47] On a similar note, the Dublin Civic Group produced a press release, signed by F. H. Walker and Kevin Nowlan, stating that the DHAC's campaign would ensure only that 'slum houses remain slums', and asking 'where was the DHAC during the recent demolition of fine houses with a high accommodation capacity in Adelaide Road, Burlington Road, Wilton Place, Northumberland Road, Pembroke Road and many other areas of considerably greater speculative appeal than Mountjoy Square. It is then permissible to demolish these houses while it is

[44] Rosita Sweetman, *On Our Knees*, 68–9.
[45] *Irish Times*, 15 December 1969, 9.
[46] *United Irishman*, January 1969, 10.
[47] *Build*, February 1969, 9.

improper to attempt the restoration of basically sound property in Mountjoy Square?'[48] The letters reveal starkly the points of convergence and divergence between campaigns for more housing and campaigns for architectural preservation. Both groups had an overwhelmingly negative conception of the effects of the modernization of the capital, and the need to preserve its urban forms. However, their conceptions of what constituted the value of these places were almost diametrically opposed. For the preservationist group, the retention of the city's spaces was an end in itself, and the removal of the local population an unfortunate corollary of the essential maintenance of the architectural features of Mountjoy Square. However, for DHAC and the extant residents, it was the community in Mountjoy Square that required preservation, and the aesthetic of the site was less important. The two groups inevitably came into direct confrontation, as ownership of the physical site of the square itself was essential to their very different aims.

The IGS's approach to saving Mountjoy Square, which focused on the authentic rehabilitation of the material remains of the eighteenth century and the social elevation of the square, was not the only approach to conservation in the locality. Uinseann MacEoin worked closely alongside the society's preservation effort of the late 1960s, but had a very different aim and approach. Described in *Hibernia* magazine in 1969 as a 'crank' and 'a rabid republican cum architect cum town planner of definite convictions cum determined preservationist and exposer of shady planning applications', MacEoin did not conform to the traditional image of the 'gentrifier', and was perhaps a surprising ally of the IGS.[49] His father, Malachy MacEoin, had been a close friend of Sean MacDermott, and was interned aboard the prison ship *Argenta* in Larne Lough during the War of Independence. Uinseann was born in Pomeroy, Co. Tyrone in 1917, later attending Blackrock College. Like his father, he was drawn towards republican politics; after producing an illegal newspaper in the 1930s, he spent three and a half years in Arbour Hill, Mountjoy, and the Curragh during the Second World War. During this time he took classes in architecture, town planning, and Irish, and after his release he combined journalism with his architecture practice MacEoin Kelly and Associates. He remained active in the republican movement, however; after losing faith in the direction of republicanism during the Border Campaign, he was involved in Clann na Poblachta and the Workers Party, and was a founding member of the Northern Ireland Civil Rights Association and the

[48] *Irish Times*, 18 January 1969, 8.
[49] *Hibernia*, 24 October–6 November 1969, 4.

Wolfe Tone Society.[50] But his place in post-war Irish history was secured by his long-term editorship of Ireland's most important architecture and construction journal, through this mouthpiece becoming a highly significant voice in shaping the reception of the modernization of Dublin in the 1960s.

Despite his markedly different politics and background, MacEoin became one of the leading figures in the IGS's campaign to preserve the Gardiner estate. The first Georgian house he bought was 5 Henrietta Street, which had a floor area of 8,500 square feet. When his wife, Margaret MacEoin, first visited the property in 1966, it was home to seventy-four people, twelve of whom were living in the front room, while the whole house shared one toilet. The landlord no longer wanted it, as he could not afford its upkeep owing to rent restrictions. The MacEoins bought it for a token sum, and converted the unmanageably large house into artists' workshops. During this period they also acquired 6 and 7 Henrietta Street and five houses on the east side of Mountjoy Square. MacEoin sought to make these houses economically viable, while retaining as far as possible the families who had lived in these houses originally, by letting out the first two floors as offices, while keeping the upper two storeys as flats.

For MacEoin, his interest in social issues and his work in preserving the eighteenth-century architecture of the city were inseparable. This left-wing approach to conservation of the built fabric, which linked the retention of buildings with the retention of community, was part of an intellectual tradition that ran from William Morris to George Lansbury and Jane Jacobs.[51] His involvement in the Wolfe Tone Society—the republican ginger group—provides another view of the rationale which underpinned his interest in the Georgian city. During the 1960s the society debated how republicanism could be renewed in a changing Ireland; it produced pamphlets on social studies, fostering folk traditions, creating a new rapport between city and western co-operatives, and Irish teaching in secondary schools.[52] This link between national culture, social reform, conservation, and nostalgia also was embodied in his campaign for the retention of the social make-up and architectural character of the city. MacEoin's interest was on the preservation and fostering of Irish vernacular culture of both rural and urban provenances, leading him to be

[50] Under MacEoin's lead the Wolfe Tone Society was involved in the saving of Tailor's Hall alongside the IGS.

[51] Patrick Wright, *A Journey Through Ruins: The Last Days of London* (London, 1991), 49.

[52] *Irish Independent*, 31 May 1968, 11.

involved in campaigns for the Irish language, folk music, and working-class culture.

MacEoin's involvement with the IGS scheme can also be read as having political overtones. In his journal, the *Irish Architect and Contractor*, MacEoin condemned the destruction of the city as resulting from a combination of cultural myopia and the Corporation's policy of creating Catholic homes in the suburbs. More importantly, however, in terms of both short- and long-term impact, he was the first to note and campaign against the government's links to property developers, and the related capitulation of the Corporation's responsibility towards the city in the face of private interests—views propounded to great effect and at great length in his editorials.[53] The use of patriotic rhetoric for the benefit of the few and to the detriment of Dublin's population was, for MacEoin, symptomatic of a wider disillusionment with the governance and direction of the twenty-six county Republic; disillusionment which he explicitly articulated through his preservationist efforts. Not only did the houses he bought within the Gardiner estate act as a bulwark against speculative development, but through making the conscious effort to rent them to low-income tenants and artists, he also aimed to challenge the reduction of low-income housing units in the city.

The recreation of an Anglo-Irish material heritage was not the only excluded narrative to be rewritten and reified through the preservation of the streets of the city. Buying, preserving, and repopulating houses in the Gardiner estate allowed MacEoin to make broader dissent with the nature of the Irish state visible. He made these links explicit with plaques he put on the houses he bought. For example, the text of a plaque put outside 6 Henrietta Street by MacEoin in the late 1960s read:

> This five bay town house, the entrance of which has long been removed was commenced in 1730 by Nathaniel Clements Member of the Irish Parliament College Green, Teller of the Exchequer and Ranger of Phoenix Park, who lived for many years here in Parisian luxury. In 1908 its fine doorcases and chimney pieces were removed by Alderman Meade who turned the houses into tenements in which more than 70 lived. *Is saoranach Eireann anois e.*

This seemingly disparate message, which condemned a nationalist Lord Mayor, while romantically describing an Anglo-Irish property developer, was united by its inversion of traditional norms of the narrative of Irish history. The last line translates as 'it is now a citizen of Ireland'; a symbolic

[53] Lionel Esher, *A Broken Wave: The Rebuilding of England 1940–80* (London, 1980), 54.

baptism of the house into the history of Ireland. His use of the Irish language on a Georgian building was a self-conscious integration of Ireland's two traditions. His use of his Georgian buildings to make tangible his political views can also be seen even more explicitly next door, on 5 Henrietta Street. In 1973, he renamed this building James Bryson House, after a young member of the Provisional IRA shot dead by the British Army that year: using the eighteenth-century building to recall not so much a sidelined past as an alternative present. The plaque, with all its connotations of legitimacy and authority, gave weight to this alternative republic. MacEoin stepped into a gap left by the lack of positive planning for the Gardiner estate. In so doing, he preserved the houses of the Protestant nation, restored them for low-income accommodation, and used them to commemorate republican dead. His Georgian houses became symbols of an alternative secular, socialist, thirty-two country republic dreamed of at independence. Therefore he was able to use the city to spatialize dissent, bring into being an alternative vision of civic and national governance, and root his marginalized politics.

Although MacEoin managed to save many eighteenth-century houses while retaining their working-class inhabitants, his was the only example of a consciously socially minded approach to preservation in the Gardiner estate. All the other attempts required the displacement of the extant population for the preservation of the built fabric; a policy often portrayed as a choice of the heritage of buildings over the heritage of communities. In many respects, though, there was no choice to be made. Although the IGS's efforts received criticism at the time, and gentrification has continued to receive negative commentary in the literature on urban space, in most cases there was rarely a clear choice between the retention of a long-standing working-class population and its replacement by a footloose middle class. Indeed, the contrast between the two groups was not so great as figures like McCarron and Sweetman portrayed it; the lower-income residents of Mountjoy Square tended to be short-term and transient even before the arrival of the IGS, while the preservationists never were, or threatened to be, such a number as to wholly denude the square of cheap accommodation. Moreover, the economic evolution of Dublin, caused in large part by increasing prices for office space, meant that, without state aid, city-centre working-class accommodation was becoming more unsustainable in the city's unregulated market. The IGS had the cultural capital to make the story of the office block in Mountjoy Square newsworthy, even as similar locations all over the city were being demolished unreported; indeed, the newspapers or planning officials would have paid little attention to the demands of the residents had it not been for their clash with the preservation group.

EIGHTEENTH-CENTURY MATERIAL CULTURE AND INTERIOR DESIGN

After reaching the agreement with Matt Gallagher, the IGS had to find twenty-two investors to purchase and restore the houses in the square. Mountjoy Estates Ltd was formed to administer the purchase of the houses and to coordinate their resale.[54] During 1970, the group issued a pamphlet detailing the specifications of each of the houses which it now owned and hoped to sell on for restoration, and offering to provide the 'link between history and commerce'.[55] It presented a jarring mix of the architectural curiosity and the harsh reality of buildings which had long been in tenements, all described in the brisk language of property sales. For example, No. 44 was described for the benefit of potential purchasers as:

> A terraced red brick, formerly residential and late tenement property, standing four storey over basement with two storey return. Now in poor order and condition. Ground floor rooms without flooring nor doors—opes sheeted up. Return building demolished. Roof and rear wall not sound. Small rear yard. No tenement lettings. Vacant possession. Frontage 23 ft, apparent depth 100 ft. Tenure: Lease to 2788 at £7.10 per an. Rateable valuation £25. Architectural particulars: Extremely pretty ceilings on the ground floor rooms, also on landing and first floor drawing room. Grisaille plaques missing from ceilings, but could be replaced. Pretty fanlight. Charming Gothic lavatory at rear. Space at rear. Fair condition.[56]

This building had been described by Mary Maher only three years before as indicative of housing problems in Dublin; from the IGS's specifications, it was still in a similarly poor condition, although the thirty-four inhabitants appeared to be no longer in residence. However, the house was not being marketed for its structural stability; it was being sold with an emphasis on the architectural features for an intended market which would be attracted by its intact eighteenth-century craftsmanship in spite of the obvious problems presented by reconstruction. 'Before' and 'after' photographs were also provided to show potential purchasers this transformation from partitioned tenement into elegant and immaculate eighteenth-century property. Thus the IGS attempted to attract purchasers who would be prepared to invest considerable amounts of money to recreate authentic eighteenth-century interiors.

[54] *Build*, July 1968, 11.
[55] IAA RW.D203, Mountjoy Square pamphlet, 1; *Irish Times*, 12 August 1970, 5.
[56] Mountjoy Square pamphlet, 11.

One of the first to successfully restore an eighteenth-century house in the Gardiner estate was Harold Clarke in North Great George's Street; indeed, the photographs released with the Mountjoy Square Estates brochure were of his already completed interiors, which showed restored plasterwork, fresh paint, and wallpaper in a room which had once been subdivided for tenement use. Having been shown the house on North Great George's Street during a lunchtime at the end of 1967, he moved in in March 1968, spending his evenings after work and weekends for the next two years on restoring the house.[57] He carefully stripped down two hundred years of wallpaper to recover the original colours, which he then faithfully reproduced, also authentically restoring the original plasterwork. In his choice of colours, Clarke was keen not to decorate the house in the 'lifeless greens and blues and greys' that had become associated with the 'Georgian palette', but instead painted the house in 'strong and positive' colours. For example, the hall was decorated in orange on a midnight blue background, and green walls with pink decorations adorned the back drawing room.[58] Clarke also collected many eighteenth-century objects with which to decorate the house, including paintings, a chandelier, a marble fireplace, a sideboard, dining table, and candelabra.

In the eighteenth century, the acquisition, display, and exchange of objects were recognized as key elements of social positioning at all levels of society; as John Styles and Amanda Vickery have stated, objects were used to 'convey a multitude of meanings, from fashion, taste and style to wealth and status, history and lineage, and from science, education, political allegiance, and religious conviction, to personality, relationships, memory, and mortality'.[59] In particular, the concept of 'taste' was a key part of Georgian cultural discourse, and provided a new way of understanding culture and society, structuring, signifying, and visualizing relationships of class and gender. In Dublin during the 1960s, eighteenth-century objects were again being collected and displayed as signifiers of taste, and cadences of these eighteenth-century discourses re-emerged in the ideas of authentic restoration of eighteenth-century property. For example, Edward Dillon's headquarters were commended in the *Cellar* magazine for the 'good taste and authenticity' of the restored plasterwork.[60]

[57] Harold Clarke, 'Do-it-yourself restoration', Harold Clarke's private collection.

[58] Harold Clarke, 'Do-it-yourself restoration'.

[59] John Styles and Amanda Vickery, 'Introduction', in J. Styles and A. Vickery (eds.), *Gender, Taste and Material Culture in Britain and North America 1700–1830* (New Haven, 2006), 12.

[60] *Sunday Independent*, 6 August 1967, 20.

However, although the objects and discourse were the same, the meaning of this collection and display were very different in a wholly new national and social context. In *Household Gods*, Deborah Cohen described antiques collecting in turn-of-the-century Britain as a 'critique of a fast living age', a retention of older forms of social hierarchy in newly shifting times. 'In a nation in which the established social hierarchy seemed increasingly imperilled, an eye for antiques became a mark of distinction not easily replicable. It signified triumph of substance over mere style.'[61] Similarly, Sharon Zukin has highlighted the importance of architectural restoration for the production of cultural capital for the new middle class in contemporary New York.[62] The IGS's bulletins were full of pleas for the acquisition of original furniture, china, and silverware to fill the houses of its members.[63] In Dublin in the 1960s, the collection, display, and restoration of objects was also invested with social and cultural meaning. With the growing prosperity of the decade, a new form of cultural capital was embodied in the expensive hobby of the acquisition, restoration, and display of eighteenth-century material culture. Even as the *Irish Press* declared in 1968, 'People come first. They want to live in modern houses and they want to work in modern factories and offices', so the spread of a mass-produced 'modern' form of living also had the reciprocal effect of privileging of craftsmanship and unique objects for a certain section of the cultural elite.[64]

Moreover, the IGS's members did not merely wish to collect eighteenth-century ornaments to furnish their empty houses, but it was of particular import that these antiques were Irish. Many doleful editorials were written in the *Quarterly Bulletin* regarding the large quantities of silverware and furnishings that had left the state since the break-up of the estates of the big houses, and calling for a halt to this trend. Harold Clarke's furnishing included a large quantity of furniture and ornaments from the break-up of the landed estates, such as vases from Ballyseedy Castle, Tralee, a toilet suite bearing the monograms of Lord Cloncurry from Lyons House, knives from Powerscourt House, and busts of Demosthenes, Homer, Cicero, and Napoleon from Ballynegall House.[65] Thus

[61] Deborah Cohen, *Household Gods: The British and Their Possessions* (London, 2006), 147.

[62] Sharon Zukin, 'Gentrification: Culture and Capital in the Urban Core', *Annual Review of Sociology* 13 (1987), 129–47.

[63] Knight of Glin and James Peill, *Irish Furniture: Woodwork and Carving in Ireland from the Earliest Times to the Act of Union* (New Haven, 2007), 1–5.

[64] *Irish Press*, 4 January 1968, 9.

[65] Christie's Auction Catalogue 19 North Great George's Street, Dublin Ireland (Dublin, 1987), 30–45.

in Ireland, the social dynamics of cultural capital invested in architectural restoration also took on national overtones. The material culture of eighteenth-century big houses, which had not been considered to be a national heritage, was newly valorized by voluntary action. In 1960s Ireland, tradition was embedded within the visual culture of the state, and so was challenged by an alternative material heritage as preserved and displayed by the IGS; in Cohen's words, 'antiques as protest'.[66]

But these domestic interiors were not wholly private worlds: each was also an amateur museum. In 1967, John and Ann Molloy opened their house charging 2s. 6d. per person, causing a peak of media interest as 'the first time a Dublin townhouse [had been] open to the public'.[67] From January 1968, Mariga Guinness's house was open daily as an architectural library and social space as the Dublin headquarters of the IGS, and Harold Clarke's home featured frequently in magazine articles and books on Irish interior design.[68] This close reproduction and display of eighteenth-century environments brought to attention the state's negligence in this regard: in 1949, Professor Thomas Bodkin had, in his *Report on the Arts in Ireland*, recommended that the state should buy a Georgian town house to exhibit Irish eighteenth-century craftsmanship, while ten years later, as we have seen, the IGS was re-formed after a campaign to have houses in Kildare Place turned into a museum failed. Indeed, throughout the 1960s, the IGS had lobbied consistently for a Georgian townhouse to be furnished and opened as a museum. For those involved in the preservation of Mountjoy Square, the rehabilitation of eighteenth-century ceilings by Michael Stapleton and the acquisition and display of Irish furniture was part of the creation of a heritage and a commodification of an aesthetic which was explicitly Irish, yet little recognised in the National Museums.[69] Owing to the duality of Ireland's cultural heritages, the group may have been looking to the past, but in so doing they were also challenging 'tradition', embedded within the political and cultural underpinnings of the state. The Georgians had renounced their effort to persuade the state to provide a museum dedicated to the eighteenth-century craft; they now took it upon themselves to create their own spaces of display, and thus a separate reading of the Irish past which valorized the culture of the eighteenth century, which they publicized through the adept usage of modern mass media. In contrast to the privacy of gentrification in London, this

[66] Cohen, *Household Gods*, 148.

[67] IAA RW.D203, Press Release.

[68] *Irish Times*, 18 December 1967, 9; Klaus-Hartmut Olbricht, *Irish Houses: History, Architecture, Furnishing* (London, 1984), 109–18.

[69] IAA RW.D203: Mountjoy Square pamphlet.

was a very public—and a very politicized—preservationism, which sought consciously to intervene in broader debates over Irishness and heritage.

Despite the IGS's emphasis on eighteenth-century material culture and aesthetics, the restored houses were not exact replicas of domestic settings from that period. For example, Clarke also furnished with modern or more recent objects, including statues from Alexandra College; a bust of Archibald William, Lord Lieutenant of Ireland, from Dublin Castle; a painting once owned by Lennox Robinson; and a 1920s chandelier from the Metropole Ballroom.[70] Mariga Guinness's house in Mountjoy Square was a similar mix of old and new; indeed, her 'effortless good taste' in combining contemporary design alongside eighteenth-century craftsmanship inspired an article in the *Irish Times* by Mary Maher.[71] Indeed, Clarke and Guinness were both self-conscious in creating intensely individual aesthetics which mixed contemporary and historicist design. Furthermore, when this mixture of old and new was overlaid on their 'authentic' eighteenth-century design schemes—rooms which were multi-coloured, opulent, and rich—this created a mixture which stood in marked, definite contradistinction to the cool palate and soft modernism of the suburbs.

TRANSCENDING DUBLIN'S TOPOGRAPHIES

The social divide between the preservationists and their neighbours was matched by the distance from their new residences to the middle-class suburbs, located to the south and east of the city centre. This double sense of alienation, from the environment in which they now resided and from the culture which they had been part of, combined to create a sense of discovery and exploration among the preservationist group regarding their new venture. Desmond Guinness advocated going on night tours of the tenements 'when marvellous plaster ceilings will come to life in the most surprising places, when the giant grey stone buildings are asleep. Then you can feel the spirit of the eighteenth century, as faithfully as in a Malton print.'[72] Similarly, David Norris told how his interest in the Georgian city came through discovering a chest of eighteenth-century leases in his great-aunt's attic, and then exploring the city to match parchment to decaying place, while Harold Clarke spoke of his enjoyment of rummaging among bric-a-brac on the quayside to buy worn and neglected

[70] Christie's Auction Catalogue 19 North Great George's Street, Dublin Ireland.
[71] *Irish Times*, 15 February 1968, 11.
[72] *Quarterly Bulletin of the Irish Georgian Society*, April–June 1965, 54.

eighteenth-century furniture for a few pounds. When John and Ann Molloy opened their house to the public, their press release played heavily on the language of the strange and the foreign. Describing the area as one of Dublin's 'least known', they used a vocabulary derived from the American frontier to describe their experiences, stating, 'It has been suggested that we are pioneers in this work. However, no pioneering spirit is required; the buffalo have long since left the parts. In fact, this is a very civilized area in close proximity to the City centre and with convenient access to the Airport, North and West.'[73] The Molloys' intention of opening the house for viewing for those from '*home* and abroad' strikingly indicated that the north bank of the Liffey was an unknown to a certain sector who lived in the suburbs beyond the Grand Canal.

This sense of pioneering, of carving out an area of civilization in an otherwise uncharted area of the city, also extended to the activities of the IGS. The headquarters at No. 50 served not only as a physical bulwark against development of the square but also as a means of opening up the area to those who would not otherwise have spent time in the north city. The top floor of the house was converted into a flat which was inhabited by an archivist, David Synott, who did research into the history of the area, while the main reception rooms were converted into a library for the study of Irish architecture. This academic focus was combined with the building's function as a social hub for parties and fundraising events for the society.[74] This mixture of the academic and social was a key motif of many IGS events; for example, for 10 shillings on 27 May 1968, there was a breakfast party at No. 50, followed by a tour of Mountjoy Square, North Great George's Street, St George's Church, Eccles Street, Nelson Street, Lower Dominick Street, and Henrietta Street.[75]

Indeed, the preservationists were also perceived as out of place in the media. For Candida, the preservationists' work was analogous to a 'beautiful woman who had lost her looks in a concentration camp and on a good food and vitamin injections was spectacularly recovering her charms', while the *Irish Press* juxtaposed the rats occupying the empty houses of one side of the square with the opening of the IGS office on the south side, describing how it was 'charmingly audacious of Mrs Desmond Guinness to set up a baptismal font in a mortuary chapel, and the lady herself has the faery like quality of the unreality which the venture demands. Do please pay her the honour of a visit.'[76] Moreover, the IGS was seen to be a

[73] IAA RW.D203, Press Release.

[74] IAA RW.D203 press cutting, *Irish Independent*, 11 January 1968.

[75] *Irish Times*, 20 May 1967, 9.

[76] *Irish Times*, 15 January 1968, 11; IAA RW.D203 press cutting, *Evening Press*, 11 January 1968.

civilizing force in this uncharted territory. When the society opened 50 Mountjoy Square at the beginning of 1968, Mariga Guinness was described in *An Irishwoman's Diary* of 18 December 1967 as, 'struggling to maintain an oasis of civilization in the doomed wastelands of Mountjoy Square'.[77]

Although Dublin was relatively compact, its spatial segregation was notable. Mountjoy Square was only a short distance from many of the principal department stores of the capital located on Henry Street and O'Connell Street, and such cultural institutions as the Abbey Theatre and the Municipal Gallery of Modern Art. Despite this, it was in many respects a different world for the Georgian enthusiasts and the journalists who reported on their actions. There would have been little reason for the preservationists ever to have entered the streets to the north and east of O'Connell Street, which were still principally occupied as tenements, before becoming involved in the area's architectural renewal. The destruction of the urban landscape only reinforced the dizzying otherworldliness of this part of the city. For example, a photo in *Country Life* showed some unspecified Georgian enthusiasts hanging out of the windows of Mariga Guinness's house in Mountjoy Square in an otherwise empty landscape. The jarring of images between the refined gentility of the IGS's building (with china and curtains visible through the windows) and the dirt and poverty of their surroundings displayed a conscious understanding of Dublin's geographies; the Georgian enthusiasts saw themselves as, and were perceived to be, a curiosity in the north city. In portraying the preservationists alone in an otherwise desolate landscape, the *Country Life* photograph visualized the group just as they described themselves, as 'pioneers' on the frontier.[78]

David Ley and Sharon Zukin have noted the importance of this idea of the frontier in constructing the city as a site of transformative potential and the achievement of personal fulfilment for those in creative professions such as artists and writers.[79] They have argued that those who moved to the city in the 1960s were rejecting the modernist landscape, the communities based around the family and the church, and the political norms of the suburbs. Instead, the city centre was repossessed by those who, in their attempts to save it, imposed their own life-narratives on decaying

[77] *Irish Times*, 18 December 1967, 9.

[78] Neil Smith, *The New Urban Frontier: Gentrification and the Revanchist City* (London, 1996), xvii.

[79] Liz Bondi, 'Gender Divisions and Gentrification: A Critique', *Transactions of the Institute of British Geographers* 16/2 (1991), 190–8.

spaces.[80] In moving away from familiar middle-class areas and into the city, those who wished to could escape these social conventions.

These social and personal freedoms permitted by central-city residency had particular significances for many of those who moved to North Great George's Street. Throughout the 1970s, the area slowly became known as a place of residence for homosexual individuals and couples. This became particularly marked after David Norris moved to the street in 1978. Norris's interest in the area began after he started running a homosexual rights group financed by a disco in 46 Parnell Street, and he walked over to North Great George's Street to look for a rival gay club in the basement of No. 37, which had been diminishing his profits.[81] His story is evocative of the urban nature of homosexual culture, a subject which has received considerable scrutiny in recent work on sexuality. More gay households were attracted to preservation as city centre housing stock suited childless couples, and with two incomes they had the time and excess capital to take on a big project such as preservation of an eighteenth-century house. However, moving to the Gardiner estate had further attractions for Dublin's wealthier gay men. As homosexuality would remain illegal until 1994, the attraction of the anonymity of the city made urban living especially suitable. This incentive, coupled with the 'push factors' of the dominance of the church and a housing stock designed for the nuclear family in the suburbs, led gay men to play a leading role in the preservation of Georgian Dublin, and in particular North Great George's Street.

Those drawn to preservation here all stood outside the political mainstream, albeit in very different ways. Uinseann MacEoin was a republican; many within the IGS were Protestants, liberals, or from an Ascendancy background; and many of those who moved to North Great George's Street were homosexuals. In moving to the city, these preservationists could reject the social, political, and religious norms which were embedded in the social and spatial structure of the suburb. They could find a form of liberation from these constraints in the heterogeneity and anonymity of the city; in particular by moving to the north city, which was only faintly known for many of those from south of the Grand Canal. Clarke, Norris, and Guinness spoke of how the preservationists helped each other and worked together to restore the houses, forming a close-knit community. Restoration became a way of asserting individuality and creating a new life. Indeed, Clarke described the experience of buying the house as a 'road to Damascus moment'.[82]

[80] Ley, *A Social Geography of the City*, 397.
[81] Interview with David Norris.
[82] Clarke, 'Do-it-yourself restoration'.

This story is common to most Western cities during the 1960s; however, in Ireland the use and recuperation of urban space became particularly politicized. The preservationists jokingly described themselves as not only 'urban pioneers' but also 'a bulwark against the hill tribes': presenting themselves not only as reclaiming the city but also as a last defence of civilization against encroaching destructive forces which surrounded the city. A place which had been destroyed by a combination of technocratic rationality and national blindness was recuperated by those who sought to fill the planning deficit left by these forces, to reconstruct and so reinterpret the space. In stepping into the gap left by the absence of a positive state-led plan for the area, the preservationists' voluntary efforts took on political dimensions. They reinterpreted the history of Ireland through the valorization of eighteenth-century architecture and material culture, thereby reinstating the Protestant Ascendancy in the narrative of the nation. Similarly, Uinseann MacEoin used his buildings to commemorate a sidelined republican past. Thus personal fulfilment, cultural opposition, and historical reinstatement combined for a small, closely knit community. In moving into the city, which they perceived as a *terra nullis*, they were able to create a new world through islands of stylized domesticity in opposition to the perceived cultural monotheism of the Dáil, the suburbs, and the countryside.

In their activities around Mountjoy Square, the IGS were attempting a hugely audacious feat: to find investors willing to sensitively restore twenty-two Georgian houses in one of the poorest locations in Dublin. However, the financial strain imposed on the society by the deal immediately gave the group a debilitating handicap even before they had started their restoration attempt. As the IGS was unable to find purchasers for the sites quickly, it soon had to abandon any hope of using the square for residential accommodation—single-occupier or flats. Moreover, although the wealthy elite of the Georgian group acted as a 'cultural vanguard', this never translated into the cultural legitimacy required to attract the numbers of middle-class families required to stabilize and preserve the area. During the 1970s, a few schemes were floated for redeveloping the houses instead as offices, but none of these were enacted.[83] In 1974, the IGS's interest in the square was sold in its entirety to a property developer, Patrick McCrea, who sought to redevelop the square sensitively, but as offices; little different to the scheme put forward by Matt Gallagher, and so adamantly resisted in 1968.[84] McCrea, however, died shortly after, and

[83] *Irish Times*, 31 May 1972, 18; *Plan*, September 1972, 8.

[84] Thanks to Jennifer McCrea for interview and access to newspaper clippings from her family archive.

as the office boom fizzled in the mid-1970s, the square remained unrepaired. The IGS's interest was finally terminated with the sale and demolition of No. 50 in 1978, leaving only the Molloy family in residence, as their property was now worth too little to sell and buy anywhere else.[85] Indeed, by 1979 more of Mountjoy Square was destroyed than ever; almost all the south and west sides had been demolished. During the 1980s, gaps in the landscape were finally filled as part of the 'Gregory deal': a programme for the social regeneration of Dublin's inner city implemented in 1982 to ensure the support of Tony Gregory, an independent Dáil member whose constituency included north inner city Dublin, for Haughey's government. However, this was a pragmatic rather than an affectionate approach to conservation, during an economically austere time, and the infill that resulted was a boxy and insensitive pastiche. Yet while Mountjoy Square is often cited as an example of 'failed preservation', this assessment is overly critical. Although the south and west sides fell into ruin, and there was a failure to attract Georgian enthusiasts to the area, the preponderance of the built stock of the square is still the original eighteenth-century construction. It has been preserved, in a functional if not exacting manner, but without the social elevation which is usually characteristic of architectural rehabilitation.

The new-found interest in the preservation of the north city from individuals and voluntary groups was part of a wider European trend. Although the word was not at this time part of an Irish lexicon, the changes to Dublin must be located within the rise of 'gentrification', which was first witnessed in London in the later 1950s and appeared throughout Western Europe and North America by the end of the 1960s. This term, coined by Ruth Glass in 1964, was used to describe the inversion of the classic Chicago-school urban model as middle-class residents returned to city centre areas which had been previously considered to be in a permanent state of decline.[86] In many respects the efforts to preserve the Gardiner estate conformed to these universal patterns of gentrification. Just as in London, New York, and Toronto, there were competing claims upon historic areas, and multiple understandings of what was under threat and worth preserving in the urban environment. However, the differences of the case-study of north city Dublin are revealing. Unlike their British counterparts, the middle classes of Dublin's suburbs never developed a taste for living in the city centre. Indeed, the only movement

[85] IAA RW.D.203 press cutting, *Hibernia*, 5 June 1980; *Irish Times*, 17 February 1978, 21; Kearns, *Georgian Dublin: Ireland's Imperilled Architectural Heritage*, 181–4.

[86] Ruth Glass, 'Introduction', in Centre for Urban Studies and Ruth Glass (eds.), *London: Aspects of Change* (London, 1964), xiii–xlii.

of people from the suburbs to the north city took place within the institutional framework of the IGS's campaign. This scheme was influenced in its conception by changes occurring in London, but ultimately suffered from a lack of 'push' factors impelling middle-class householders to return to the city. Moreover, in a country divided by national as well as social fissures, the built stock of the capital did not represent a unified cultural inheritance, and could not command mass popular support for its preservation. The cultural capital of city living in older property never gained enough adherents to secure the preservation of Georgian Dublin.

While the IGS's venture in Mountjoy Square became an expensive failure for the group, there were preservationist successes in the Gardiner area. Uinseann MacEoin's properties on the east side of Mountjoy Square and in Henrietta Street remained intact. In North Great George's Street, Harold Clarke remained in residence for twenty years, joined by Desiree Short in 1974, and David Norris in 1978, among many others. During the 1970s and 1980s, the street became the sole area of middle-class owner occupancy in the north city, and one of the few complete streets in a crumbling landscape.

7

Office Politics, 1965–70

At 4 a.m. on 7 June 1970 a group of fifty men assembled silently in the half-light in St Stephen's Green. Yellow helmets and batons were distributed among the group; at 4.20 a.m. the order was given, and the men moved together towards the east side of the square. All of a sudden, the Sunday morning silence was disturbed as the men used their batons to smash down the front door of an eighteenth-century house. They entered, and dragged the four people who had been sleeping inside—Duncan Stewart, George Hodnett, Rosemarie McCallion, and Marie McMahon—out on to the street. The squad then began to demolish the house: stripping the roof off the building, and destroying doors, floors, plasterwork, and fittings.[1] The occupants phoned for help, and, alongside reinforcements, attempted to regain entry and to prevent the lightning demolition. By the time the demolition crew drove away at 11.15 a.m. they had successfully stripped the roofs off three buildings, 44 and 45 St Stephen's Green and 18 Hume Street, had partially destroyed many of the eighteenth-century doors, windows, and staircases, and demolished some of the walls.[2] As news spread of the violence in St Stephen's Green, people began to gather to offer help and to show solidarity; at 4 p.m., supporters of the students addressed the crowd, which by then numbered a thousand people. The speakers included Garret FitzGerald, Justin Keating, Mary Bourke, and Noel Browne; each in turn called for the houses to be preserved, condemning the violence and the government's role in allowing the buildings' destruction.[3]

This was the dramatic climax to the 'Battle of Hume Street'; a controversy regarding the preservation of six eighteenth-century houses on the corner of Hume Street and St Stephen's Green. This four-year-long standoff between the property developer and conservation bodies ultimately resulted in a six-month-long occupation of the houses by a group of architectural students. In many respects, the controversy regarding the

[1] *Irish Times*, 8 June 1970, 1; *Irish Press*, 8 June 1970, 1; *Irish Independent*, 8 June 1970, 1.
[2] *Irish Press*, 8 June 1970, 3.
[3] *Irish Times*, 8 June 1970, 15; *Irish Press*, 8 June 1970, 3.

houses at Hume Street was no different to many other demolitions and speculative constructions taking place all over the city at this time; indeed, the chronology of the planning battle and protest ran parallel to the IGS's campaign at Mountjoy Square and DHAC's protests across the city. However, the student group were more skilled at utilizing the media than other preservationists had been up to this point: they employed visual protests and press statements to ensure a broader and more sustained coverage of their campaign, and attracted the interest of spectators eager to construct the occupation as Ireland's photogenic answer to protests in Paris and America. Indeed, Hume Street's prominent position on Dublin's principal square, its totemic position as 'Dublin's last complete Georgian street', and the involvement of the government and a British development firm meant that the development scheme was frequently used as a synecdoche of the growing pains of national and urban modernization. Although the campaign to preserve the buildings ultimately failed, it achieved widespread support, and marked an important turning point in the history of twentieth-century Dublin.

The story of Hume Street, from planning application to occupation and eventual eviction, provides a way to examine the cultural politics of the later 1960s; in particular, regarding the intersection of forms of protest, ideas of the nation, and urban theory. During this period, initial popular enthusiasm surrounding modernization was slowly dissipating as employment rates fell and the Second Programme for Economic Expansion stumbled, just at the moment when these economic shifts were becoming newly apparent and tangible through the wave of building in the city. Although the controversy took place only four years after the demolition of Fitzwilliam Street, the form the debate took, and the options considered feasible for the future, had undergone a transformation, reflecting shifts within both architecture and ideas of national authenticity. This not only led to the preservationist group winning much popular support regarding the street, but also called into question the logic which had sustained the modernization of the city since the late 1950s.

During the 1960s, St Stephen's Green became Ireland's most sought-after location for new office developments. On its north-west corner, Grafton Street was Ireland's most exclusive shopping area, Leeson Street to the south-east led to the prosperous residential areas of Dublin 4, while the state institutions were clustered around the Dáil and Merrion Square to its north-west. Many office blocks, including Colmstock House and Hainault House, were already in construction on the square when Green Properties identified Hume Street, a late eighteenth-century residential enclave on the east of the square, as the location for its next prestige office development (Map 7.1).[4] The British development firm first bought Nos. 44, 45, and 47–9 (the Dominican Hall) St Stephen's Green, and 18 and 19 Hume Street.[5] Having acquired these properties, they then applied to Dublin Corporation for outline planning permission, granted in 1966, to redevelop the southern corner of Hume Street (being Nos 46–9 St Stephen's Green and Nos 1 and 2 Hume Street) as a modern office block.[6] On receipt of this, they also purchased 2 Hume Street and 46 St Stephen's Green.[7]

But the modernization of Dublin consisted of two conflicting developments. At the same time as the Green Property Company was acquiring property in this area for new offices, An Taisce and Dublin Corporation were also drawing up plans for the city's preservation. During its first years, An Taisce had concentrated on the preservation of natural heritage

Map 7.1. Map of the Hume Street area.

[4] Craig, *Dublin 1660–1860,* 233 and 323; *Irish Times*, 19 December 1969, 17.

[5] Green Properties was the Irish subsidiary of the British development company Marcus Leaver & Co. Its managing director was John Corcoran. *Irish Press*, 11 June 1970, 10; *Build*, May 1966, 16; *Build*, April 1967, 17.

[6] Designs in the Irish Architectural Archive.

[7] On the planning process: Dublin Corporation file 2158–7 (still held at Dublin Civic Offices); *Irish Builder and Engineer*, 10 January 1970, 1.

sites, such as the Burren and the North Bull bird sanctuary, but with increasing awareness of threats to Dublin's eighteenth-century environment during the 1960s, its membership increasingly turned towards campaigning for the preservation of the city.[8] In November 1966, An Taisce published its *Study of Amenity Planning Issues in Dublin and Dun Laoghaire*, which set out its recommendations for the 'absolute minimum' which should be preserved under Dublin Corporation's development plan.[9] The only streets on this minimum list were Henrietta Street, Fitzwilliam and Merrion Squares, Hume Street, and Ely Place. The Hume Street–Ely Place area was described as 'possessing some interiors of distinction, [they] remain the only smaller streets of the city to retain their good classical quality largely intact. It is vital that no further intrusion in this small area be permitted.'[10] When Dublin Corporation finally published its list for preservation as part of the 1967 Draft Development Plan, it followed An Taisce's recommendations closely. Indeed, it listed all properties in Hume Street, and 41–6 St Stephen's Green for preservation.[11] Yet this ongoing process of definition and regulation had little force in law, as Dublin's development plan remained unimplemented until 1971.

Alongside this effort to define the historic environment, preservationist groups also campaigned for the retention of Hume Street. Both An Taisce and the IGS celebrated Hume Street as the 'last complete eighteenth-century street in Dublin' and therefore particularly worthy of preservation, because of its status as the final remnant of a disappearing city.[12] When, in late 1966, the government put the houses it owned on Hume Street and St Stephen's Green up for sale, the IGS and An Taisce combined to form a committee for the preservation of these houses. The Dublin Civic Group (DCG), led by Kevin Nowlan, professor of history at UCD, held its first press conference on 12 December 1966, and was described in the *Irish Times* as the 'vanguard of the major societies formed to act more urgently on cases where somebody is about to sell what they think is Dublin's beauty'.[13]

Undeterred by the campaign of the DCG and Dublin Corporation's embryonic listing procedure, the Green Property Company continued to acquire buildings on the east side of St Stephen's Green. In 1967, the company applied for detailed planning permission for a much more ambitious scheme than that for which they had received initial planning

[8] O'Loughlin Kennedy, 'Introduction', in Bond (ed.), *An Taisce*, 20.
[9] An Taisce, *Amenity Study of Dublin and Dun Laoghaire* (Dublin, 1967).
[10] An Taisce, *Amenity Study of Dublin*, 13.
[11] Dublin Draft Development Plan 1968, 31; An Taisce, *For Demolition?*
[12] An Taisce, *For Demolition?*; *Irish Times*, 19 December 1969, 17.
[13] *Irish Times*, 13 December 1966, 11.

permission. This second proposal was for a design by Sam Stephenson; it consisted of office blocks on both the north and south corners of Hume Street, faced with concrete, with recessed windows, being very similar in form and materials to Hainault House, which was already in construction on the north side of St Stephen's Green. Under the terms of the recently completed Draft Development Plan, this new scheme was refused planning permission by Dublin Corporation.[14] However, Green Properties did not accept this decision, as it had bought many sites in the area based on the conditional planning approval of 1966, and the company appealed against Dublin Corporation's refusal to the Minister for Local Government. At a hearing in December 1967, Boland overturned the Corporation's decision, counteracting the terms of the development plan and An Taisce's recommendations, by granting the Green Property Company permission to proceed with their development.[15]

Though repulsed in all their efforts up to this point to block the development, the preservationist lobby had one final avenue to pursue. Planning permission covered the whole site; this included No. 1, which was still in government ownership. If the government decided not to sell No. 1, the permission for the whole site would have been invalidated.[16] The coalition of preservationists now turned their attention to persuading the government to halt this sale.[17] On 17 July 1969, An Taisce, the IGS, and the DCG organized a joint meeting at the Wolfe Tone Memorial, on the north-east corner of St Stephen's Green, with the aim of stopping the Hume Street development as 'an area of the highest importance in the struggle to preserve Dublin's Georgian Heritage'.[18] The resolutions were passed:

> the Government should refuse to sell these state-owned houses;
>
> the Government should respect promises already made by their spokesman to abide by the Dublin Development Plan, which calls for the preservation of these houses;
>
> the Government should establish a positive clear policy on preservation of certain buildings and streets in Dublin city.[19]

These resolutions give an indication of why Hume Street became so much more contentious than the many other similar developments in

[14] An Taisce, *For Demolition?*

[15] An Taisce, *For Demolition*; *Irish Builder and Engineer*, 10 January 1970, 1.

[16] *Irish Times*, 16 January 1970, 11; *Build*, November 1969, 5; *Plan*, January 1970, 6.

[17] *Build*, July/August 1969, 38.

[18] Flyer (n.d.), Uinseann MacEoin papers.

[19] An Taisce, *For Demolition?* See MacEoin papers for newspaper reports and transcript of MacEoin's speech.

train in the city. Importantly, processes of development and conservation were in conflict: just as much of the city was being reconstructed as offices, the 'historic' areas of the capital were also being defined, listed, and cordoned off from development. Developers and preservationists both wished to lay claim to the same area of the city, centred on the Pembroke estate. For preservationists, the style of the late eighteenth-century buildings conformed to their notions of the aesthetic value of the city, and the prosperity of the area meant that the built stock had remained in good condition. However, these qualities also attracted developers, as the area could command high rentals, it had good transport links, and the eighteenth-century streets were wide and well proportioned. At Hume Street, preservationists and speculator clashed as both the development proposal and listing procedure were in process, subject to interpretation, and therefore competed to lay claim to the same territory. Most important, however, was the role of the government in sanctioning the development. As ministers had both overridden Dublin Corporation's refusal of planning permission and authorized the sale of state-owned property to a development firm, the houses became a locus for discontent regarding corruption, and Fianna Fáil's relationship to property speculators. The intimate relationship between developer and politician, and the government's obstinate refusal to entertain the concerns of the conservation lobby, now seemed to indicate that legal planning channels existed only to validate the interests of private property investors. Direct action therefore seemed to be the only viable and practicable means of preventing the development.

RADICAL ACTION FOR A GOOD ENVIRONMENT

On Thursday 11 December 1969, a group of students noticed workmen in the controversial Hume Street houses: lifting floorboards, ripping out fireplaces, and stripping the roofs of the eighteenth-century buildings.[20] They persuaded the demolition men to withdraw, and, joined by more friends, they occupied No. 45 to protest against the destruction of the six houses (Fig. 7.1).[21] They contacted the writer and journalist Lionel Fleming, and he described the occupation in his column in the *Irish*

[20] IAA RW.D.138 press cutting: *Building*, 9 January 1970; *Irish Times*, 19 December 1969, 17; *Irish Times*, 12 December 1969, 15; *Irish Times*, 16 December 1969, 1; *Irish Press*, 12 December 1969, 5; *Irish Builder and Engineer*, 10 January 1970, 1.

[21] *Irish Times*, 12 December 1969, 15; *Irish Times*, 16 December 1969, 1; IAA RW.D.138 press cutting: *Building*, 9 January 1970.

Fig. 7.1. Hume Street, 1970. Image courtesy of RTÉ Stills Library.

Times the next day: 'The students were in cheerful but belligerent mood when I called on them yesterday afternoon, making my way up the stairs past placards bearing such inscriptions as "save our heritage", and "stop this destruction", and "this is an occupied area". At the doorway they handed out An Taisce leaflets calling for the preservation of Hume Street while upstairs they got ready to camp out till further orders.'[22] From this beginning, the group continued to make a conscious effort to make their campaign and concerns visible, and to link their protest through their vocabulary of action to other student protests taking place across Europe and North America. Three weeks after moving in, on New Year's Day, the first day of European Conservation Year, the group marched to the offices of Green Properties with placards bearing slogans such as 'Demolition is demoralisation', '£££££', '1970—Conservation Year?', 'A city without old buildings is like a man without a memory'.[23] Upon reaching the offices they ascended the roof and hung a banner reading, 'Corcoran is a traitor. Is Boland? Is Haughey? The Hume Street occupiers'.[24]

[22] *Irish Times*, 12 December 1969, 15.
[23] *Irish Times*, 2 January 1970, 13; *Irish Builder and Engineer*, 10 January 1970, 1.
[24] *Irish Times*, 2 January 1970, 13; *Irish Builder and Engineer*, 10 January 1970, 1.

The Hume Street 'garrison' was based around Radical Action for a Good Environment (RAGE), which had been set up a year before by Duncan Stewart, a UCD architecture student, to protest against the plans to run a motorway along the line of the Grand Canal. The group was predominantly composed of architecture students from UCD and Bolton Street, joined by some others from Trinity College and the Grafton Academy of Art. This was not the first piece of radical action that UCD architecture students had been involved in: when it seemed that the department was to be stripped of its RIBA recognition in 1968, many of the same students had been at the centre of UCD's Gentle Revolution. This altercation had led to the head of architecture, Professor Desmond FitzGerald, being quietly removed from his chair, with Ivor Smith—architect of Sheffield's Park Hill—employed to improve standards in the department.[25]

Officially the group had no leader, although Deirdre McMahon, who was older than the rest and had a background of activism, often led discussions. However, their decisions were always made with a meeting and a vote. But 45 St Stephen's Green was not lacking in rules despite its lack of hierarchy. People could not stay in the house at random; everyone who stayed had to earn their right to be there by doing restoration work on the house, and there was a rota for staying overnight, which was compulsory to ensure that at least four people were in the house at any given time. The *Irish Builder and Engineer* painted a picture of a committed and diligent protest: 'They are inside day and night in substantial numbers, replacing floor boards, window surrounds, doors, etc., and have re-covered the stripped roof.'[26] They also attempted to make the building homely, by procuring Christmas trees and a dartboard, picking flowers from St Stephen's Green, and obtaining a plaque for above the mantelpiece that said 'Home Sweet Hume'.[27]

The house became a centre of youth culture. George Hodnett, the jazz critic from the *Irish Times*, moved in, musicians played in the students' living room, and students, even those not involved in preservation, came to drink and talk politics after the pubs shut. During this period, Stewart was also organizing the Dublin Arts Festival, so 45 St Stephen's Green became the festival's offices. Groups from all over Ireland and Britain, including the Ronnie Scott Band, Sean O'Riada, the Chieftains, rock

[25] Duncan Stewart, one of the leaders of the Hume Street group, was also the Auditor of the Architectural Society during the 'Gentle Revolution', and central to protests that led to the replacement of Professor Desmond FitzGerald. See *Plan*, October 1969, 28; *Plan*, September 1970, 13; *Irish Builder and Engineer*, 14 December 1968, 810. More on this, including manifestos of the protestors and minutes of meetings, in MacEoin papers.

[26] *Irish Builder and Engineer*, 10 January 1970, 1.

[27] See photograph in *Hibernia*, 9 January 1970, 3.

poets, flamenco dancers, and classical guitarists, came to perform in Dublin and visited the house. Through the creation of domestic space in the centre of the city, the students were able to take on many of the trappings of alternative lifestyle politics of protest. By moving back into the centre of the city, an area that had long been vacated by the middle class, they were able to move away from the community from which they originated, and find liberation through the creation of alternative domestic environments. In these spaces of protest they were able to engage with a global network of student protest, and fashion themselves as part of a worldwide environmental campaigning movement.

The group received much popular support. The *Irish Times*, *Plan*, and *Irish Builder and Engineer* were all explicit in their backing for the students, and devoted considerable space to covering the protest and helping them raise funds. Indeed, 300 members of the RIAI signed a declaration to state that they considered 'the preservation of the entire Hume Street area of the utmost importance and wholeheartedly support[ed] all efforts towards this end'.[28] They also received many visitors; for example, on 7 February, a group of over 50 members of 'The Congress of Geography Students of Ireland', representing 'universities, colleges and schools in Dublin, Cork, Galway and Belfast and includ[ing] a large number of clerical students', made an organised visit to the house.[29] Moreover, Hume Street became a locus of protest for a range of critical and controversial public voices; Garret FitzGerald, Noel Browne, Justin Keating, Owen Sheehy Skeffington, Mary Bourke (later Robinson), Liam de Paor, Conor Cruise O'Brien, and Austin Flannery all spoke out in support of the students' actions.[30]

But the students' links were not confined to Ireland: they positioned themselves as part of a global movement of protest, and formed networks with other environmental groups across Europe, links which played a key part in their conception of the protest. *Agenor*, a magazine based in Brussels which aimed to 'break down barriers to communication in Europe', and was 'concerned with direct political involvement by pressure groups

[28] RIAI release, 2 February 1970, Montgomery papers.

[29] *Irish Builder and Engineer*, 21 February 1970, 119.

[30] Garret FitzGerald (1926–2011), UCD economist and Fine Gael politician, later serving two terms as Taoiseach; Noel Browne (1915–97), doctor and Labour politician, remembered for his part in the Mother and Child scheme; Justin Keating (1930–2009), veterinary surgeon, lecturer at Trinity College and Labour politician; Owen Sheehy Skeffington (1909–70), lecturer in French at Trinity College and senator; Mary Bourke (1944–), lecturer in Law at Trinity College, Labour politician, later President of Ireland; Liam de Paor (1926–98), historian at UCD; Conor Cruise O'Brien (1917–2008), Labour politician and writer; Austin Flannery (1925–2008), Dominican priest, presenter of RTÉ's current affairs programme, *Outlook*.

in order to bring about social change', commissioned an article.[31] They exchanged letters with a group of students in Stockholm, who were campaigning to save elm trees in the historic Kungsträdgården from destruction. A group of students from Austin, Texas collected 300 signatures in support of the students at Hume Street, and eight of them and one of their lecturers came to stay to show their solidarity.[32] Benjamin Spock, in Ireland to address the Society of Citizens for Civil Liberties, also visited the house and told them: 'Young people had fought for their ideals in America and it was wonderful to come to Dublin and find young Irish people doing so too. You are demonstrating for justice and I'm with you. It's wonderful, keep it up. This is the way that countries are saved.'[33]

'Something beyond architecture': urban theory and the students' protest

On 12 December, Fleming published the manifesto of the students in occupation in full:

> We, as conscientious students of the environment, have occupied this building to bring once again to the attention of the general public the callous indifference the government has shown to the architectural heritage of Dublin, the corporation city plan, and its own promises. We condemn the arrogant action of the Government in this issue, which shows more concern for the financial welfare of the Green Property Company than to the environment of the people of Dublin. We call on the government, the architect and all others involved in this destruction to examine their conscience and their duty to society on this issue and above all, we call on the citizens of Dublin to resist the assault upon their environment with all the means at their disposal.[34]

As this manifesto attests, the student group did not limit the scope of their concerns to the protection and restoration of the houses they inhabited. They made a considerable effort, through their banners, placards, speeches, and letters to the press to link their occupation to a range of issues, regarding the interplay between economic modernization and national culture.

In particular, developments within urban theory during the 1960s played a central role in the way that the students understood their grievances

[31] Letter from John Lambert (co-editor) to the occupiers of 45 St Stephen's Green, 5 January 1969, Montgomery papers.

[32] *Irish Times*, 21 January 1970, 8; NAI 2002/19/78, Letter from O. Bret Peaden, Box 834, Florida Presbyterian College, St. Petersburg, Florida to Irish Embassy, New York, 22 May 1970.

[33] *Irish Times*, 10 June 1970, 7.

[34] *Irish Times*, 12 December 1969, 15; *Irish Times*, 16 December 1969, 1.

and justified their protest. In the place of the authority of modernism, the pronouncements of writers such as Jane Jacobs and Kevin Lynch were moving to form a new orthodoxy in urban theory during this period; this led to a new emphasis on qualities such as atmosphere, tradition, identity, and above all community, as the tenets upon which the 'success' of a city would be judged. In contrast with the emphasis which had previously been laid on the technocrat's ability to mould the city, it was no longer self-evident that the expertise of an architect or the scientific methods of a planner could improve on the environment; rather, as McMahon argued, 'any form of planning which destroys a good environment is bad planning'.[35] Instead, there was a new understanding within European architectural circles that the processes through which a model city would take shape would be through complexity, disorder, and even 'non-planning'.[36] Hume Street marked an important point in the slow collapse of public confidence in the values of modernist town planning in Ireland; indeed, the influence of Jane Jacobs can be witnessed in a letter published by *Hibernia* from Deirdre McMahon:

> What is [Sam Stephenson] doing to keep this a living city? What are his associates in Marcus Lever and Corcoran etc. doing? They are slowly robbing this lovely city of its character and what is worse, by their ruthless speculation doing what many cities in the world are desperately trying to undo. Emptying it of its citizens...While Mr Stephenson can afford the enjoyment of living in the city while planning to turn it into an office zone, those of us who are in danger of being pushed out of our city by these same office zones, will not sit back and let him. We are there because we love Dublin. We don't want a city which opens at 9am and closes at 5.30pm.[37]

It was the distance and tensions between the newer body of literature and the values which had structured the modernization of the capital during the preceding decade which made this reading of urban theory particularly contentious. In her letter, McMahon situated the development at Hume Street as part of a larger process whereby commercial property, zoning, and 'ruthless' speculation were brutalizing the landscape, ridding the city centre of its inhabitants, and creating an anonymous 'office zone' in place of the diversity and life implicit in the idea of a 'city'. In *Agenor*, she followed this theme, stating that 'our capital city' was turning into 'a mass of poorly designed office blocks'.[38] Thus the city centre was becoming a place that was inhabited only by suited clerical workers during the

35 *Agenor*, June 1970, 14.
36 Peter Hall, *Cities of Tomorrow*, 260.
37 IAA RW.D.138 press cutting, *Hibernia* (n.d.).
38 *Agenor*, June 1970, 14.

day, and which was empty of people and life during the rest of the week. In tandem with this process of creeping desolation at the centre of the city, the people who had previously inhabited these spaces also had their lives compromised by the dictates of planning: former residents of the city centre were being moved to the suburbs 'in the flat, uninteresting west side of the city. These estates are badly laid out with no community centres, no proper parks, or playgrounds, no variety. Mile after mile of identical houses. Long bus-rides to and from work, or to cinemas and theatres.'[39] Through this analysis, McMahon created a Marcusian image of the banality of Fordist rationalities when applied to work, leisure, and urban space; the city became less than the sum of its parts, as both centre and suburb suffered from the lack of what the other had in excess.

Furthermore, successful urban spaces would not just be the product of buildings and roads but a holistic approach to the city; the students saw themselves as not just preservationists but as 'conscientious students of the environment', who called on the people of Dublin to 'resist the assault upon their environment'. This emphasis was indicative of a sea-change which was taking place in the study of architecture: while the word 'environment' had never been part of the lexicon of previous preservation efforts, it was central to RAGE's conception of their protest.[40] In 1968, Michael Scott described the term as 'a word we come to hear more and more each day. Environmental and environmentalist are words in common usage... It is because it is a word which describes something beyond architecture.'[41] The students' emphasis on the protection of the environment meant that they did not attempt to justify the preservation of the buildings because of their intrinsic historical worth, or the craftsmanship of plasterwork and features. Rather, the protest was now tied into broader themes relating to the city; the prevention of the demolition of the eighteenth-century buildings was part of the amelioration or prevention of systemic problems such as traffic, pollution, and urban blight. This environmental discourse allied their protest at Hume Street to the growing conservation movement, which focused primarily on the retention of rural spaces and wildlife. In so doing, they rhetorically distanced their efforts from social and national connotations which had damaged the preservationist campaign at Fitzwilliam Street, and instead positioned architectural heritage as an essential part of a healthy, sustainable environment which was beneficial to all.

[39] *Agenor*, June 1970, 14–15.

[40] Simon Gunn, 'The Buchanan Report, Environment, and the Problem of Traffic in 1960s Britain', *Twentieth Century British History* 22/4 (2011), 522–3.

[41] *Irish Builder and Engineer*, 1 June 1968, 361.

The discontent relating to the nature of town planning was allied to a mounting disaffection with the nature of the financial relationships which had enabled these physical transformations. On 16 January, Green Properties attempted a conciliatory gesture towards the Hume Street preservationists, by offering to sell them the entire site for £250,000.[42] The students and their supporters could not afford to pay this amount to preserve the site; however, they used the offer as an example of how speculation was destroying more than just the older buildings of the city. As a flyer they produced pointed out, because of property speculation and the profit to be made from office construction, at Green Properties' valuation, each of the six houses of the Hume Street development was worth close to £50,000. This they compared with a fully restored town house in Westminster, which, owing to 'no speculation being involved', only cost £19,500.[43] It was not only the dictates of town planning which were leading to the segregation of the city, but also the logistics of capital associated with these processes: the city was simply becoming too expensive to live in. Thus the students combined their critique of problems of multinational capital and contemporary urbanism to fight 'speculation in Hume Street because through speculation it is becoming impossible for people to live in the city centre, and, because of speculation, only the rich can afford to buy houses near the city or mountains as the speculators have moved to these areas too and forced up land prices sky high'.[44] This inflated 'land prices to such a degree that people can no longer afford to live in the city, and only the rich can decide where they will live outside it'.[45]

But it was not only the property developers who were vilified for their role in forcing up land prices in the city centre; the government's part in allowing, and even enabling, this process was also called into question. From the middle of the 1960s, it became clear that high-profile individuals within the government were profiting from the construction boom: enabling property developers through re-zoning land, and guiding planning approvals through the bureaucratic process in return for cash bribes. A new, mutually beneficial elite was in formation, composed primarily of builders and politicians. At the centre of this nexus of capital and power was Charles Haughey, rising swiftly through the ministerial ranks during the 1960s, and accumulating vast debts in financing his extravagant

[42] *Plan*, June 1970, 2.
[43] Flyer (n.d.), MacEoin's papers.
[44] *Agenor*, June 1970, 14–15.
[45] *Agenor*, June 1970, 14–15.

lifestyle and expensive tastes along the way. Haughey was a unique figure, and his ambitions led him to the top of Irish politics, serving as Taoiseach for four terms between 1979 and 1992. The full extent of his illegal and barely legal financial involvements would not be exposed for more than thirty years; however, he was representative of the new type of politician who arose out of the prosperous 1960s, known for their wealth and 'mohair suits'. These new tendencies within the party were symbolized, reinforced, but ultimately brought to public attention by the Taca scandal. Taca was a Fianna Fáil party organization, created in 1966 with the object of raising money from the business community. Members—who were overwhelmingly involved in the construction industry—made an annual payment of £100 towards the party's electoral fund, while the interest on the fund was used to hold dinners at which members could mix with cabinet ministers. The organization's elitism, and undercurrent of corruption, were vocally criticized within Fianna Fáil as being symptomatic of the party's abandonment of its founding principles, and the party underwent a long-running and embittered struggle between 'new'- and 'old'-style politicians and politics.[46] These links between speculators and politicians were vocally condemned by an increasingly efficacious media, and ultimately became a great source of popular disaffection with economic liberalization. Hume Street was part of this; in the words of McMahon, the occupation was a demonstration 'against a system which allows a Minister to break planning laws to suit these speculators and to protest about the inadequacies of the planning laws themselves'.[47]

The role that British speculators played in these flows of capital had a strong emotive resonance. McMahon 'objected strongly when 95 per cent of modern buildings are offices, and mainly built by British companies, for government departments. In other words, the Irish taxpayer is paying British property speculators rentals of 30s to 40s per square foot, and in return he gets driven out of his own city.'[48] In similar terms, MacEoin saw Hume Street as primarily not a conservation matter at all, but 'one of the brashest little deals in surrendering control of important urban sites to cross channel development corporations that has occurred in recent times'.[49] Indeed, MacEoin wrote to the *Architects' Journal* to invite its readership to come to Dublin to 'marvel at our fourth-rate office blocks built by a new horde of English (?) landlords and inhabited by docile little

[46] Keogh, *Jack Lynch*, 117.
[47] *Agenor*, June 1970, 14.
[48] *Agenor*, June 1970, 14.
[49] Letter from Uinseann MacEoin to the *Irish Times*, 12 July 1969.

Irish civil servants'.[50] As McMahon and MacEoin's rhetoric shows, much popular support for the students at Hume Street derived from a sense that modernization was leading to the revival of older colonial relationships through new forms, as British property developers bought up land in the capital, leased it back to Irish tenants, and in so doing worsened living standards for the majority of inhabitants.

During the 1960s, the 'developer' became one of the folk-devils of the decade, alongside the 'man in the mohair suit', both symbolic of the new ethos of wealth creation and capital accumulation which surrounded a small, Dublin-based group. By 1970, the impact of international capital, clientelism, and malleable planning laws was already visible on the streets of Dublin; in the preceding decade, forty-eight office blocks were completed, with another eighty-five finished by 1975, concentrated in the south-eastern quadrant of the city within the canals and in Ballsbridge.[51] The axes of the city, which had been laid down by the Wide Streets Commissioners, had been overlaid by a matrix of speculative office blocks, which dominated the skyline and reshaped the landscape of the city.[52] Buildings built and planned in this period included Setanta House on Nassau Street, the Bank of Ireland on Baggot Street, the Central Bank on Dame Street, the Civic Offices on Wood Quay, Apollo House on Tara Street, and Hawkins House on Poolbeg Street. However, contemporary construction in Ireland had lost touch with the doctrine of progress which had brought the modern style into fruition in the early years of the twentieth century. Most of the new buildings in the city were constructed in the international form which had come to be accepted as expressive of the power of multinational corporations; these constructions had little, in terms of either style or usage of materials, which was experimental or new about their design. For example, the Bank of Ireland building on Baggot Street, designed by Ronnie Tallon and opened in 1973, was clad in bronze with tinted windows and composed around a plaza, being strongly influenced by the 1950s work of Mies van der Rohe. The building was criticized by Lance Wright, writing in the *Architectural Review*, as a small-scale replica of the Segram building executed in tripartite that, rather than being modern in ethos, looked back to an era of twenty years before.[53] Moreover, as shown in Chapter 2, this proliferation of office accommodation

[50] Letter from Uinseann MacEoin to editor of the *Architects' Journal*, 24 November 1969.

[51] Malone, *Office Development in Dublin 1960–80*, 54–6; also Desmond Gillmor and Michael Bannon, 'The Changing Centre of Gravity of Office Establishments within Central Dublin, 1940 to 1970', *Irish Geography* 6/4 (1972), 480–4.

[52] Gold, *The Practice of Modernism*, 86–9.

[53] *Plan*, March 1973, 6–7.

had not been envisaged by modernism's foundational proponents; indeed, the shift in international economics, land prices, and industrial practices which caused the rush of office building had been wholly unforeseen. Thus the function of these buildings, which bore the aesthetic hallmarks of modern design, and which were very visible in the landscape of central Dublin, stood in marked contrast to both the agenda of social reformism of the early Modern Movement internationally and to ideals of national renewal in the domestic architectural profession.

The rational dereliction of the environment, the replacement of distinctive Dublin buildings with an anonymous officescape, and the profiteering and corruption associated with these processes were taken up by those campaigning at Hume Street as indicative of the ideological vacuity at the heart of the Lemassian project of modernization. As Delaney has noted, 'individualistic self-interest was seen as the defining feature of this "new" Ireland, replacing the common interest of the common good'.[54] These anxieties were reified by changes taking place to the city; for example, the Labour politician and doctor Noel Browne, who had been at the centre of the Mother and Child controversy twenty years previously, made a speech from the window of 45 Hume Street, protesting that prosperity had led only to a destruction of Irish identity. To him, Ireland had 'become a society whose whole purpose is profit making. Anything was for sale and we had sold out on everything, artistically, intellectually, spiritually, physically, and politically. After half a century of our best efforts we had become a nation of cultural pygmies, enjoying all the vulgarity and hedonistic pleasures of a blatantly materialistic and decadent society.'[55] Browne's language and argument echoed the writings of D. P. Moran in the *Leader* in the early years of the twentieth century. He positioned Irish culture as both traditional and unmaterialistic, and thus challenged by economic modernization and the emergence of a consumer society during the 1960s. He was joined in this view by Owen Sheehy-Skeffington, the son of the nationalists Francis and Hanna Sheehy-Skeffington, who in a letter to the *Irish Times* positioned the altercation at Hume Street as a battle between the forces of greed and avarice and a traditional national character: 'Whether the order to sacrifice eighteenth-century Dublin on the altar of Mammon is signed by John Bull or Kevin Boland is quite immaterial. What is essential is that the sacrifice should not take place; and that the students are now most effectively holding the fort against the Philistines.'[56]

[54] Enda Delaney, 'Modernity, the Past, and Politics in Post War Ireland', 103.
[55] *Irish Times*, 24 December 1969, 6.
[56] *Irish Times*, 30 December 1969, 5.

Whereas at Fitzwilliam Street the preservationists struggled to define how the streetscape formed part of a 'national' heritage, at Hume Street the axes of culture were orientated very differently. Rather, the students positioned themselves as the 'true' protectors of the nation in the face of the corrupted rhetoric and practices of government and finance. For example, in a letter to *Hibernia* McMahon protested against Kevin Boland's attacks on preservationists and asserted the protestors' authentic national identity:

> Of the people taking part in the occupation, three of them, including myself were pupils of Scoil Bhríde, the late Louise Gavan Duffy's school, and received their primary education completely through Irish. Two others were pupils of Coláiste Mhuire and yet another has recently won the best young actor of the year award in the Taibhdhearc na Gaillimhe. At our demonstration on New Year's Day, a large percentage of our placards were in Irish. It seems to me that Mr Boland has been caught with his finger in the proverbial pie and his only way out seem to be to launch attacks on all sides to obscure the real issue; that this so called Republicanism is selling his (and our) capital city to British speculators.[57]

McMahon used the students' competence with, and dedication to, the Irish language as symbolic of their commitment to a true Irishness as understood by Browne and Sheehy-Skeffington. Moreover, she argued that the students were acting in defence of this national culture in their attempt to preserve the houses, while the symbols and discourse of this culture had been expropriated and undermined by an alliance of government and speculators for callous financial gain. Indeed, her statement that Boland's 'so called Republicanism' was selling the 'capital city to British speculators' played on her perception of the contradiction inherent in Boland's position: he used nationalist rhetoric to condemn the campaign, while in sanctioning the development in Hume Street he was also enabling the further ownership of Irish land by British business.

In 1970, Hilary Jenkins described the Gentle Revolution in terms that also applied well to the Hume Street students; she averred that it was characterized by 'a puritan and socialist tone but not libertine. A controlled hippiness—that expresses its distaste for middle-class materialism in a form for which Catholicism and rural character form the chief inspiration.'[58] Indeed, the students' rhetorical adherence to national symbols carried through their modes of protestation; they made a conscious effort

[57] *Hibernia*, 11 April 1970, 9.

[58] Hilary Jenkins, 'Where the Revolution is At', in Philip Pettit (ed.), *The Gentle Revolution* (Dublin, 1969), 72.

to construct their identity around traditional and vernacular notions of Irish culture. They flew a tricolour from the building; played Irish music in the house; wrote many of their banners in Irish; and did not replace the staircase which had been destroyed while the house was vacant, instead using a ladder which could be pulled up in case of attack, 'like Celtic monks hiding from marauding Vikings'.[59] They also rewrote the lyrics to traditional Irish tunes, which they distributed in support of their cause. For example, the students distributed the 'Ballad of Hume Street', a song arranged to the tune of the 'Old Orange Flute', which played on the idea of British speculators as a new incarnation of the Black and Tans.[60] This unity of discourses between cultural forms associated with a traditional Ireland and opposition to urban modernization was not confined to Hume Street; in 1979, Luke Kelly wrote 'Dublin in the Rare Old Times', which linked traditional music and the disappearance of an established Dublin way of life, and became a classic of the genre.[61]

At the end of the 1960s, preservation of the eighteenth-century city came to be part of a host of causes, such as Irish language militancy and the folk music revival, which sought to save the culture of Ireland from the globalizing effects of modernization. At Fitzwilliam Street, architectural theory and nationalism had combined to give the new ESB building an apparently unassailable logic; the future city would be rational and modern, and this rationality would come through the reconstruction of older streets. Moreover, in so doing, national culture, which was constructed through the oppositions between ideas of 'Irish' and 'British' and 'Catholic' and 'Protestant' forms, would also be reinforced. However, at Hume Street, owing to the evolution of both national ideals and urban theory, these two discourses combined with very different effect. The students' conception of a successful urban environment did not stress rationality or functionality, but rather the inverse of these values; instead they looked to the value of the city as residing in its community in the city, and in the eighteenth-century buildings' 'handmade' characteristics. Similarly, although discourses of Irishness were still central to validating the houses' intrinsic worth, the constructions of national culture at Hume Street differed significantly from those used five years earlier. Although the protestors utilized traditional cadences of Irishness, and drew upon the lexicon of nineteenth-century cultural nationalism to call for the street's preservation, the emphasis was now on the 'traditional', 'vernacular', and 'unmaterialistic'

[59] RTÉ Archives, Wednesday Report, 21 January 1970.

[60] Flyer (n.d.), MacEoin papers.

[61] On folk revival, Gerry Smyth, *Noisy Island: A Short History of Irish Popular Music* (Cork, 2005), 22.

nature of Irish culture, which was under threat from the homogenizing impact of international capitalism. The 'other' through which authentic Irish culture was defined was still symbolized by Britain; however, this was no longer embodied by the architecture of colonialism but the contemporary threat of the British speculator and his supporters within the Irish government. Thus the international urban ideals aspired to by the student group had much in common with their notions of the essentialized nation. In this schema, preservation had an intellectual and theoretical coherency: the Georgian houses were part of a broader vernacular and traditional Irish culture, which had to be preserved in the face of the threat of the 'global' and 'rational' impact of modernism. In this context of these new dangers, the extant architecture of Dublin was reconstituted as an authentic Irish cultural production which needed to be defended from modernization, which threatened to make Dublin 'a bit more soulless, a bit more like a tin pot Birmingham'.[62]

'What happened in 1922?': Niall Montgomery's speech

The focus was not the same for all those who protested at Hume Street; in particular the significances that Niall Montgomery saw in the street were very different to the students' concerns. Montgomery's contribution to Irish post-war culture has been largely overlooked. He received training as an architect, but was also an accomplished artist, poet, Joyce scholar, and cultural critic. He was a close friend of Flann O'Brien's, and frequently wrote O'Brien's famous *Irish Times* column, Cruiksheen Lawn, in his absence. He published a vast amount on the subject of the future of Dublin from the 1950s to the 1970s as the Dublin correspondent to the *Architects' Journal*; however, his position altered substantially during this time. For example, in 1955, full of optimism at the changes Le Corbusier's urban revolution could bring, he had described the extant city as an 'empty tomb of... the Unknown Nobleman', and called those who wished it preserved 'rubbernecks' (see Chapter 2). However, this confidence had wholly dissipated by 1970, when his vocal support for the preservation of Hume Street revealed a new cynicism about the changes which had taken place in the city.

On 23 December 1969 Montgomery gave a speech from the window of 45 Hume Street, which was widely reproduced in newspapers, and precipitated an enormous positive reaction. He began by describing how property developers sought to use patriotic rhetoric to position their

[62] Uinseann MacEoin, 'An Open Letter to Sam Stephenson' (n.d.), MacEoin papers.

construction projects as creating a new, more Irish capital for the independent state. Montgomery referred to the practice whereby development firms used the lexicon of Irish nationalist hagiography in an attempt to provide a legitimating vocabulary for their business transactions, and anchor property speculation to ideas of national rejuvenation. This was achieved through the use of names in Irish or from Irish mythology for office blocks, and by publishing planning notices solely in the Irish language.[63] However, he believed that,

> Some of these patriotic characters wouldn't care if George I, George II, George III, George IV, and the old Duke of Cumberland, Billy the Butcher himself were to come back in the morning, provided that they kept their hungry Hanoverian hands off the sacred property market.[64]

Montgomery condemned the use of 'patriotic' rhetoric to justify the destruction of the extant city. He mocked the sincerity of the developers' patriotism, arguing that discourses of Irishness were instrumentalized in order to disguise planning appeals, suppress criticism, and provide a positive sheen to profiteering. A similar position was taken by Uinseann MacEoin, who wrote with regard to a developer named Setanta's office project in Nassau Street that, 'if ever a development group hiding under the patriotic name of the young Cuchulainn, represented a powerful phalanx of wrap-the-green-flag-round-me boys Irish nationalism and the know-how of London finance this is one'.[65] For Montgomery and MacEoin, 'national' images were turned on their head as patriotic rhetoric was used for the profit of the political elite and the construction industry, while the destruction of the city was leading to unliveable landscapes, housing shortages, and the evacuation of inner-city populations.

While this condemnation of the 'selling out' of national rhetoric echoed Mahon's concerns, it led Montgomery to different conclusions. Instead of condemning the government for having reneged on foundational national ideals, he instead questioned the validity of this ideology. He did this by challenging traditional notions of Dublin as a 'colonial city' or being less 'Irish' than the rest of the country:

[63] The most famous use of Irish to conceal the intent of the applicant was the case in which the Phoenix Assurance Company applied for permission to demolish a portion of the Kildare Street Club, the Victorian masterpiece in Venetian Gothic style by Benjamin Woodward. The planning notice appeared in Irish in the *Irish Times* on 15 February 1967. For a contemporary discussion of this see *Hibernia*, 13 December 1968–2 January 1969, 2.

[64] Correspondence and notes regarding speech, Montgomery papers. Also published in full *Irish Times*, 31 December 1969, 10.

[65] *Build*, September 1968, 9.

> No one who has ever set foot in Manchester or Leeds or Sheffield will think of Dublin as an English city. No one who has ever seen the glories of Bath and Cheltenham will pretend that it is a Georgian city and maybe no one who has been to Galway will call it an Irish city. But to hell with that. This is something else. This is Dublin city, made by Dublin men and lived in by Dublin men for hundreds and hundreds of years. I won't go in for the sentimentality of saying that the city was built by ordinary Dublin men. There was nothing ordinary about them. They were most superior men—bricklayers, masons, carpenters, joiners, plasterers, plumbers, slaters, tilers.[66]

In his eulogization of the city, its architecture, and craftsmen, Montgomery made a pointed criticism of traditional constructions of nationalism which had framed political rhetoric since the state's foundation. By laying emphasis on the 'Dublin' rather than the 'Irish' nature of the houses, his campaign for the preservation of Hume Street discarded the categorization that would rank the urban terraces as less 'Irish' than rural cottages. Montgomery recognized the city's heterogeneity as a distinct facet of the city's identity rather than a mark of its foreignness; his declaration that 'no one who has been to Galway will call it an Irish city' was a bold statement of Dublin's ambiguous position as the historic nexus and dissemination point of British culture. In so doing, Montgomery articulated a distinct Dublin sense of identity which, in his view, had been sidelined by the monolithic cultural dogmatism of cultural nationalism. This was a steady theme throughout his work at the end of the 1960s; in a similar piece on Dublin Corporation in 1969, he wrote cynically of the destruction of the city as the result of the 'success of Fianna Fáil's cultural revolution—in which the Irish Petronius, Jimin Mháire Thaidhg, is the analogue of Chairman Mao', which forced the citizens of Dublin to 'keep quiet about their history and their traditions'.[67]

Finally, he ended the speech with a long meditation on what he termed the 'prostitution' of the country: the government-sanctioned destruction of the country's natural and material heritage for profit. He ended by linking this profiteering to the wholesale corruption of the ideals of independence:

> It's reasonable, it's not sentimental—I'm not making any apology for it—at this stage to look at the spirit of Ireland today, the spirit of a rich country, and to contrast it with the spirit of the Irish in servitude. It's reasonable and not sentimental now to think about the men that went out in '98 and '48 and '67 and '16 and '22. What were the poor old angashores[68] thinking

[66] *Irish Times*, 31 December 1969, 10.
[67] 'Dublin Corporation's Dublin', Montgomery papers.
[68] 'Angashore': from the Irish 'ainniseoir', meaning a miserable, wretched person.

> about at all? What happened in 1922? Was there a revolution or just a take-over of the machinery of government by a lot of hard faced business men? What happened to the revolution?[69]

Like Mahon, Montgomery had lost faith in the project of urban modernization. This had important national implications. As seen in Chapter 4, throughout the 1960s, the reconstruction of Dublin had been linked to broader images of national renewal. As the project of urban modernization faltered in the latter part of the decade, the national rhetoric with which it was associated was called into question. Moreover, developers' use of discourses of Gaelic culture to justify speculative office development and the dispossession of communities from the city centre showed how a rhetoric which had been associated with the movement for national independence had been expropriated by elites and foreign investors to use for profit. However, Montgomery's final point went further than this. His concluding paragraph, in particular his final sentence, 'What happened in 1922? What happened to the revolution?', linked the destruction of these houses to wider corruption and wider failings of independence.[70] For Montgomery, the profiteering and corruption so visible at Hume Street was a resultant of the failure of a social revolution to take place alongside the political revolution; in making this connection, he went further than any other protestor in using the situation at Hume Street to question the very validity of the form independence had taken.

Montgomery linked a range of seemingly disparate themes in this speech, and used Hume Street to make broader criticisms of Irish politics and culture. For him, the destruction of the houses represented abandonment of the ideals of the state's founders: housing shortages; a narrow definition of the nation; the corruption of the political elite; and the corrosive impact of modern architecture and town planning in creating dehumanising environments in which communities failed to develop. Montgomery simultaneously looked back to a less materialistic Ireland reified in the landscape and condemned the destruction and dispossession which had been validated by these same ideals. Thus, the Georgian houses—once the homes of the elite—came to symbolize those dispossessed by the political, social, and cultural norms of the 1960s. For Montgomery, their preservation symbolized a heterogeneous Irishness; a Jane Jacobs-style organic approach to town planning; the preservation of working-class communities; and resistance to corruption. In Dublin, where the historic city lacked a state-led interpretation, a range of causes

[69] *Irish Times*, 31 December 1969, 10.
[70] *Irish Times*, 31 December 1969, 10.

could be articulated through the preservation of the eighteenth-century streets. Montgomery's campaign for the preservation of the houses, like those living in the Gardiner estate, interrogated the teleology of Irish history and constructions of national identity, prefiguring the crisis in the writing of the history of the island that would take place in the following decade. While conservation of the historic fabric of a city has often been read as a reactionary response to social and spatial modernization, for Montgomery and many others, preservationism became a progressive, oppositional cause, which revealed the contradictions inherent in Irish life.

VIOLENCE AND EVICTION

The student group stayed in the house for six months, and continued to clean and restore the property as media attention slowly died away. But they could not remain indefinitely undisturbed. In May, the Arms Crisis was a fundamental turning point, precipitating a changing of the guard in the upper echelons of government: Haughey, Boland, and Blaney left their posts, and it was widely assumed that Lynch's government would fall. This political crisis had an impact on the continuing stand-off at Hume Street. An election now seemed probable, and was commonly expected to depose Fianna Fáil from power. Green Properties could not be assured that a new administration would be as accommodating towards their plans; indeed, many Labour and Fine Gael politicians had been prominent supporters of the students' protest. In response to this evolving political landscape, on the morning of 7 June, the company acted decisively to remove the students from the house.

The fighting, which began on Sunday morning, continued over three days. The students built barricades in Hume Street and the laneways behind, which they manned in an effort to prevent the demolition team reaching the house, while legal injunctions were sought to prevent the buildings' destruction.[71] On Tuesday afternoon, Conor Cruise O'Brien and Benjamin Spock gave speeches in support of the students' stand.[72] When the assembled crowd was asked to join in the defence of the buildings, 'hundreds of those listening moved forward and sat down outside the houses. The footpaths were completely covered by seated people and the alleyways at the rear were jammed tight with crowds.'[73] But even as

[71] *Irish Times*, 8 June 1970, 13; *Irish Times*, 9 June 1970, 3.
[72] *Irish Times*, 10 June 1970, 7.
[73] *Irish Press*, 10 June 1970, 4.

Spock and Cruise O'Brien addressed the students and their supporters, a meeting was taking place between the Minister for Finance, George Colley, the developers, and representatives of RIAI, An Taisce, and the DCG. They agreed that the houses would be returned to Green Properties.[74] Later that night, the student group finally left the house; with substantial sections of the eighteenth-century buildings now destroyed after three days of demolition work, they had little left to fight for. Upon their exit, they released a statement which thanked a diverse group of allies, including 'Sinn Féin, the Georgian Society, An Taisce, and the Bricklayers Association'.[75]

The students' condemnation of urban modernization was reinforced by images of the protest reproduced across the country. During the three days of violence in St Stephen's Green, the clashes between the students and the security firm filled the front pages of all the national newspapers, accompanied by images of crowds, shattered buildings, and bruised students. The pictures of the Gardaí standing by during this attack by a private security firm on the unarmed, sleeping students was an obvious and unsettling image of how the violent power of the state was implemented. In particular, photographers focused on images of female students with tear-stained faces, in the nightgowns which they had been wearing when the demolition squad arrived. The *Irish Press* described the 'silent and embarrassed' crowd 'as golden haired Marie McMahon, wearing a soiled orange frock and with plasters on her arms, burst into tears as she described the incidents'.[76] Indeed, some of the images of female students were so exploitative that they were ridiculed for their sexual content in the following issue of *Hibernia*. The discourse of 'rape' was frequently used to describe the destruction of the city, and now this metaphor took on a new reality through these images of violence against women. Discourses of the rape of the city were tangibly manifested, as the forced entry into Hume Street in the night was portrayed as a bodily assault, revealing the destructive impact of urban modernity through an emotive visual lexicon.

The architectural solution which eventually resolved the confrontation was first suggested in an editorial in the *Irish Times* on 4 March 1970:

> In London, modern offices have been built behind the Nash facades of Regent's Park, and the same has happened with many picturesque old buildings along the Amsterdam canals ... This could be done in the case of Hume Street. It is true that it would represent a compromise. Conservationists could lament the disappearance of the interiors, and say that the facades

[74] *Irish Builder and Engineer*, 13 June 1970, 377; *An Tasice News*, Summer 1970, 2.
[75] *Irish Times*, 10 June 1970, 1; *Irish Times*, 11 June 1970, 15; *Irish Press*, 10 June 1970, 1.
[76] *Irish Press*, 8 June 1970, 3.

> which needed rebuilding were 'fake Georgian'. Those concerned with housing could object to yet another street being turned over to office use. Green Properties could say that a more modern treatment would bring a greater return for their money. But the original purpose of the battle would have been achieved, and are there other alternatives?[77]

The next day, the Green Property Company released a statement saying it would be happy to follow the suggestion in the *Irish Times*. Although the *Times*'s proposal was for the retention of the original façades with the construction of new offices behind them, the Green Property company offered—grudgingly—to construct the new building with replica façades:

> Mr Sam Stephenson has been engaged as our architect for the development and we have perfect confidence in his ability to design a building which would be homogeneous with the area. We do not know of any reason why our company should interfere with his design. If however, Mr Stephenson feels that he could consider a change in the elevational treatment we would not interfere.[78]

The proposal to change the 'elevational treatment' indicated that the adherence to an eighteenth-century aesthetic would be of the most superficial nature, and the suggestion immediately split conservationists. Kevin Nowlan welcomed the idea, as did Joe McCullough of An Taisce, who stressed the need for an 'authentic' treatment of the elevation. He stated that any such restoration 'would naturally have to ensure that materials and details should either be careful reproductions of the existing ones or that the original fanlights, balconies and so on should be incorporated from the demolished building'.[79] However, not all those who campaigned for the preservation of Hume Street were united in support of this solution. Uinseann MacEoin stated in his journal that, 'if the buildings are knocked and a massive pastiche Georgian put up on both corners it will not be a compromise, it will be a standing public ridicule'.[80] Moreover, this solution was denounced by the students in occupation. Describing this as a 'meaningless compromise', their statement said: 'we are amazed that An Taisce, the Dublin Civic Group and the *Irish Times* should entertain such a solution. Is Hume Street to become a stage set? We will not let this happen.'[81] Although the *Irish Times* had stated that 'the original purpose

[77] *Irish Times*, 4 March 1970, 11.
[78] *Irish Times*, 5 March 1970, 5.
[79] *Irish Times*, 5 March 1970, 5.
[80] *Plan*, April 1970, 10.
[81] *Irish Times*, 6 March 1970, 6.

of the battle would have been achieved' in the construction of an office block with neo-classical façades, rather the inverse was true.[82] For those concerned with the retention of eighteenth-century architecture, the pastiche building would have no value whatsoever. Furthermore, popular support for the campaign had coalesced around opposition to speculation, planning corruption, and decreasing central city housing, which would not be ameliorated by the building's reconstruction as 'Georgian' offices.[83] Despite these problems, it was this scheme which was eventually put into action, as the student group was left out of the negotiations which ended the violence of the final days, and the rapid demolition of the houses by the demolition team meant that some form of reconstruction was necessary. The agreement reached between government, speculators, and conservation bodies stated that 'the façade will be in a manner which will maintain as far as possible the existing quality, character and features of the streetscape'.[84] Thus the two corners of Hume Street and St Stephen's Green were finally rebuilt as luxury offices in an eighteenth-century idiom.

Only five years earlier, a reproduction façade was considered totally unfeasible by groups on both sides of the debate regarding Fitzwilliam Street, as pastiche lacked the 'honesty' and 'authenticity' demanded by both preservationists and modern architects. But architecture's intellectual climate had changed profoundly since the early 1960s. Robert Venturi's claim in 1972 that 'architects can no longer afford to be intimidated by the puritanically moral language of orthodox Modern architecture' heralded a new interrogation of the formerly canonical maxims of modernism.[85] In this period, the architectural community began to reject the self-evidence of the 'truth' of functionalist design, which had made modernism a doctrine rather than a style, and began to question whether it had more intrinsic worth than any other mode of construction. Not only was pastiche economically viable, but this questioning of the tenets of modernism also made it morally justifiable. This alteration in architectural theory, alongside the declining confidence in Ireland's project of modernization, the fracturing of national discourses, and the rise of the importance of ideas of 'authentic' and 'local' cultures, meant that it became feasible to construct the new office block in the neo-classical idiom. This was the first time pastiche had been used for such a large and

[82] *Irish Times*, 4 March 1970, 11.
[83] Harvey, *The Condition of Postmodernity*, 85–7.
[84] *An Taisce News*, Summer 1970, 2.
[85] Robert Venturi, *Complexity and Contradiction in Architecture* (New York, 1972), 12.

high-profile development, and it set a precedent for 'Georgian' office developments in much of the central area during the 1970s and 1980s.

The Battle of Hume Street may have been, ultimately, a demoralizing failure for many of those most committed to saving the site, but it also resulted in the formation of two groups which became important and dynamic forces in the campaign for the improvement of the city's environment. Deirdre McMahon—better known as Deirdre Kelly—went on to found the Living City Group alongside Niall Montgomery and Aidan Kelly (her husband and partner of Uinseann MacEoin in MacEoin Kelly Architects) in 1972.[86] The group campaigned for the regulated growth of the city and for the protection of working-class communities. The statement released upon their foundation emphasized the centrality of people to the retention of place: 'The essence of a city is its people, living in communities which have developed from generation to generation, giving character each to its own neighbourhood. The city's true life is in the life of such communities. In Dublin, private enterprise is destroying those communities, expelling inhabitants to the old suburbs and to new reservations outside the city, replacing the citizens and their houses with offices and warehouses empty at night of all life and all activity.'[87] Throughout the 1970s and 1980s, the group was active in supporting what had by then been defined as 'inner city' communities, and protesting against developments that would have an impact upon the life of the city.

For twenty years after the Battle of Hume Street, the DCG continued to meet every second Monday, and became a highly significant voice in shaping the future of Dublin's landscape. The organization was led by Professor Kevin Nowlan, who had first become involved in conservation after being invited to a meeting regarding the preservation of Tailors' Hall by the historian Professor Theo Moody of Trinity College Dublin.[88] Alongside Nowlan, F. H. Walker, Sheila Carden, Desmond and Mariga Guinness, Uinseann MacEoin, Ivor Underwood, Austin Dunphy, Con Maxwell, and Donald Keoghan were all active in the organization.[89] But the group was much more informal than the other conservationist bodies, having neither a structure, a constitution, nor a membership fee. The group met in F. H. Walker's optician's shop at 38 Grafton Street; they would go down the lists of planning applications issued by both Dublin and Dun Laoghaire corporations and pick out the applications which appeared to be complex or large-scale.[90] A volunteer would then go to the

86 Living City Group correspondence, Montgomery papers.
87 Living City Group, *Dublin – A Living City* (Dublin, 1972), 5.
88 Interview with Kevin Nowlan.
89 Interview with Sheila Carden and F. H. Walker.
90 Interview with Kevin Nowlan.

planning office to look up further information, and report to the group at the next meeting. If a planning application was deemed to be environmentally or socially damaging, objections would be lodged, statements would be made to the press, and the developer would be approached directly.[91] Their concerns were more diverse than those of the IGS and An Taisce, encompassing not only historic preservation but also low-income housing, green spaces, and the provision of amenities.[92] Having no formal membership and no 'expert' qualifications was part of their platform; they expressed an opinion as citizens, not as experts or planners.[93] In this citizen-based, amateur approach to regulating the city that gained its authority from a feeling for the city rather than professional qualifications, the group paralleled the growth of many similar environmental movements across Europe. However, despite this self-proclaimed amateurism, the group developed an expertise in how planning mechanisms functioned in order to effectively challenge developments.[94]

During the Hume Street occupation, Sheila Wheeler wrote to Niall Montgomery:

> Last time I was in Dublin I took a taxi and asked the driver what he felt about all the demolitions going on, and he burst into a magnificent speech himself, about how he and his family had lived in an old house where 'the plasterwork of the ceilings was so beautiful you never got tired of looking at it', and however much money you had now you wouldn't be able to buy a house like that or find a plasterer who could do it for you. So it seems to be only the bureaucrats and the businessmen who are happy with what is going on.[95]

By 1970, the view Wheeler expressed had become a commonplace: that the rationality of the bureaucrat and the profiteering of the businessman were having only a detrimental effect on the urban environment. This was, however, a new interpretation of city space. From the foundation of the state, modern design had been a way of pushing forward an Irish form of progress. Modern architecture was understood to bring into being a new society which was simultaneously forward-looking and yet, liberated from British influence, acting as the inheritor of 'true' Irish culture. Furthermore, modernism also supplied answers to the chronic problems of

[91] Interview with Carden and Walker.

[92] IAA Dublin Civic Group papers, 'A Future for Our Past': Report on Seminar 'The Changing City' held on 4 October 1975 as part of European Architectural Heritage Year 1975.

[93] Interview with Carden and Walker.

[94] See Lionel Fleming, *Head or Harp?* (Dublin, 1965).

[95] Letter from Sheila Wheeler, secretary of the *Architects' Journal*, to Niall Montgomery, 27 January 1970, Montgomery papers.

poverty and underdevelopment. In the early 1960s, Lemass had made the physical transformation of the environment central to his rhetoric. However, the consensus surrounding this Irish modernity slowly corroded throughout the later 1960s; Lynch was unable to sustain the popular enthusiasm for modernization that Lemass had generated. Modernism may have provided the conduit to better housing and new forms of wealth creation, but it was also seen to create housing shortages, new inequalities, and corruption. Wheeler's anecdotal exchange with her taxi driver was symptomatic of these shifts; his emphasis on the craftsmanship of his former home revealed a city which not only had value in its construction but also a value which could not be replicated through contemporary technologies.

During the week of the stand-off at Hume Street between students and demolition team, the three national daily papers led with the story of the protest every day. Violent images of young girls screaming as they were attacked by demolition men dominated the coverage, visualizing the destructive impact of the modernization of the city and gaining mass attention. The preservation of the city was no longer a minority campaign, and its members could no longer be dismissed as 'belted earls and intellectuals' or republican activists. Instead, the profile and positioning of the students was middle-class and middle-of-the-road. While the students engaged with the memes of global protest, their anti-capitalism was lukewarm in tone, and derived more from a parochial rejection of the economic reforms of the 1960s than from the Frankfurter school. Similarly, their conception of the Hume Street affair was in general conservative; they used it as a platform to criticize the government for reneging on the nation's foundational values rather than for the limitations of that vision. However, theirs was not the only interpretation of the stand-off. Niall Montgomery's speeches and letters were published in all the main newspapers, and his understanding of why the houses were demolished was widely disseminated. He went further than the students in arguing that national constructions had served only to ignore and undervalue the heritage of the people of Dublin, leading to the demolition of the city and the degradation of their environment. Notwithstanding the variety of interpretations, the protest had an important impact. Through positioning themselves as a more authentic voice of a true Irish culture, the protesters expropriated ownership of national ideals from the government, and through linking preservation of the city to protests against corruption and modernization, they broadened its appeal to a wider audience. Hume Street was by no means the last eighteenth-century building to be the subject of controversy in the city, but it represented the moment when the popular mood towards changes to the city shifted definitively.

Conclusion

The Invention of Georgian Dublin

The Corporation's first development plan was instituted in 1971, for the first time formally acknowledging the existence of the city's eighteenth-century built environment:

> The Planning Authority is aware of the great quality and value of Dublin's architectural heritage and in particular of those buildings, streets and squares which constitute a unique example of eighteenth-century architecture. It is also conscious of its responsibilities to secure the preservation of this heritage which constitutes an essential element in the character and historical development of the city.[1]

Not only did the plan recognize the importance of Dublin's historic built environment, but it also constituted the first formal attempt made by Dublin Corporation to define which parts of the city were worthy of preservation. It was also the first time that a list of protected buildings was given legal authority. The selection of structures was compiled by Richard Llewelyn-Davies, the British architect who earned his place in British history as the planner of Milton Keynes. However, it was based substantively on a list compiled by An Taisce in 1967.[2] Three types of buildings were specified. The buildings in List B were given the most protection, with the planning scheme stating that it was the 'objective of the Planning Authority, in the interests of amenity, to secure the preservation of the buildings and other structures of the groups of buildings specified' in this list. Furthermore, it was 'the intention of the Planning Authority, in the event of an application being made for permission to alter or demolish any of the buildings or other structures specified in List A, to consider the preservation of such buildings or groups of buildings'.[3] List C detailed state-owned buildings which the Corporation wished to secure for preservation, but as they were in the ownership of the Office of Public Works, it was unable

[1] Dublin Corporation, *Dublin City Development Plan 1968* (Dublin, 1968), 23.
[2] *Dublin City Development Plan*, 24.
[3] *Dublin City Development Plan*, 25.

to do more than indicate this wish.[4] The area covered by these listed buildings was approximately 16 per cent of the central area within the canals and 2.5 per cent of the area within the city boundary.[5] These lists included not only Ely Place and Fitzwilliam Street on List B, but also less well-known or wealthy areas of the city on List A, such as selected buildings in Eccles Street, Dominick Street, Mountjoy Square, and Harcourt Street.[6]

Although the scheme was a great step forward for those who wished to preserve Dublin's built environment, it contained many flaws. In listing individual buildings for preservation, it ignored the fact that the aesthetic impact of much of Dublin came from the appearance of the buildings in groups; it also meant that those buildings not listed had no means of preservation. Importantly, the list was compiled solely from external appearance, so a great deal of fine plasterwork was destroyed in the following years. In defining the 'value' of Dublin as lying in the late eighteenth-century architecture of the east of the city, it also meant denying legal protection to many important buildings which did not match the appearance of the neo-classical Pembroke Estate, which came to define a 'postcard' image of Dublin. Indeed, in selecting, designating, and defining where the 'historic' value of the city lay, it created a static image of the city's value which contrasted with the fluidity with which the city was used and understood by its inhabitants and residents. Despite these drawbacks, this was a key moment for preservationists, as it provided them with a formal list of buildings which had to be protected, and a starting point from which to campaign for further development controls.

However, even as the 1971 scheme was implemented, the nature of town planning was changing. In 1975, the London-based Lance Wright and Kenneth Browne published *A Future for Dublin*, originally as a report in the *Architectural Review*, and later as a book under the same name. This document provides a useful counterpoint for exploring Irish state planning and the evolution of the ideas of the city in the later twentieth century. Wright and Browne approached the city as a totality, and used town planning to create a fluid schema which would evolve as the city evolved, rather than an 'end-state' vision of the city. Although their report recommended the preservation of much more of the city than extant town plans, its focus was not upon conservation but instead on 'urbanism'. This reflected a new attitude to urban space, which was constituted in both new language and new approaches. Indeed, the report was concerned not only with Dublin but rather used the city as a case study of the problems

4 *Dublin City Development Plan*, 26.
5 *Dublin City Development Plan*, 26.
6 *Dublin City Development Plan*, 27–34.

of the modern city, and to propose a world-wide reconceptualization of urban design.

Wright set up his study of Dublin by posing a question about the future of the city which presaged Marshall Bermann's vision of modernity as a unity of creative and destructive forces. 'The "problem" of Dublin is primarily the problem of the central area: "can she become a truly modern capital city without destroying herself?"'[7] He went on to provide the answer to his own question:

> If you take the conventional interpretation of the 'modern city' the answer to this question must be 'No'; for the conventional interpretation of a modern city centre is one in which the motor car is free to penetrate at high speed to any part of the centre; in which the central area buildings are very large indeed (to justify all this accessibility); and in which the main components of the city—the commercial core, the industry, the housing, are all in large dollops and separated from one another. Dublin has already been manipulated to some extent in these three directions: she has her over-big office buildings, she has her patches of industrial blight, she has her big municipal housing estates right out in the blue; but these manipulations have been to her disadvantage. The argument that we want to put in this issue is that this conventional image of the modern city is in fact wrong. It is wrong because it destroys the urban community, dividing it up into one-class ghettos; because it creates an intolerable environment—both to experience (fumes and danger) and to look at (impersonal spirit crushing buildings); and because, by putting the various components so far from one another (homes, workplaces), it *creates* a traffic problem which no system of transport can solve satisfactorily.[8]

For Wright, the values which defined the modern city were not creating an ideal environment but rather something intrinsically destructive. Zoning was creating inhuman environments; cars and inner city motorways were seen to be polluting the inner city; and skyscrapers and office blocks were destroying communities. He went on to identify Dublin's five main problems, which had arisen from the imposition of these modern values: planning blight, destructive motorways, dispersed housing, an over-concentration of offices in the central area, and dirty industry. Thus Wright saw the modern city—with Dublin as the instructive paradigm—as caught in a destructive bind: in trying to fulfil the unassailable criteria of full car ownership, low-density segregated living in the suburbs, and high-density offices in the centre, the city was ultimately destroying itself.

[7] Lance Wright and Kenneth Browne, *A Future for Dublin* (London, 1975), 270.

[8] Wright and Browne, *A Future for Dublin*, 270.

As a solution, Wright proposed a very different idea of urban form to that advocated throughout the 1960s and inscribed in the 1971 town plan. Indeed, in following through his train of thought, he proposed a revolution in the way that cities were designed and understood. 'The aim of any sane urbanism must surely be to undo this disastrous process and, by a mixture of civic power and civic inducement to draw the magnets back into the city; so that we see a steady return to a mixed community.'[9] In Dublin he saw a precedent close to home for the ideal mixed community which he advocated. 'The great social virtue of the Georgian city fabric is that it enclosed a mixed society. Though the inequalities of fortune were far more gross than they are today, the spectrum of classes were never far removed from one another. Furthermore, the various work places, the places where things are made and the places where things are sold, were all closely related, so that no one had far to go to the shops or to work.'[10] Thus for Browne and Wright, the eighteenth-century city stood in contradistinction to the scientifically planned twentieth-century city, and represented much more than an architectural entity. The eighteenth-century city represented an unplanned, unmodernized, unrationalized alternative future based on a rejection of brutalist solutions and quantitative planning mechanisms.

Wright's manifesto also reflected a major shift in attitudes towards technology. He argued that up to this point society had 'given [itself] up to [technology] regardless of consequences', leading to many negative results. Instead of this approach, he advocated a change of tack, using 'skills and knowledge to restore the values that have been accidentally destroyed'.[11] However, this was by no means an anti-modern position. Indeed, the advent of telecommunications technology allowed cities to modernize without being rebuilt:

> Thus the admiration which everyone instinctively feels for Georgian Dublin is not only an *architectural* admiration; much of the satisfaction these streets and squares inspire comes from their being an exemplar of a satisfactory sort of city life. Thus it is that the saving of eighteenth-century Dublin is not really a matter of saving bricks and mortar for their own sake, but of saving Dublin's community life; and of defending the 'ideal of a city' that Dublin represents against the distortions which we have been wrongly told are the price of modernity.[12]

[9] Wright and Browne, *A Future for Dublin,* 284.
[10] Wright and Browne, *A Future for Dublin,* 284.
[11] Wright and Browne, *A Future for Dublin,* 282.
[12] Wright and Browne, *A Future for Dublin,* 284.

Wright's conception of modernity was thus far more subtle and more receptive to the pasts implicit in its construction than that which had guided Dublin's planners. This city of the future envisaged by Wright was therefore also a 'modern' city, but it was one which was very different to that planned by Myles Wright and Nathaniel Lichfield. It was a city which preserved more than it replaced, but did so by utilizing the developments of the 'telecommunications revolution' to minimize the need for offices in the central area and inner-city motorways. Indeed, he went full circle to evoke the heterogeneity and diversity of eighteenth-century Dublin as the model of the city of the future.

From the late 1950s to the mid-1960s, the modernization of the capital was, in general, well received. Economic reforms were introduced, and the offices, widened roads, and suburbanization of the city were understood to be the spatial concomitants of these changes. But this spatial transformation also had an ideological impetus. Through the imposition of new macro and micro urban forms on the old city, town planners and politicians alike realized a vision of a city populated by producers, consumers, and churchgoers. The new urban landscape brought into being a society better suited for participation in the European economic world, centred on the family, and still defined by the symbolisms of independence. Indeed, it spatialized the economic ideology of the Lemass years, and was an important, if yet unrecognized, constituent of Ireland's modernization.

However, the consensus which surrounded this process of modernization began to fracture from the middle of the decade, and had collapsed by its end. Housing shortages, residential displacement, cleared sites, planning blight, and imposing office developments seemed to be the most visible manifestations of a partially finished project of urban renewal. Moreover, an architectural style which had promised a new society was soon co-opted by a wholly different process: rather than bringing social justice or national renewal, it became part of an international financial system based on speculation on land prices in a rising market; and this gap between aspiration and practice led to controversy and dissent. From the middle of the decade, there was a continuous, highly charged debate in the media and opposition on the streets to the impact of modernization and the visible loss of old buildings. Related to this, there was a new-found awareness of the 'heritage' of the city. Indeed, 'Georgian Dublin' was invented during the 1960s. It was in this period that the phase began to be used to describe not only Gandon's landmark buildings but also the 'characteristic' streets and squares of the city. That is not to say, however, that all opposition to urban change took the same path. Indeed, it is notable just how malleable notions of the value of the city and ideas of the past were. During the 1960s, Dublin was a place where there were multiple, jarring, and overlapping readings of urban space, and where history and meaning were unfixed. In each of the streets discussed, geographical location and present politics combined to bring differing sets of issues to the fore; notions of authenticity were in constant flux, determined by the shifting cultural politics of modernization. Indeed, the future of Dublin was by no means predetermined by its past, but rather the past was constantly reformulated as the product of contemporary debates and historical memory.

Opposition took a variety of forms. Letters were written, applications were lodged through formal planning mechanisms, petitions signed, meetings held, as well as marches, demonstrations, squats, and sit-ins. Over the course of the 1960s, the modes of opposition changed as protestors both responded to the increasingly bureaucratic state and became more militant in their tactics. Urban protest also took in a heterogeneous collection of individuals and groups. The Irish Georgian Society, the Dublin Housing Action Committee, the Dublin Civic Group, and the residents of North Great George's Street were united in their opposition to the changes taking place to the city, but separated in their approach and final goals. It is notable that women, almost invisible in political and planning circles, were central to the campaigns for the preservation of housing and architecture in the inner city. The working-class communities of the inner city, however, although most affected by the processes shaping Dublin, were least represented in the public debates surrounding the form the new city should take. Their voice was frequently ignored altogether or, when it appeared, was mediated though the discourse of political activists and journalists for a variety of purposes. This shift in methods and growth in campaigning groups reflected Ireland's swift evolution in this decade. In this time the country both became a more modern polity and participated in an international decline of deference, and this change in tone and type of protest reflected this. Indeed, this study of the evolution of the profile of urban preservationism vividly indicates how much Ireland changed between the Whitaker Report and entry into the EEC.

An examination of the debates regarding the built form of Dublin provides a fresh understanding of the 1960s as a period rich with debate regarding the nature of the nation and the state. A turn towards urban politics also demonstrates that protest and dissent was far more diverse and complex than allowed by the historical profession's conventional focus on tracing the roots of the rebirth of violence in Northern Ireland; indeed, many of the very active and influential protest movements of the decade have been ignored by this present-centred approach to the past.

But just as the city envisaged by town planners imposed an ideologically imbued urban form on the capital, so in challenging these physical changes, preservationists and other urban protestors challenged the substance of modernization. When families refused to leave their tenements, they raised awareness of the negative effects of modernization; when DHAC campaigned against housing shortages and the residential denudation of the inner city, they challenged the place of capitalism and traditional republican ideology in Irish life; in preventing an eighteenth-century house being turned into an office block, the Hume Street group contested the globalization of the Irish economy. Through turning to an examination of the politics of urban space in the 1960s, we discover a society where people were engaged in a vigorous debate regarding the nature of state and nation, and reveal new complexities to the process and reception of modernization.

It was not only Ireland's contemporary situation which was interrogated by urban activism but also the politics of the Irish past. The cultural clash between Irish-Ireland and Anglo-Ireland, which had, in the early years of the century, produced a tension leading to creative effervescence, had by the 1960s become a stultifying bind, whereby architecture and artistic production could be judged on national and sectarian criteria. But this evolved throughout the decade as the city changed. When the eighteenth-century streets of the inner city were destroyed to make way for office blocks, shopping precincts, and motorways, the destruction disturbed and brought to the surface the dormant pasts which had taken place in these streets. These included not only a Protestant nation but also working-class Dublin life, and republican-socialist political activism. Thus urban protest came to represent not only the problems of the present but also dissonant national trajectories. Urban activism became a means by which sidelined groups both spatialized dissent and recreated their own vision of Ireland's past and future. This was reinforced by those, such as the Hume Street students, who approached urban preservation from a different angle, seeing it as the logical conclusion of a traditional nationalism which had been abandoned by the state's government and elite. The culmination of this activism had a corrosive impact on Ireland's national modernity. A nation which had been defined by its search for the authentic Gaelic spirit of the western isles was fundamentally challenged in the later 1960s through the politics of urban heritage.

Bibliography

PRIMARY SOURCES

1. Manuscript and archival sources

Private collection

Uinseann MacEoin

National Library

Niall Montgomery Acc. 6475

Irish Architectural Archive

Dublin Civic Group
Frederick Rogerson
Raymond McGrath
RD.D.110: North Great George's Street
RP.C.28.3: *Architects' Journal*
RP.D.307.8: St Catherine's Church, Thomas Street, Dublin 8
RP.D.2.5: Tailors' Hall
RP.D.202.6: ESB Architectural Competition for a Head Office Building
RW.B.88: Irish Georgian Society
RW.D.15: Tailors' Hall
RW.D.98: Fitzwilliam Street
RW.D.99: Lower Fitzwilliam Street–ESB Head Office
RW.D.130: Henrietta Street
RW.D.203: Mountjoy Square
RW.D.355: Gardiner Street
RW.D.569: Kildare Place

Dublin Corporation Archive

Minutes of the Corporation of Dublin 1950–80
Reports and Printed Documents of the Corporation of Dublin 1950–80

National Archive of Ireland

Department of the Taoiseach
S2123D: Royal Hospital Kilmainham, Acquisition and Use
S5004C: National Monuments, Buildings of Historical Importance etc
S5004D/94: National Monuments, Buildings of Historical Importance etc
S5004E/ 61: National Monuments, Buildings of Historical Importance etc
S5004 E/62: Society for the Preservation of Historic Ireland

S14922B: Arts Council Establishment
S16682B: Folk Museum Proposal
S16851A: Powerscourt Estate General
S16851B: Powerscourt Estate General
S16904B/95: Canals: Maintenance etc. Grand Canal: Future of Dublin Section
S16968D/95: Local Government Planning and Development Act 1963
S17096A: ESB Building Fitzwilliam Street
S17096/A/1/63: ESB Building Fitzwilliam Street
S17096 A/2: ESB Building Fitzwilliam Street
S17096/95: ESB Building Fitzwilliam Street
S17096/95B: ESB Building Fitzwilliam Street
S17486/63: Dangerous Buildings Public Inquiry Dublin 1963
S17486/95: Dangerous Buildings Public Inquiry Dublin 1963
S17537 A/63: Housing Legislation
97/6/88: Dangerous Buildings
97/6/101: Department of the Taoiseach–Housing Legislation
99/1/406: Housing Legislation
99-1-535: Housing Act 1969
2000/6/423: Department of Taoiseach (1) Dublin Housing Action Committee: Agitation 1968–; (2) National Housing Committee
2000/6/599: Housing Legislation
2000/6/633: Housing Act 1969
2001/6/262: Building Industry (including Housing)

Office of the President
PRES 2000/15/55: Tailors' Hall
PRES 2005-160-63: Riverstown House–Restoration by Irish Georgian Society

2. Printed primary sources

a. Journals and newspapers
Agenor
Architects' Journal
Architectural Review
Build
Building
Business and Finance
Christus Rex
Communist Comment
Country Life
Evening Herald
Evening Press
Forgnán

Hibernia
Irish Architect and Contractor
Irish Builder and Engineer
Irish Contractor
Irish Independent
Irish Press
Irish Socialist
Irish Times
Irish Times Pictorial Weekly
National Observer: A Monthly Journal of Current Affairs
New Statesman
Plan
Royal Institute of Architects of Ireland Yearbook
Studies
Sunday Independent
The Bell
The Cellar
The Green Book: The Journal of the Architectural Association of Ireland
The Red Mole
The Squatter
United Irishman

b. Parliamentary Debates
Parliamentary Debates Dáil Éireann

c. Websites
Central Statistics Offices: www.cso.ie

3. Secondary literature

Aalen, F. H. A., and Whelan, Kevin, *Dublin City and County: From Prehistory to Present* (Dublin, 1992)

Abercrombie, Patrick, *Greater London Plan* (London, 1945)

Abrams, Charles, *Forbidden Neighbours: A Study of Prejudice in Housing* (New York, 1955)

Abrams, Charles, *Urban Renewal in Ireland (Dublin)* (Dublin, 1961)

Abrams, Charles, *Man's Struggle for Shelter in an Urbanising World* (Cambridge, Mass., 1964)

Abrams, Charles, *The City is the Frontier* (New York, 1967)

Andrae, Sophie, 'From Comprehensive Development to Conservation Areas', in Hunter, Michael (ed.), *Preserving the Past: The Rise of Heritage in Modern Britain* (Stroud, 1996), 135–55

An Taisce, *Amenity Study of Dublin and Dun Laoghaire* (Dublin, 1967)

An Taisce, *For Demolition?* (Dublin, 1969)

Appadurai, Arjun, 'Introduction: Commodities and the Politics of Value', in Appadurai, Arjun (ed.), *The Social Life of Things* (Cambridge, 1986), 3–63

Arensberg, Conrad, *Family and Community in Ireland* (Cambridge, Mass., 1948)

Ashworth, G. J., and Larkham, P. J. (eds.), *Building a New Heritage: Tourism, Culture and Identity in the New Europe* (London, 1994)

Balshaw, Maria, and Kennedy, Liam, 'Introduction: Urban Space and Representation', in Balshaw, Maria, and Kennedy, Liam (eds.), *Urban Space and Representation* (London, 2000), 1–21

Banham, Reyner, *Theory and Design in the First Machine Age* (London, 1960)

Bannon, Michael, 'Development Planning and the Neglect of the Critical Regional Dimension', in Bannon, Michael (ed.), *Planning: The Irish Experience 1920–88* (Dublin, 1989), 122–57

Bannon, Michael. (ed.), *Planning: The Irish Experience 1920–88* (Dublin, 1989)

Bannon, Michael, 'Dublin Town Planning Competition: Ashbee and Chettle's "New Dublin—A Study in Civics"', *Planning Perspectives* 14/2 (1999), 145–62

Becker, Annette, Olley, John, Wang, Wilfried, *Twentieth-Century Architecture: Ireland* (Frankfurt, 1997)

Beckett, J. C., *The Anglo-Irish Tradition* (London, 1976)

Behan, Dominic, *Tell Dublin I Miss Her* (Dublin, 1962)

Bender, Barbara, 'Introduction: Landscape–Meaning and Action', in Bender, Barbara (ed.), *Landscape: Politics and Perspectives* (Oxford, 1993), 1–17

Benjamin, Walter, *One Way Street and Other Writings* (London, 1997)

Benjamin, Walter, *The Arcades Project* (Cambridge, Mass., 1999)

Berman, Marshall, *All That is Solid Melts into Air: The Experience of Modernity* (London, 1983)

Bew, Paul, *Ireland: The Politics of Enmity 1789–2006* (Oxford, 2007)

Bew, Paul, and Patterson, Henry, *Sean Lemass and the Making of Modern Ireland, 1945–66* (Dublin, 1982)

Blackwell, John, and Convery, Frank (eds.), *Replace or Retain? Irish Policies for Buildings Analysed* (Dublin, 1988)

Bluestone, Daniel, 'Preservation and Renewal in Post-World War II Chicago', in Waldheim, Charles, and Ruedi Ray, Katerina (eds.), *Chicago Architecture: Histories, Revisions, Alternatives* (Chicago, 2005), 61–81

Bodkin, Thomas, *Report on the Arts in Ireland* (Dublin, 1951)

Bond, Valerie (ed.), *An Taisce: the First Fifty Years* (Meath, 2005)

Bondi, Liz, 'Gender Divisions and Gentrification: A Critique', *Transactions of the Institute of British Geographers* 16/2 (1991), 190–8

Bord Fáilte, *National Monuments of Ireland in the Charge of the Commissioners of Public Works in Ireland* (Dublin, 1964)

Bourdieu, Pierre, *Distinction: A Social Critique of the Judgement of Taste* (London, 1986)

Bowen, Kurt, *Protestants in a Catholic State: Ireland's Privileged Minority* (Dublin, 1983)

Bowman, John, *Window and Mirror: RTÉ Television 1961–2011* (Dublin, 2011)

Boyce, D. G., *Nationalism in Ireland* (London, 1995)

Boyd, Gary A., *Dublin 1745–1922: Hospitals, Spectacle and Vice* (Dublin, 2006)

Brand, C. M., *Modern Legislation for the Protection of History: The Ancient Monuments and Archaeological Areas Act 1979* (Glasgow, 1989)

Brett, David, 'The Construction of Heritage', in Cronin, Michael, and O'Connor, Barbara (eds.), *Tourism in Ireland: A Critical Analysis* (Cork, 1993), 183–202

Brown, Terence, *Ireland: A Social and Cultural History 1922–2002* (London, 2004)

Browne, Noel, *Against the Tide* (Dublin, 1986)

Buechler, Steven, 'New Social Movement Theories', *Sociological Quarterly*, 36/3 (1995), 441–64

Bullock, Nicholas, *Building the Post-War World: Modern Architecture and Reconstruction in Britain* (London, 2002)

Burke, Peter, *Eyewitnessing: The Uses of Images as Historical Evidence* (London, 2001)

Butler, Hubert, *Escape from the Anthill* (Dublin, 1985)

Butler, Tim, *Gentrification and the Middle Classes* (Aldershot, 1997)

Campbell, Hugh, 'The Emergence of Modern Dublin: Reality and Representation', *Architectural Research Quarterly* 2/4 (1997), 44–53

Campbell, Hugh, 'Modern Architecture and National Identity in Ireland', in Cleary, Joe, and Connolly, Claire (eds.), *Cambridge Companion to Modern Irish Culture* (Cambridge, 2005), 285–303

Carens, James, *Surpassing Wit: Oliver St. John Gogarty, his Poetry and Prose* (New York, 1979)

Casey, Christine, *Dublin: The City Within the Grand and Royal Canals and the Circular Road including the Phoenix Park* (London, 2005)

Castells, Manuel, *The City and the Grassroots: A Cross-Cultural Theory of Urban Social Movements* (London, 1983)

Cerulo, Karen, 'Identity Construction: New Issues, New Directions', *Annual Review of Sociology*, Vol. 23 (1997), 385–409

Cherry, Gordon, *The Evolution of British Town Planning* (Leighton Buzzard, 1974)

Cherry, Gordon, 'Reconstruction: Its Place in Planning History', in Diefendorf, Jeffry (ed.), *Rebuilding Europe's Bombed Cities* (London, 1990), 209–20

Childers, E. S. E., *The Story of the Royal Hospital, Kilmainham* (London, 1921)

Choay, Francoise, *The Invention of the Historic Monument* (Cambridge, 2001)

Christie's, *Auction Catalogue 19 North Great George's Street, Dublin Ireland* (Dublin, 1987)

Civics Institute of Ireland, *Dublin of the Future: The New Town Plan, Being the Scheme Awarded the First Prize in the International Competition by Patrick Abercrombie, Sydney Kelly & Arthur Kelly* (Dublin, 1922)

Civics Institute of Ireland, *The Dublin Civic Survey Report* (London, 1925)

Clarke, Brendan, 'The Environment', in Lee, J. J. (ed.), *Ireland 1945–70* (Dublin, 1979), 96–110

Cleary, Joe, 'Introduction: Ireland and Modernity', in Cleary, Joe, and Connolly, Claire (eds.), *The Cambridge Companion to Modern Irish Culture* (Cambridge, 2005), 1–24

Cleary, Joe, and Connolly, Claire (eds.), *The Cambridge Companion to Modern Irish Culture* (Cambridge, 2005)

Clifford, Brendan, *The Dubliner: The Lives, Times and Writings of James Clarence Mangan* (Belfast, 1988)

Cohen, Deborah, *Household Gods: The British and their Possessions* (London, 2006)

Cole, David, 'Gentrification, Social Character and Personal Identity', *Geographical Review* 75/2 (1985), 142–55

Cole, David, 'Artists and Urban Redevelopment', *Geographical Review* 77/4 (1987), 391–407

Collins, Stephen, *The Haughey File: The Unprecedented Career and Last Years of The Boss* (Dublin, 1992)

Collins, Stephen, *The Power Game: Ireland under Fianna Fáil* (Dublin, 2001)

Colquhoun, Alan, *Modern Architecture* (Oxford, 2002)

Connolly, Linda, and Hourigan, Niamh (eds.), *Social Movements and Ireland* (Manchester, 2007)

Coogan, Tim Pat, *Disillusioned Decades: Ireland 1966–87* (Dublin, 1987)

Cook, Matt, *London and the Culture of Homosexuality 1885–1914* (Cambridge, 2003)

Le Corbusier, *The Radiant City: Elements of a Doctrine of Urbanism to be Used as the Basis of our Machine-Age Civilisation* (London, 1933)

Cornforth, John, *The Inspiration of the Past: Country House Taste in the Twentieth Century* (Harmondsworth, 1985)

Cosgrave, Denis, and Daniels, Stephen (eds.), *The Iconography of Landscape: Essays on the Symbolic Representation, Design and Use of Past Environments* (Cambridge, 1988)

Craig, Maurice, *Dublin 1660–1880* (Suffolk, 1980)

Cronin, Anthony, *Dead as Doornails: Bohemian Dublin in the Fifties and Sixties* (Oxford, 1986)

Cronin, Michael, and O'Connor, Barbara, *Tourism in Ireland: A Critical Analysis* (Cork, 1983)

Cullen, Gordon, *Townscape* (London, 1961)

Cullen Owens, Rosemary, *A Social History of Women in Ireland 1870–1970* (Dublin, 2005)

Curtis, William, *Modern Architecture since 1900* (Third edition: London, 2007)

Daly, Mary, *Dublin The Deposed Capital: A Social and Economic History 1860–1914* (Cork, 1984)

Daly, Mary, (ed.), *County and Town: One Hundred Years of Local Government in Ireland* (Dublin, 2001)

Daly, Mary, 'Less a Commemoration of the Actual Achievements and More a Commemoration of the Hopes of the Men of 1916', in Daly, Mary, and O'Callaghan, Margaret (eds.), *1916 in 1966: Commemorating the Easter Rising* (Dublin, 2007), 18–85

Daly, Mary, and O'Callaghan, Margaret (eds.), *1916 in 1966: Commemorating the Easter Rising* (Dublin, 2007)

Daly, Mary, and O'Callaghan, Margaret, 'Introduction—Irish Modernity and "the Patriotic Dead" in 1966', in Daly, Mary, and O'Callaghan, Margaret (eds.), *1916 in 1966: Commemorating the Easter Rising* (Dublin, 2007), 1–17

Davis, John, 'Rents and Race in 1960s London: New Light on Rachmanism', *Twentieth-Century British History* 12/1 (2001), 69–92

Davis, John, 'Simple Solutions to Complex Problems': The Greater London Council and the Greater London Development Plan, 1965–73', in Harris, Jose (ed.), *Civil Society in British History: Ideas, Identities, Institutions* (Oxford, 2003), 249–73

De Certeau, Michel, *The Practice of Everyday Life* (London, 1984)

Delafons, John, *Politics and Preservation: A Policy History of the Built Heritage 1882–1996* (London, 1997)

Delaney, Enda, 'Modernity, the Past, and Politics in Post War Ireland', in Hachey, Thomas (ed.), *Turning Points in Twentieth-Century Irish History* (Dublin, 2011), 103–18

Delaney, Patrick (ed.), *Architectural Survey (Dublin) 1958–1966* (Dublin, 1966)

Desrochers, Brigitte, 'Ruins Revisited: Modernist Conceptions of Heritage', in Madge, James, and Peckham, Andrew (eds.), *Narrating Architecture: A Retrospective Anthology* (London, 2006), 189–200

Diefendorf, Jeffry (ed.), *Rebuilding Europe's Bombed Cities* (London, 1990)

Donleavy, J. P., *The Ginger Man* (Dublin, 1955)

Douglas, Mary, *Purity and Danger: An Analysis of the Concepts of Pollution and Taboo* (London, 2003)

Dublin Corporation, *County Borough of Dublin and Neighbourhood Town Planning Report Sketch Development Plan by Professor Patrick Abercrombie, Sydney A. Kelly, Manning Robertson* (Dublin, 1941)

Dublin Corporation, *County Borough of Dublin Draft Planning Scheme* (Dublin, 1955)

Dublin Corporation, *Planning Scheme Book 'A' Land Reservations* (Dublin, 1957)

Dublin Corporation, *Articles of the Planning Scheme* (Dublin, 1957)

Dublin Corporation, *Draft Dublin Development Plan* (Dublin, 1967)

Dublin Corporation, *Dublin City Development Plan* (Dublin, 1968)

Dublin Corporation, *Dublin Development Plan* (Dublin, 1968)

Dyos, H. J., 'The Slums of Victorian London', in Cannadine, David, and Reeder, David (eds.), *Exploring the Urban Past: Essays in Urban History by H. J. Dyos* (Cambridge, 1982), 129–53

Elwall, Robert, *Building a Better Tomorrow: Architecture in Britain in the 1950s* (Chichester, 2000)

English, Richard, *Armed Struggle: The History of the IRA* (Oxford, 2003)

English, Richard, *Irish Freedom: The History of Nationalism in Ireland* (London, 2006)

Esher, Lionel, *A Broken Wave: The Rebuilding of England 1940–80* (London, 1980)

Evans, Robert, and Harp, Richard (eds.), *Frank O'Connor: New Perspectives* (West Cornwall, CT, 1998)

Fahey, Tony, 'Housing and Local Government', in Daly, Mary (ed.), *County and Town: One Hundred Years of Local Government in Ireland* (Dublin, 2001), 121–35

Fallon, Brian, *An Age of Innocence: Irish Culture 1930–60* (Dublin, 1998)

Fanning, Bryan, *The Quest for Modern Ireland: The Battle of Ideas, 1912–86* (Dublin, 2008)

Farrell, Brian, *Chairman or Chief? The Role of Taoiseach in Irish Government* (London, 1971)

Ferriter, Diarmuid, *The Transformation of Ireland 1900–2000* (London, 2004)

Fink, Carole, Gassert, Philipp, and Junker, Detlef (eds.), *1968: The World Transformed* (Cambridge, 1998)

Fitzgerald, Desmond, and Peill, James, *Irish Furniture: Woodwork and Carving in Ireland from the Earliest Times to the Act of Union* (New Haven, 2007)

Fleming, Lionel, *Head or Harp?* (Dublin, 1965)

An Foras Forbartha, *Transportation in Dublin* (Dublin, 1971)

Foster, R. F., *Modern Ireland, 1600–1972* (London, 1989)

Foster, R. F., *Luck and the Irish: A Brief History of Change c. 1970–2000* (London, 2007)

Foucault, Michel, *Madness and Civilisation: A History of Insanity in the Age of Reason* (London, 1971)

Foucault, Michel, *Discipline and Punish: The Birth of the Prison* (London, 1977)

Frampton, Kenneth, *Modern Architecture: A Critical History* (London, 1992)

Fraser, Robert, *1968: A Student Generation in Revolt* (London, 1988)

Garvin, Tom, 'The Destiny of Soldiers: Tradition and Modernity in the Politics of De Valera's Ireland', *Political Studies* 26/3 (1978), 328–48

Garvin, Tom, *Preventing the Future: Why was Ireland so Poor for so Long?* (Dublin, 2004)

Georgian Society, *The Georgian Society Records of Eighteenth Century Domestic Architecture and Decoration in Dublin,* Vols. 1–5 (Dublin, 1909; republished Dublin, 1969)

Gillmor, Desmond, and Bannon, Michael, 'The Changing Centre of Gravity of Office Establishments within Central Dublin, 1940 to 1970', *Irish Geography* 6/4 (1972), 480–4

Girvin, Brian, *Between Two Worlds: Politics and Economy in Independent Ireland* (Dublin, 1989)

Girvin, Brian, *From Union to Union: Nationalism, Democracy and Religion in Ireland—Act of Union to EU* (Dublin, 2002)

Girvin, Brian, and Murphy, Gary (eds.), *The Lemass Era: Politics and Society in the Ireland of Sean Lemass* (Dublin, 2005)

Girvin, Brian and Murphy, Gary, 'Whose Ireland? The Lemass Era', in Girvin, Brian, and Murphy, Gary (eds.), *The Lemass Era: Politics and Society in the Ireland of Sean Lemass* (Dublin, 2005), 1–11

Glass, Ruth, 'Introduction', in Centre for Urban Studies and Glass, Ruth (eds.), *London: Aspects of Change* (London, 1964), xiii–xlii

Glendinning, Miles, and Muthesius, Stefan, *Tower Block: Modern Public Housing in England, Scotland, Wales and Northern Ireland* (New Haven, 1994)

Gold, John, *The Practice of Modernism: Modern Architects and Urban Transformation 1954–72* (Oxford, 2007)
Goldhagen, Sarah Williams, and Legault, Réjean (eds.), *Anxious Modernisms: Experimentation in Postwar Architectural Culture* (Cambridge, Mass., 2000)
Gogarty, Oliver St John, *Rolling Down the Lea* (Dublin, 1950)
Graham, Brian, 'Heritage Conservation and Revisionist Nationalism in Ireland', in Ashworth G. J., and Larkham, P. J (eds.), *Building a New Heritage: Tourism, Culture and Identity in the New Europe* (London, 1994), 135–58
Graham, Brian, 'The Imagining of Place: Representation and Identity in Contemporary Ireland', in Graham, Brian, *In Search of Ireland: A Cultural Geography* (London, 1997), 192–212
Graham, Brian, *In Search of Ireland: A Cultural Geography* (London, 1997)
Graham, Brian, 'Ireland and Irishness: Place, Culture and Identity', in Graham, Brian, *In Search of Ireland: A Cultural Geography* (London, 1997), 1–13
Grist, Berna, 'Local Authorities and the Planning Process', in Daly, Mary (ed.), *County and Town: One Hundred Years of Local Government in Ireland* (Dublin, 2001), 130–41
Guinness, Desmond, 'Introduction', *The Georgian Society Records of Eighteenth Century Domestic Architecture and Decoration in Dublin* (Dublin, 1969), v–ix
Gunn, Simon, 'The Spatial Turn: Changing Histories of Space and Place', in Gunn, Simon, and Morris, Robert (eds.), *Identities in Space: Contested Terrains in the Western City since 1850* (Aldershot, 2001), 1–14
Hachey, Thomas (ed.), *Turning Points in Twentieth-Century Irish History* (Dublin, 2011)
Hall, Peter, *Great Planning Disasters* (Harmondsworth, 1981)
Hall, Peter, *Cities of Tomorrow: An Intellectual History of Urban Planning and Design in the Twentieth Century* (Oxford, 1992)
Hamnet, Chris, *Unequal City* (London, 2003)
Hanley, Brian, and Millar, Scott, *The Lost Revolution: The Story of the Official IRA and the Workers Party* (Dublin, 2009)
Harbinson, Peter, Potterton, Homan, and Sheehy, Jeanne, *Irish Art and Architecture: From Prehistory to Present* (London, 1993)
Harvey, David, *The Urban Experience* (Oxford, 1989)
Harvey, David, *The Condition of Postmodernity: An Enquiry into the Origins of Cultural Change* (London, 1990)
Harvey, David, *Paris, Capital of Modernity* (London, 2003)
Hayden, Dolores, *The Power of Place: Urban Landscapes as Public History* (London, 1995)
Hebbert, Michael, and Sonne, Wolfgang, 'History Builds the Town: On the Uses of History in Twentieth-Century City Planning', in Monclús, Javier, and Guardia, Manuel (eds.), *Culture, Urbanism and Planning* (Aldershot, 2006), 3–21
Henige, David, *Oral Historiography* (New York, 1982)
Hewison, Robert, *The Heritage Industry: Britain in a Climate of Decline* (London, 1987)

Hill, Jacqueline (ed.), *A New History of Ireland VII: Ireland 1921–84* (Oxford, 2003)

Hillman, Judy (ed.), *Planning for London* (Harmondsworth, 1971)

Hilwig, Stuart, 'The Revolt Against the Establishment: Students Versus the Press in West Germany and Italy', in Fink, Carole, Gassert, Philipp, and Junker, Detlef (eds.), *1968: The World Transformed* (Cambridge, 1998), 321–50

Holohan, Carole, 'More than a Revival of Memories? 1960s Youth and the 1916 Rising', in Daly, Mary, and O'Callaghan, Margaret (eds.), *1916 in 1966: Commemorating the Easter Rising* (Dublin, 2007), 173–97

Horgan, John, *Sean Lemass: The Enigmatic Patriot* (Dublin, 1997)

Horgan, John, *Irish Media: A Critical History* (London, 2001)

Horn, Gerd-Rainer, *The Spirit of '68: Rebellion in Western Europe and North America, 1956–76* (Oxford, 2007)

Houlbrook, Matt, *Queer London: Perils and Pleasures of the Sexual Metropolis, 1918–1957* (Chicago, 2005)

Hourihane, Jim (ed.), *Engaging Spaces: People, Place and Space from an Irish Perspective* (Dublin, 2003)

Humphreys SJ, A. J., 'Migration to Dublin: Its Social Effects', *Christus Rex* IV/2 (1955), 199–205

Humphreys SJ, A. J., *New Dubliners: Urbanisation and the Irish Family* (Dublin, 1966; reprinted London, 1998)

Hunter, Michael, *Preserving the Past: The Rise of Heritage in Britain* (Stroud, 1996)

Hurley, Richard, and Cantwell, Wilfred, *Contemporary Irish Church Architecture* (Dublin, 1985)

Hurley, Richard, and Larmour, Paul (eds.), *Sacred Places: The Story of Christian Architecture in Ireland* (Dublin, 2000)

Jackson, Alvin, *Ireland 1798–1998: Politics and War* (Oxford, 1999)

Jackson, Peter, *Maps of Meaning: An Introduction to Cultural Geography* (London, 1989)

Jacobs, Jane, *The Death and Life of Great American Cities* (Harmondsworth, 1994)

Jacobs, Jane, *Edge of Empire: Postcolonialism and the City* (London, 1996)

Jager, Michael, 'Class Definition and the Esthetics of Gentrification', in Smith, Neil, and Williams, Peter (eds.), *Gentrification of the City* (London, 1986)

James, Dermot, *From the Margins to the Centre: A History of the Irish Times* (Dublin, 2008)

Jenkins, Hilary, 'Where the Revolution is At', in Pettit, Philipp (ed.), *The Gentle Revolution* (Dublin, 1969), 67–75

Johnson, Nuala, 'Where Geography and History Meet: Heritage Tourism and the Big House in Ireland', *Annals of the Association of American Geographers* 86/3 (1996), 551–66

Johnson, Nuala, 'Framing the Past: Time, Space and the Politics of Heritage Tourism in Ireland', *Political Geography* 8/2 (1999), 187–207

Johnston, Roy, *Century of Endeavour: A Biographical and Autobiographical View of the Twentieth Century in Ireland* (Dublin, 2006)

Jokilehto, Jukka, *A History of Architectural Conservation* (Oxford, 1999)

Joyce, Patrick, *The Rule of Freedom: Liberalism and the Modern City* (London, 2003)

Kearns, Kevin, *Georgian Dublin: Ireland's Imperilled Architectural Heritage* (Newton Abbott, 1983)

Keenan-Thomson, Tara, *Irish Women and Street Politics 1956–73: 'This Could be Contagious'* (Dublin, 2010)

Kennedy, B. P., *Dreams and Responsibilities: The State and the Arts in Independent Ireland* (Dublin, 1991)

Kennedy, B. P., 'The Irish Free State 1922–49: A Visual Perspective', in Gillespie, Raymond, and Kennedy, B. P. (eds.), *Ireland: Art into History* (Dublin, 1996), 132–54

Keogh, Dermot, *Jack Lynch: A Biography* (Dublin, 2008)

Keogh, Dermot, and McCarthy, Andrew, *Twentieth Century Ireland: Revolution and State Building* (Dublin, 2005)

Keogh, Dermot, O'Shea, Finbarr, Quinlan, Carmel (eds.), *The Lost Decade: Ireland in the Fifties* (Cork, 2004)

Kincaid, Andrew, *Postcolonial Dublin: Imperial Legacies in the Built Environment* (London, 2006)

King, Geoff, *Mapping Reality: An Exploration of Cultural Geographies* (Basingstoke, 1996)

Klemek, Christopher, *The Transatlantic Collapse of Urban Renewal: Postwar Urbanism from New York to Berlin* (Chicago, 2011)

Koven, Seth, *Slumming: Sexual and Social Politics in Victorian London* (Princeton, 2004)

Lawford, Valerie, *Vogue's Book of Houses, Gardens, People, Photographed by Horst,* (London, 1968)

Lee, J. J., 'Continuity and Change in Ireland 1945–70', in Lee, J. J. (ed.), *Ireland 1945–70* (Dublin, 1979), 166–77

Lee, J. J. (ed.), *Ireland 1945–70* (Dublin, 1979)

Lee, J. J., *Ireland: Politics and Society 1912–85* (Cambridge, 1989)

Lefebvre, Henri, *The Production of Space* (Oxford, 1991)

Lefebvre, Henri, *The Urban Revolution* (Minneapolis, 2003)

Legg, Charles, and Allen, Judith, 'The Origins of Gentrification in London', *History Workshop Journal,* 17(1) (1984), 164–6

Lennon, Hilary (ed.), *Frank O'Connor: Critical Essays* (Dublin, 2007)

Ley, David, *A Social Geography of the City* (London, 1983)

Ley, David, 'Alternative Explanations for Inner-City Gentrification: A Canadian Assessment', *Annals of the Association of American Geographers* 76/4 (1986), 521–35

Ley, David, *The New Middle Class and the Remaking of the Central City* (Oxford, 1996)

Lincoln, Colm, 'City of Culture: Dublin and the Discovery of Urban Heritage,', in Cronin Michael, and O'Connor, Barbara, *Tourism in Ireland: A Critical Analysis* (Cork, 1983), 203–30

Living City Group, *Dublin—A Living City,* (Dublin, 1972)

Lowenthal, David, *The Past is a Foreign Country* (Cambridge, 1985)
Lumley, Robert, *States of Emergency: Cultures of Revolt in Italy from 1968 to 1978* (London, 1999)
Lynch, Claire, *Irish Autobiography: Stories of Self in the Narrative of a Nation* (Bern, 2009)
Lyons, F. S. L., *Ireland Since the Famine* (Dublin, 1963)
McCamley, Bill, *Dennis Dennehy: Socialist Agitator* (Dublin, 1985)
McCarthy, Cormac, *Modernisation, Crisis, and Culture in Ireland, 1969–92* (Dublin, 2000)
McCullough, Niall, *Dublin: An Urban History* (Dublin, 1989)
McCullough, Niall, *Dublin: The Plan for the City* (Dublin, 2007)
McDonald, Frank, *The Destruction of Dublin* (Dublin, 1985)
MacDonnell, Randal, *The Lost Houses of Ireland* (London, 2002)
McDowell, R. B., *Crisis and Decline: The Fate of Southern Unionists* (Dublin, 1997)
McKellar, Elizabeth, 'Populism versus Professionalism: John Summerson and the Twentieth-Century Creation of the "Georgian" ', in Arciszewska, Barbara, and McKellar, Elizabeth, (eds.), *Articulating British Classicism: New Approaches to Eighteenth-Century Architecture* (Aldershot, 2004), 35–56
MacLiammóir, Micheál, *Put Money in Thy Purse* (London, 1950)
MacManus, Ruth, 'Heritage and Tourism in Ireland—an Unholy Alliance?' *Irish Geography* 30/2 (1997), 90–8
McManus, Ruth, *Dublin 1910–40: Shaping the City and Suburbs* (Dublin, 2002)
McParland, Edward, *The Royal Hospital, Kilmainham, Co. Dublin: A National Centre for Culture and the Arts in Ireland* (Dublin, 1985)
McParland, Edward, *A Bibliography of Irish Architectural History* (Dublin, 1989)
McParland, Edward, *Public Architecture in Ireland, 1680–1760* (New Haven, 2001)
Maguire, Martin, ' "Our People": The Church of Ireland and the Culture of Community in Dublin since Disestablishment', in Gillespie, Raymond, and Neely, W. G. (eds.), *The Laity and the Church of Ireland: All Sorts and Conditions* (Dublin, 2002), 277–303
Malone, Patrick, *Office Development in Dublin 1960–90* (Dublin, 1990)
Mandler, Peter, 'John Summerson (1904–92): The Architectural Critic and the Search for the Modern', in Pederson, Susan, and Mandler, Peter (eds.), *After the Victorians: Private Conscience and Public Duty in Modern England* (London, 1994), 231–48
Mandler, Peter, 'New Towns for Old: The Fate of the Town Centre', in Conekin, Becky, Mort, Frank, and Waters, Chris (eds.), *Moments of Modernity: Reconstructing Britain 1945–64* (London, 1999), 208–27
Manning, Maurice, and McDowell, Moore, *Electricity Supply in Ireland: The History of the ESB* (Dublin, 1984)
Marcuse, Harold, 'The Revival of Holocaust Awareness in West Germany, Israel and the United States', in Fink, Carole, Gassert, Philipp, and Junker, Detlef (eds.), *1968: The World Transformed* (Cambridge, 1998), 421–38

Marwick, Arthur, *The Sixties: Cultural Revolution in Britain, France, Italy, and the United States, c.1958–c.1974* (Oxford, 1998)

Marwick, Arthur, 'Youth Culture and the Cultural Revolution of the Long Sixties', in Schildt, Axel, and Siegfried, Detlef (eds.), *Between Marx and Coca-Cola: Youth Cultures in Changing European Societies, 1960–80* (Oxford, 2006), 38–59

Massey, Doreen, 'Places and their Pasts,' *History Workshop Journal* 39/1 (1995), 182–92

Mawhinney, Kenneth, 'Environmental Conservation: Concern and Action 1920–70', in Bannon, Michael (ed.), *Planning: The Irish Experience 1920–88* (Dublin, 1989)

Mayer, Harold, 'Urban Geography and Chicago in Retrospect', *Annals of the Association of American Geographers* 69/1 (March 1979), 114–18

Meller, Helen, *Towns, Plans and Society in Modern Britain* (Cambridge, 1997)

Melucci, Alberto, 'A Strange Kind of Newness; What's "New" in New Social Movements?', in Johnston, Hank, Laraña, Enrique, and Gusfield, Joseph (eds.), *New Social Movements: From Ideology to Identity* (Philadelphia, 1994), 101–32

Monclús, Francisco, and Guàrdia, Manuel (eds.), *Culture, Urbanism and Planning* (Aldershot, 2006)

Morris, Ewan, '"God save the King" versus "the Soldier's Song": The 1929 Trinity College National Anthem Dispute and the Politics of the Irish Free State', *Irish Historical Studies* 31/121 (1998), 72–90

Mort, Frank, 'Fantasies of Metropolitan Life: Planning London in the 1940s', *Journal of British Studies* 43/1 (2004), 120–51

Mort, Frank, and Ogborn, Miles, 'Transforming Metropolitan London 1750–1960', *Journal of British Studies* 43/1 (2004), 1–14

Mulholland, Marc, *The Longest War: Northern Ireland's Troubled History* (Oxford, 2002)

Mullin, Stephen, 'Change, Conservation and the Tourist Trade', in Hillman, Judy (ed.), *Planning for London* (Harmondsworth, 1971), 112–23

Nowlan, Kevin, 'The Evolution of Irish Planning 1934–64', in Bannon, Michael (ed.), *Planning: The Irish Experience 1920–88* (Dublin, 1989), 71–85

O'Brien, Flann, *At Swim-Two-Birds* (New York, 1939)

O'Brien, Justin, *The Modern Prince: Charles J. Haughey and the Quest for Power* (Dublin, 2002)

O'Brien, Mark, *The Irish Times: A History* (Dublin, 2008)

O'Connor, Deirdre, *Housing in Dublin's Inner City* (Dublin, 1979)

O'Connor, Frank, *Irish Miles* (Dublin, 1947)

O'Connor, Kevin, *Sweetie* (Dublin, 1999)

O'Connor, Ulick, *Oliver St. John Gogarty* (London, 1963)

Ó Dochartaigh, Niall, 'Housing and Conflict: Social Change and Collective Action in Derry in the 1960s', in O'Brien, Gerard (ed.), *Derry and Londonderry, History and Society: Interdisciplinary Essays on the History of an Irish County* (Dublin, 1999), 625–46

O'Donovan, Donal, *God's Architect: A Life of Raymond McGrath* (Bray, 1995)

O'Dwyer, Frederick, *Lost Dublin* (Dublin, 1981)

Ó'Faoláin, Seán, *An Irish Journey* (Dublin, 1940)

Office of Public Works, *An Introduction to the Royal Hospital Kilmainham: Its Architecture, History and Restoration* (Dublin, 1987)

Olbricht, Klaus-Hartmut, *Irish Houses: History, Architecture, Furnishing* (London, 1984)

Olley, John, 'Weaving the Fabric of the City: Urban Design and Dublin', in Becker, Annette, Olley, John, and Wang, Wilfried (eds.), *Twentieth Century Architecture: Ireland* (Frankfurt, 1997), 42–7

O'Mahony, Patrick, and Delanty, Gerald, *Rethinking Irish History: Nationalism, Identity and Ideology* (London, 1998)

O'Malley, Padraig, *The Uncivil Wars: Ireland Today* (Boston, 1997)

O'Regan, John (ed.), *Michael Scott 1905–89* (Dublin, 1993)

O'Regan, John (ed.), *Scott Tallon Walker Architects: 100 Buildings and Projects 1960–2005* (Kinsale, 2005)

O'Regan, John, and Dearey, Nicola (eds.), *Michael Scott: Architect in (Casual) Conversation with Dorothy Walker* (Cork, 1995)

O'Reilly, Seán, *Irish Houses and Gardens: From the Archives of Country Life* (London, 1998)

Orwell, George, *Down and Out in Paris and London* (London, 1933)

Orwell, George, *The Road to Wigan Pier* (London, 1937)

Patterson, Henry, *Ireland Since 1939: The Persistence of Conflict* (London, 2006)

Pendlebury, John, 'Planning the Historic City: 1960s Plans for Bath and York', in Monclús, Javier, and Guàrdia, Manuel (eds.), *Culture, Urbanism, and Planning* (Aldershot, 2006), 149–64

Pendlebury, John, *Conservation in the Age of Consensus* (London, 2008)

Pettit, Philip (ed.), *The Gentle Revolution* (Dublin, 1969)

Piccinato, Giorgio, 'Words and History: Controversies on Urban Heritage in Italy', in Monclús, Javier, and Guàrdia, Manuel (eds.), *Culture, Urbanism and Planning* (Aldershot, 2006), 113–27

Pinder, David, *Visions of the City: Utopianism, Power and Politics in Twentieth-Century Urbanism* (Edinburgh, 2005)

Portelli, Alessandro, 'What Makes Oral History Different', in Perks, Robert, and Thomson, Alistair (eds.), *The Oral History Reader* (London, 2006), 32–42

Powell, Martyn, *The Politics of Consumption in Eighteenth-Century Ireland* (Basingstoke, 2005)

Power, Anne, *Estates on the Edge: The Social Consequences of Mass Housing in Northern Europe* (Basingstoke, 1997)

Power, Sinead, 'The Development of the Ballymun Housing Scheme, Dublin 1965–69', *Irish Geography* 33/2 (2000), 199–212

Powers, Alan, *Britain: Modern Architectures in History* (London, 2007)

Powers, Alan, *Modern: The Modern Movement in Britain* (London, 2007)

Priestley, J. B., *English Journey* (London, 1934)

Prince, Simon, *Northern Ireland's '68: Civil Rights, Global Revolt and the Origins of the Troubles* (Dublin, 2007)

Prunty, Jacinta, *Dublin Slums 1800–1925: A Study in Urban Geography* (Dublin, 1999)

Purdie, Bob, *Politics in the Streets: The Origins of the Civil Rights Movement in Northern Ireland* (Belfast, 1990)

Rafter, Kevin, *Neil Blaney: A Soldier of Destiny* (Dublin, 1993)

Ravetz, Alison, *The Government of Space: Town Planning in Modern Society* (London, 1986)

Ravetz, Alison, *Council Housing and Culture: The History of a Social Experiment* (London, 2001)

Rohan, Marc, *Paris '68: Graffiti, Posters, Newspapers and Poems of the Events of May 1968* (London, 1988)

Rossi, Aldo, *Architettura della città* (1966) (published in English as Rossi, Aldo, *The Architecture of the City* (Cambridge, Mass., 1982))

Royal Institute of Architects of Ireland, *Recommendations and Observations on the City of Dublin Planning Scheme* (Dublin, 1957)

Ryan, Liam, 'Social Dynamite: A Study of Early School Leavers', *Christus Rex* 21/1 (1967), 1–54

Ryle Dwyer, T., *Haughey's Forty Years of Controversy* (Cork, 2005)

Sacks, Paul, *The Donegal Mafia: An Irish Political Machine* (New Haven, 1976)

Samuel, Raphael, *Theatres of Memory, Volume 1: Past and Present in Contemporary Culture* (London, 1994)

Savage, Michael, and Warde, Alan, *Urban Sociology, Capitalism and Modernity* (London, 1993)

Savage, Robert, *Irish Television: Its Political and Social Origins* (Westport, CT, 1996)

Savage, Robert, 'Introducing Television in the Age of Sean Lemass', in Girvin, Brian, and Murphy, Gary (eds.), *The Lemass Era: Politics and Society in the Ireland of Sean Lemass* (Dublin, 2005), 191–214

Savage, Robert, *A Loss of Innocence? Television and Irish Society 1960–72* (Manchester, 2010)

Schaechterle, Karl-Heinz, *Traffic Investigation Concerning the Future Main Road Network* (Ulm/Donau, 1965)

Seidman, Michael, *The Imaginary Revolution: Parisian Students and Workers in 1968* (New York, 2004)

Shapely, Peter, *The Politics of Housing: Power, Consumers and Urban Culture* (Manchester, 2007)

Siegfried, Detlef, '"Don't Trust Anyone Older Than 30?" Voices of Conflict and Consensus between Generations in 1960s West Germany', *Journal of Contemporary History* 40/4 (2005), 727–44

Simmel, Georg, 'The Metropolis and Mental Life', in Wolff, Kurt (ed.), *The Sociology of Georg Simmel* (New York, 1976), 409–26

Smith, Neil, 'Blind man's Bluff, or Hamnett's Philosophical Individualism in Search of Gentrification', *Transactions of the Institute of British Geographers* 17/1 (1992), 110–15

Smith, Neil, *The New Urban Frontier: Gentrification and the Revanchist City* (London, 1996)

Smyth, Gerry, '"The Natural Course of Things": Matthew Arnold, Celticism, and the English Poetic Tradition', *Journal of Victorian Culture* 1/1 (1996), 35–53

Soja, Edward, *Postmodern Geographies: The Reassertion of Space in Critical Social Theory* (London, 1989)

Somerville-Large, Peter, *Dublin: The Fair City* (London, 1979)

Sontag, Susan, *On Photography* (London, 2002)

Stanford, W. B., and McDowell, R. B., *Mahaffy: A Biography of an Anglo-Irishman* (London, 1971)

Styles, John, and Vickery, Amanda, 'Introduction', in Styles, John, and Vickery, Amanda (eds.), *Gender, Taste and Material Culture in Britain and North America 1700–1830* (New Haven, 2006), 1–34

Summerson, John, *Georgian London* (London, 1948)

Summerson, John, *Heavenly Mansions and other Essays on Architecture* (New York, 1963)

Sweetman, Rosita, 'The Right (H)on', in *On Our Knees* (London, 1972), 67–75

Thomas, Nicholas, *Protest Movements in 1960s West Germany: A Social History of Dissent and Democracy* (Oxford, 2003)

Thomas, Nicholas, 'Protests against the Vietnam War in 1960s Britain: The Relationship between Protesters and the Press', *Contemporary British History* 22/3 (2008), 335–54

Tobin, Fergal, *The Best of Decades: Ireland in the Nineteen Sixties* (Dublin, 1984)

Tonkiss, Fran, *Space, the City and Social Theory: Social Relations and Urban Forms* (Cambridge, 2005)

Torchiana, Donald, *W. B. Yeats and Georgian Ireland* (Washington, 1992)

Townshend, Charles, *Ireland: The 20th Century* (London, 1999)

Travers Morgan Partnership, *Central Dublin Traffic Plan* (London, 1973)

Tunbridge, J. E., and Ashworth, G. J., *Dissonant Heritage: The Management of the Past as a Resource in Conflict* (Chichester, 1996)

Venturi, Robert, *Complexity and Contradiction in Architecture* (New York, 1972)

Vernon, James, *Hunger: A Modern History* (London, 2007)

Vickery, Amanda, *Behind Closed Doors: At Home in Georgian England* (New Haven, 2009)

von Dirke, Sabine, *'All Power to the Imagination!': The West German Counterculture from the Student Movement to the Greens* (Nebraska, 1997)

Walker, Simon, 'Architecture in Ireland 1940–75', in Becker, Annette, Olley, John, and Wang, Wilfried (eds.), *Twentieth Century Architecture: Ireland* (Frankfurt, 1997), 23–7

Walkowitz, Judith, *City of Dreadful Delight: Narratives of Sexual Danger in Late-Victorian London* (London, 1992)

Ward, Conor, Galligan, Mary, Glynn, Margaret, and Hodkinson, Katherine, *New Homes for Old: Report* (Dublin, 1969)

Ward, Stephen, *Planning and Urban Change* (London, 1994)

Wates, Nick, *The Battle for Tolmers Square* (London, 1976)

Whelan, Yvonne, *Reinventing Modern Dublin: Streetscape, Iconography and the Politics of Identity* (Dublin, 2003)

White, Jack, *Minority Report: The Protestant Community in the Irish Republic* (Dublin, 1975)

White, Jerry, *London in the Twentieth Century: A City and its People* (Harmondsworth, 2001)

Whiteley, Nigel, *Reyner Banham: Historian of the Immediate Future* (London, 2002)

Whittaker, Andrew, *Bright, Brilliant Days: Douglas Gageby and the Irish Times* (Dublin, 2006)

Whyte, John, *Church and State in Modern Ireland* (London, 1971)

Whyte, John, 'Economic progress and political pragmatism, 1957–63', in Hill, Jacqueline (ed.), *A New History of Ireland VII: Ireland 1921–84* (Oxford, 2003), 294–308

Whyte, William, 'The Englishness of English Architecture: Modernism, and the Making of a National International Style, 1937–57', *Journal of British Studies* 48/2 (2009), 441–65

Wierling, Dorothee, 'Generations and Generational Conflicts in East and West Germany', in Klessman, Christoph (ed.), *The Divided Past: Rewriting Post-War German History* (Oxford, 2001), 69–90

Wills, Clair, *That Neutral Island: A History of Ireland During the Second World War* (London, 2008)

Wiltshire, Elinor, and Fitzpatrick, Orla, *If You Ever Go to Dublin Town* (Dublin, 1999)

Wright, Lance, and Browne, Kenneth, *A Future for Dublin* (London, 1975)

Wright, Myles, *Advisory Regional Plan and Final Report Part I: The Dublin Region* (Dublin, 1966)

Wright, Myles, *The Dublin Region: Advisory Regional Plan and Final Report Part II* (Dublin, 1967)

Wright, Patrick, *On Living in an Old Country: The National Past in Contemporary Britain* (Cambridge, 1985)

Wright, Patrick, *A Journey through Ruins: The Last Days of London* (London, 1991)

Young, Michael, and Wilmott, Peter, *Family and Kinship in East London* (Harmondsworth, 1962)

Zukin, Sharon, 'Gentrification: Culture and Capital in the Urban Core', *Annual Review of Sociology*, Vol. 13 (1987), 129–47

Zukin, Sharon, *Loft Living: Culture and Capital in Urban Change* (London, 1988)

Zukin, Sharon, *Naked City: The Death and Life of Authentic Urban Places* (Oxford, 2010)

Index